translation
Richard Sadleir
documentary research
Cecilia Colombo
editorial coordination
Giovanna Crespi
editing
Gail Swerling
graphic design
Tassinari/Vetta
(CODEsign)
page layout and cover
CODEsign
technical coordination
Andrea Panozzo
quality control
Giancarlo Berti

Acknowledgments
Silvana Annichiarico and Roberto Giusti, Milan Triennale
Permanent Collection of Italian Design
Francesca Appiani, Museo Alessi, Omegna (Verbania)
Danièle Archambault, Musée des Beaux-Arts
de Montréal, Quebec (Canada)
AV Mazzega
Francesca Balena Artista, Poltronova
Giuseppe Baldini, UpGroup
Maristella Bonalumi, Fontana Arte
Massimo Bovi, Barovier&Toso
Brunati Italia
Caimi Brevetti
Cappellini International
Paola Silva Coronel
Maria Grazia Corsucci, RB Rossana
Gemma Curtin, Design Museum, London (Great Britain)
Bernadette De Loose, Design Museum, Ghent (Belgium)
Edilkamin
Alessandra Fossati, Adi, Milan
Fragile
Fiorella Ghilardi and Roberto Poloni, Alias
Anna Grabowska, The National Museum, Poznan (Poland)
Adele Guerini and Brigitte Heinrich, Rosenthal
Emiliana Martinelli, Martinelli Luce
Simona Maspero, Clac, Cantù (Como)
Laurence Mauderli, Museum für Gestaltung, Zurich (Switzerland)
Alberto Morini, Floor Gres
Michiel Nijhoff, Stedelijk Museum of Modern Art,
Amsterdam (The Netherlands)
Alberto Novelli
Marika Omenetto, Cleto Munari
Simona Palella, Sambonet
Lanfranco Perotti
Marco Pogliani, Moccagatta Pogliani & Associati
Simona Romano, MuseoKartell, Noviglio (Milan)
Marialaura Rossiello Irvine, Danese Milano
Alessandra Simioni, PBA
Giovanna Solinas, Artemide
Ambrogio Spotti, Tisettanta
Studio Azzurro
Akiko and Tadao Takaichi
Mario Trimarchi
Simona Trizio, Glas Italia
Frank Ubik and Irma Hager, Vitra Design Museum,
Weil am Rhein (Germany)
Unifor
Stefania Vitali, Poltrona Frau
Ietvart Zarmanian, Zarmanian Associati

special thanks go to:
Cecilia Colombo, for her invaluable help
Mara Corradi, for her conscientious work and patience
Monica Del Torchio, for her constant support
and infinite availability
Michele De Lucchi, for having provided his precious time
and archive
Angelo Micheli, for the useful information
and all staff members of the Studio aMDL, for their
collaboration

Alberto Bassi, because without him this book would never
have been possible

The dates of the works that appear in the titles
of the entries and the captions refer to the
project year.

Distributed by Phaidon Press
ISBN 1-904313-39-6

www.phaidon.com

www.electaweb.it

Printed in Hong Kong

architecture

from here to there and beyond
MICHELE DE LUCCHI
fiorella bulegato sergio polano

Electaarchitecture

contents

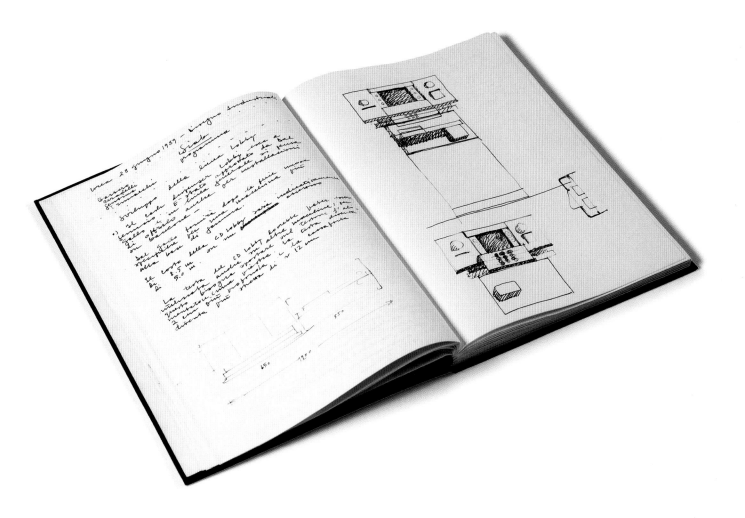

01

Just one work: designer, in general

Sergio Polano

To start with, it is worth yet again pointing to a distinctively Italian trait, or rather a fertile quality. The country's industrial system is dominated by small rather than medium-sized firms and at the same time it has a singularly large number of skilled craft workers. Until a few years ago, nearly all Italian designers were trained in schools of architecture. Though this education was compatible with a general design culture, it essentially focused on the building as a unique object built on a specific site. In terms of working method, this was the complete opposite of industrial design, which is supposed to aim at series production of identical, reproducible machine-made objects. In fact even the best-known products by Italian designers could be described, with rare exceptions and not too paradoxically, as examples of "craft design" (since they are produced in small, sometimes very small, production runs), rather than examples of industrial design proper. "Craft design" is an apt term for the most prominent kinds of useful and functional products manufactured in Italy (such as furniture and home fittings). They are made all the more conspicuous because of the limited interest the dedicated literature takes in major industrial products— such as forms of transport and machinery (which are generally relegated to separate, specialist publications). By contrast, the training of designers in many other countries, especially the English-speaking world, though it oscillates between the legacy of the applied arts and the engineering-driven cult of performance, has long since branched off on a path of its own, clearly separate from other professions, and it lays great stress on the understanding of technology, materials and methods of production. This affects the working relationship between designers and industry and frequently influences its principles and the forms it takes.

The originality and richness of Italian design in the second half of the twentieth century grew out of a fruitful encounter between the distinctive features of our production system and the special aptitudes of architects. They tend to be detached from the specifics of technology and the constraints of serial production, but attracted by the cultural and behavioral implications of design treated as an extension of architecture. On the other hand they take a lively interest in uninhibited experiment, intuitive yet effective composition. They explore the ways products interact with people and their setting, ways of combining form, function and materials with expressive and cultural values, and show due respect for commercial requirements and business strategies. It is as part of this picture (no more than a quick sketch but providing the essential background for any detailed assessment of the culture of Italian industrial design) that we need to view Michele De Lucchi, a figure in many ways exemplary and in others symptomatic.

"Industry was always my stumbling block. [...] The very first thing I learned and which I'd like to teach is that, despite everything, we have to learn to love industry," he explained in an academic address he gave in Venice in 2002, confirming an opinion he frequently expressed (perhaps in an effort to convince himself). "I found it tough [...] but there's good reason why we should do so: there's no alternative! [...] The role of the designer is very complicated [...] in a civilization, industrial civilization, meaning our own [...] in a system where industry is rarely willing to put itself out for design, or even for the world."

In the press as in the conventional wisdom, the figure of Michele De Lucchi appears quite straightforward, contained within a simple and reassuring definition as a brilliant industrial designer with a typical Italian pedigree, and as such not immune to systematic, increasingly frequent forays into interior design and architecture. As appears in the rich bibliography, the pen and the eye of the commentators, in both the specialist press and the general media, have followed his progress closely ever since his debut, through what now amounts to thirty years' work, an extraordinary achievement by its range and quantity alone. The importance of many of his clients, combined with the stir caused by certain projects and products and backed up by an impressive list of awards, have all added something to the solid professional image of Michele De Lucchi and his firm. Here nothing could be easier or more pleasant than to follow his career step by step and browse in the lush pastures of his work (a detailed and analytic account follows in this same volume): you arrange the pieces on the chessboard of time, slot them neatly into the relevant categories, and the work is done.

Everything in fact seems more or less to pan out in his immense and many-sided work as a designer; and all the more so in that the specialist literature has already traced (as noted above) a path that is on the whole straightforward and crystal clear. All the same, if we take a broad critical view of Michele De Lucchi's achievement, we are prompted to ask ourselves a question. Isn't one of the qualities of his work that is most marked a courteous reticence, the words he leaves unspoken, the elliptical suspensions, which allow him to cultivate and modestly preserve his profound convictions and personal inclinations, which lie behind his evident inventiveness and his equally evident powers of organization, and leave faint traces that are discernible to the eye that is willing to look for them? To explore this question, without being able to give a final answer, we need to turn to the fascinating series of albums, notebooks and drawing pads, jealously preserved and occasionally exhibited, in which De Lucchi has traced with passionate intensity over the years sketches and drawings, memories and reflections, rapid jottings and ideas captured as they surfaced. A statement he made in 1999 clearly illustrates their role. "They were my sheet anchor, my 47 notebooks of drawings, a line that runs through all my work and makes its development comprehensible through the succession of changes. I'm still using number 48! I keep them in my bookcase together with the small notebooks, the diaries, the folders where I organize the drawings using various systems." In the same place De Lucchi stated even more explicitly: "I've always liked drawing and the most important choices of my life have been strongly influenced by this urge. The work I chose derived surely from the hope of being able to hold a pencil in my hand every day."

"Listen to me!" he had already proclaimed in 1973, in a performance of candid irony. "Listen to me! I am a Designer in General and in General a Designer. I give the world the beauty of useful things [...] I am with you in the search for balance and harmony between artistic beauty and natural beauty [...] I design you!"

So designer as draughtsman, in general; design as drawing, to the extent that "drawing" is both a highly tangible form of expression, the visible line traced, and the projection of the mental-conceptual purpose, foreshadowing of an image that guides the hand. Seen in these terms, Michele De Lucchi is following the traditional (though no less respectable) path of the artist-architect, of Renaissance origin, which rested on the practice and mastery of drawing, the fruit of his Italian university training. "Today the designer is rather like the artist in the olden days," claimed De Lucchi, in the same academic address, "when the artist's task was to enable people to see how beautiful nature was. [Today the designer] has to show people the beauty of the artificial world, the beautiful things that industry is capable of making with technology. [...] We live in a full period of fears and, rightly enough, technology should not be a further cause for fear."

"Leave technology to me, because I know how to use it," he promised in his 1973 performance, "so it will be useful, not harmful." Though piecemeal and in different ways, along his personal path of experiment and development, De Lucchi's work as a designer has continuously and distinctively embodied attempts to pacify technology, domesticate products and make spaces more homelike. He has created a serene and archaic landscape of forms, frugal and sober, restrained and austere, as shown in the first place by his sketchbooks, which trace a "line that runs through all my work." They form a secluded world, in a certain sense secret (or rather tacit), and express a pre-industrial atmosphere made up of an ideal countrified rusticity and a vital inner restraint. They include simple, ironic mechanical devices (set in states of dynamic equilibrium), as well as reflecting a fascination with the organic and a love for agrarian nature. There are also rare moments of self-indulgence, reflected and transmitted through the discreet yet sensitive reflexes that emerge from the most varied projects, being modulated and transfigured to reveal, quite without rhetoric, "the beauty of the artificial world" and a timeless architecture.

Running parallel with this subterranean vein (perceptible as repeated outcroppings in the background of his work), there is a tenacious level of experimental thinking (which strikes out in different and sometimes contradictory directions over the years), together with a pleasure in being provocative and intellectually challenging. These are the outstanding features of De Lucchi's achievement, to which this note will have to confine itself. They are clearly present in his earliest

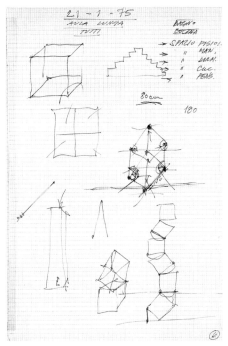

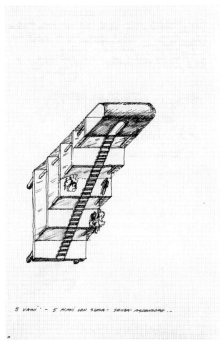

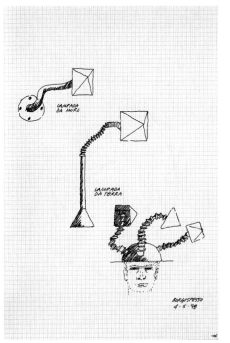

1975–76
Drawings for *Vertical
Architecture*, January 21, 1975.
*5 rooms - 5 floors with stairs -
no elevator*, drawing of vertical
housing, 1976.
Inventions of inhabitable holes,
drawing of underground
dwelling, Milan,
August 30, 1977.
Drawings of lamps,
Via Borgospesso, May 4, 1978.

work, in the mid-seventies, as in the housing he designed, when radicalism in architecture was at its height, under the banner of Cavart (a militant design group formed with other students). They also appear in his ideas for vertical housing in his degree dissertation, which he took in Florence under Adolfo Natalini (himself an outstanding figure in the contemporary scene and an enduring influence on De Lucchi, beginning with his sensuous passion for drawing).

The young De Lucchi translated the radicals' surreal-serious global critique into assertive theoretical declarations and conceptual reconstructions of elementary and primordial forms of housing in spare, abstract models. He created a sequence of problematic enunciations of architecture that ranged from the dynamic stability of a vertical S-shaped structure, made out of five cubes stacked to form an (in)finite ribbon-like development anchored, *malgré soi*, to the ground but soaring skyward, to the nomadic mobility of a sedan-chair/house, like a primitive stilt-house, the image of a dwelling in (temporary) conflict with its own foundations. It is significant that "Culturally Impossible Architecture" was the title of a seminar on design and criticism organized by Cavart at Monselice in 1975. Equally significantly, the name De Lucchi gave the practice he opened in Florence after graduating was *Architetture ed Altri Piaceri* ("Architecture and Other Pleasures"). The need to re-examine first principles, typical of the generation of cultural and political protest to which De Lucchi belonged, sometimes led to a general abdication of responsibility. In other cases, like his, and in other circles, like those he frequented, it became radicalized as the effort to create new foundations for the discipline and seek new professional horizons. In 1977 he moved to Milan and gradually formed contacts in radical circles, already evident in his work for Gaetano Pesce, Superstudio and Andrea Branzi. He focused his interest on "other pleasures." His immediate commitment was to Alchymia, where Alessandro Mendini and Ettore Sottsass, among others, were active. De Lucchi soon earned their esteem. The conceptual quality of his earlier statements about housing now appeared in affable, playful designs; they were not lacking in irony but went much further by stripping everything down to the bare essentials (even the color schemes) and freeing them from functional qualities by systematically banalizing them. A proof of this lies in objects like the Sinerpica table lamp, designed in 1979, a metaphor for a rarefied domestic phyto-mechanical device (with distant Futurist origins). The base is a cylindrical vase, of which grows a tubular stem with an elastic flex coiled around it and terminating in a cylindrical bulb-fitting, with the light bulb a naked glowing bud. Then there was its sister lamp Sinvola, which formed a surreal counterpoint to Sinerpica by the prickly pointlessness of its outsize pin-cushion (another homely old memory), quite alien to its slender stem, from which blossoms a little cone-shaped bulb-fitting that sheds an equally harsh light. A similar "gentle spirit" animates the series of models made for Girmi, again in 1980, with a strong family likeness running through them. A vacuum cleaner, kettle, iron, toaster, fan and similar objects are recomposed in smooth, simple pastel-colored volumes that make them look like characters out of post-modern cartoons: a set of fairy-tale toys that personify tame-looking electrical appliances for a doll's house, devoid as they are of all technological exhibitionism or aggressive form, with the emphasis wholly on their plastic shapes and fanciful associations.

In 1979 he began his first consultancy work for Olivetti, developing under the watchful eye of Ettore Sottsass. They also began designing together in the same year (in 1981–83 for Fiorucci, among others). In 1981 another significant step came when he joined Memphis, for which he was an active organizer and assiduous exhibitor. He provided his own assessment of this experience in 2001. "It was the event that shook off the conventions and prejudices I had accumulated—imagining I was doing the right thing—in the early years of my work. What luck Memphis was for me! It taught me the value of being provocative, the need to always try something new and different, the importance of questioning everything, especially habits, and not only aesthetic and formal habits, and it made me realize you can carry out some sort of revolution even while designing plates, tables and chairs." By the beginning of the eighties, De Lucchi's process of peacefully paring down the domestic landscape to elementary forms suddenly took a turn towards decorative intensification, with zebra-stripes, spots, textured surfaces, unusual combinations of materials and geometrical hybrids, with effects that were sometimes cloying.

This vaguely déco and obliquely allusive decorative quality was embodied in a well-known series of designs for mobile hi-fi sets in 1981 (lumpy clusters of tattooed boxes, little colored blocks, lights, buttons and dimples), as well as in his provocative designs for Memphis: they ranged from Oceanic, a table lamp presented in 1981 (a little creature made of candy sticks/liquorice and children's building blocks captured in movement), to the coeval, lumpy Kristall side table (a serviceable alien crouching on four blue feet, waiting to move), to First, a chair-proclamation of 1983 (a spartan stool, enhanced by a circular aureole that serves as decoration for arms and head, in a virtual transfiguration of the idea of a chair) and so on down to all the variegated variations (above all on the relations between elementary geometrical figures, primary colors, gestalt-organic textures) explored as part of the collegial undertaking of Memphis.

In this way De Lucchi played his part in the reaction against the form/function objectivity of Good Design and the rational International Style (Ulm above all) of the postwar period, fostering the emotional crystallization that made the fortune of the Nuovo Bel Design Italiano (an expressiveness with childlike overtones and an immoderate tactile cheerfulness, a consciously banal simplification and an explicit emotional quality highly responsive to the feelings inspired by objects). However, this never prevented him from exploring other parallel and far-reaching paths of design. In 1997 he was to write: "I believe that design means not just finding attractive forms for objects and choosing fine materials to match. It certainly means a lot more: for example, it's a system of communication, a means of expression, a business tool and above all a form of education."

De Lucchi's work for Olivetti grew rapidly and eventually led to him taking over from Sottsass as director of design until the new millennium. It went through various significant phases: the project, in collaboration with Sottsass, for the Icarus office system for Olivetti Synthesis in 1981; in 1985, the Delphos system for Olivetti Synthesis, again with Sottsass, and a series of computer monitors in 1985–87, his first contribution to product design. The next decade opened with the Sangirolamo system for Olivetti Synthesis (1990), in partnership with Achille Castiglioni, another of the tutelary spirits of Italian design. It continued (to mention only the major achievements) with the notebooks Philos (1992–93) and Echos (1993–94), the multimedia kiosks of 1993–94, the printers of 1994–98 (from PR2 to Artjet 20) and the fax machines of 1994–2000 (from OFX 1000 to 300). In the same period he organized workshops with Philips (1993) and Domestic Chips (1996), which also produced outstanding results.

In 1981 he started developing intelligent office systems for Olivetti Synthesis. They reflected his formal inventiveness (like the seemingly mannered design of the curved legs that gave a touch of dynamism to Sangirolamo), a gift for creating highly adaptable configurations, a refined technological perspicacity and great restraint in the use of materials (avoiding the dreariness of all-purpose systems). They also led him to think continually about the needs and qualities of workplaces. One result was that De Lucchi developed a very broad conception of furniture, which remains an important part of his work: this is furniture as a form of caring for the human environment, which starts from the set of objects that compose it and is then integrated and fused with an idea of architecture as the conformation of space, first taking the form of a protective inwardness and eventually embracing its overall configuration as construction.

This was the period of the rapid decline and tragic end of the extraordinary saga of Olivetti, with the disruption on many levels of its unique industrial system. The company proved incapable of devising a strategy in the digital field even vaguely comparable to those that guided its triumphal progress in the days of mechanical and electromechanical products. De Lucchi designed with a deliberate concern for the company's tradition. (This is especially evident, given their affinities with the designer's own interests, in the inclusive organic qualities of the monitors, multimedia kiosks and Artjet 20, as well as the soft textures of their cabinetry). However, the company's line of consumer electronics seems to have suffered from a fatal flaw: the products were either too advanced or too backward, in a market dominated by rapid change. This is confirmed by the remarkable insights to be found in the records of the workshops mentioned above. The eighties saw the start of a series of other important commissions, with a steady expansion

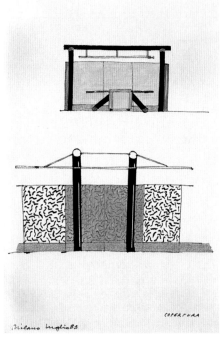

MDL85

COPERTURA

Drawing of a skyscraper,
August 26,1983.
Drawing for the exhibit
at the Milan Triennale,
"Research into an Office
Environment," July 1983.
Drawing of an apartment block,
Paris, January 3, 1981.
Drawing of apartment block,
1981.

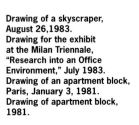

PARIGI 3.1.1981

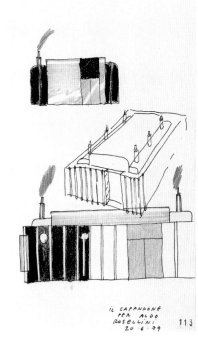

Factory shed for Aldo Rosellini,
drawings of architecture,
June 20, 1979.
Drawing of store interior
in Japan, July 6, 1986.
Drawing of architecture,
August 11, 1986.
Journey to Polynesia,
August 1984.

and diversification of De Lucchi's client base in Italy and abroad. They included interior design projects (e.g. the Nuovo Banco Ambrosiano in 1985–88, the Credito Commerciale in Mantua, in 1987–88, and the store systems for Renown, Americanino and Maconde Moments at the end of the decade), exhibition installations (e.g. exhibit designs for the shows organized by Memphis from 1981 to 1987, followed by various trade-fair stands and in 1989 his involvement in the museum of Groningen), as well as some architectural works (e.g. the La Fenice building in Osaka, 1989–91 and the Sanpo House of Marble at Gumma in 1990–91). In product design, De Lucchi has worked for firms ranging from Fontana Arte to Vistosi, Bieffeplast, Cleto Munari, Abet Print, Unilever, RB Rossana, Kartell and Pelikan (his invention of the Kleberoller in 1987 was outstanding). In particular, his work for Artemide brought him to tackle one of the classic design themes: the various types of artificial illumination (ranging from the first Cyclos of 1982–85 to the recent Logico and Castore). In the perpetual challenge to nearly every designer of lighting devices to measure up to an irreplaceable classic such as Luxo, De Lucchi succeeded in an undertaking that is usually not so much extraordinary as unique in a designer's career. His poised and elegant Tolomeo table lamp of 1986 became a runaway worldwide success and eventually proliferated into a whole family of lamps. It first took over the place held by Richard Sapper's Tizio and then became an icon among contemporary lamps, to the point where it now appears in all sorts of settings, contexts, situations and representations of interiors, and has almost made De Lucchi a household name. It is difficult to identify the reasons for such truly universal approval; we can confine ourselves to recognizing that its objective qualities, like its elegant design and the technical sophistication of the components (from the pudding-basin shape of the shade, with its broad chimney, its tapered stems and the housing which conceals the tensing mechanism) are combined with apparent simplicity (including a suggestion of voluptuous gadgetry, the fruit of the designer's love for mechanisms in precarious dynamic equilibrium). To which we should add that this was one of those unpredictable phenomena that become embedded in the recesses of the technical and collective imagination and help propel the oscillations of taste. Something of the same magic returned significantly at the end of the following decade, in the project that De Lucchi (working with Achille Castiglioni) submitted to a competition for the design of pylons for the state electricity company Enel, which are one of the peaks in his career: simple, innovative and graceful.

At the start of the nineties, all these activities defined and consolidated De Lucchi's international standing. The structure of his design office was unusual compared with the professional scale common in Italy. When we write "De Lucchi" we are actually invoking a firm of large though variable dimensions (rich in individual talents, some only briefly present before departing on their own paths), a specific business logic (with its corollary of strategies, balances and risks), an organization based on teamwork and disciplined by the collaborative-charismatic leadership of its owner. The successful balance between these elements, plus the ability to focus conceptually on the central issues and find solutions with economical formulas enabled De Lucchi to respond in the nineties with the appropriate skills and successfully measure up to demanding challenges and pressing requests (often replacing other architects) to redesign the buildings and spaces of major corporations, such as Deutsche Bank (1989), Deutsche Bahn (1995), Enel (1997–), Poste Italiane (1998–2003), Telecom (1999–).
Along the way, De Lucchi has embraced new challenges. One example is his recent work for Mandarina Duck, with a sophisticated ambience (including "sensorial styling") for a chain of stores for which he first began working back in 1987. It reflects his awareness that communication and expression are increasingly closely bound up with construction and performance, on all scales of design, for better or worse. He stated as much in 2003: "Though involved in different disciplines, I do just one work. I interface with industry in all the issues connected with communication, but above all corporate identity and character. In all these years I have learned to understand industry, succeeding in relating appropriately to all aspects of business functions, conferring character and an identity on the various ways a firm expresses itself, regardless of whether they are products or showrooms, posters or buildings, offices or something

quite different." In the nineties, in other words, De Lucchi increasingly refined an approach to design in terms of system and identity, with highly complex implications. He designed objects (exquisite and casual like the phytomorphic Palme outdoor lamp for Artemide's DZ Licht in 1999–2001, or awkward and inhibited like the grim-looking Enel electricity meter of 2001) and furnishings (with significant products for Moroso in 1991, Mauser Office in 1994–99, and Poltrona Frau in 1998–2001, with his work for Olivetti always in the background). It would be impossible and pointless to list his whole client base: names like Alias, Bull, Ciba, Compaq, Decaux, Ferrari, Fusital, Ideal Standard, Poltronova, Rhea Vendors, Rosenthal, Vorwerk and Wang give some idea of the range. This new experience embodies a distinctive working method, which is quite separate from the scale, though skillfully explored, of installations, whether for exhibitions (such as those in 2000–02 for the agency for the Holy Year in Rome or his work in the trade-fair sector), offices (such as his design for Carigi in 1989, the Banco Portogues do Atlantico in 1990–93, for the Banca Popolare di Lodi in 1998–99, and for Banca 121 and Armani in 2000–01), interiors (from the mannered Manager Restaurant in Tokyo in 1991 to the lucid parterre for the Milan Triennale in 2002, and including the ticket hall of Termini station in Rome in 1999), and the relatively less frequent works of architecture (from the massive Olivetti research center in Bari in 1989–91 to the Conrad Seminar House in 1996–98, the competition for the maritime terminal at Yokohama in 1994, the competition for the Centro per le Arti Contemporanee in Rome in 1998, and so down to the various projects still under way).

In addition to projects already tried and tested for over two decades, the start of the new millennium finds De Lucchi busily engaged in camouflaging electric power stations and substations to blend with their setting, the modernization (long overdue) of the immense network of post offices in Italy (with a palette of acid colors), and redesigning the headquarters of a major telecommunications company. This suggests that his future design ambitions will lead him into fields that offer a more tangible and durable "hope of being able to hold a pencil in my hand every day."

At the end of this note (and as a provisional conclusion) we can see a special significance in a firm, still functioning and successful, that De Lucchi launched in 1990: He called it Produzione Privata and gave it the form of a small business. Here the designer experiments with exquisite ceramic and glass products, reinventing the ancient traditions with delicate innovations and original configurations, revealing an elegantly ironic strategy and a quiet sense of humor. But he also produces extraordinary prototypes of industrial artifacts, above all chairs and lamps: chairs that look as if they have always existed; lights that mostly (not all, out of respect for the spirit of the business: some are playful replicas of designs by Munari, others are airy Leonardesque machines) seem to have been assembled out of ready-made components, even using the new and often rather gawky-looking bulbs available on the market to good effect.

Despite the self-effacing modesty that shelters his convictions, one might say that with Produzione Privata De Lucchi is seeking subtly to stir thought and raise questions among those who have the time to think about these things. To carry out his experiments at Produzione Privata, De Lucchi formed a close alliance with the outstanding tradition of Italian *botteghe* and craft workshops. For the country's future, as it faces the global challenge, mightn't it be a good idea to consider more carefully the contribution they make to innovation and development? At the same time, we are left with the paradox that these simple and economical artifacts, austere and expressive, these prototypes of chairs and lamps, instead of being mass produced, are confined to the limited editions of "private production." Is this because they aspire to be anonymous, to achieve "the Uncommon Beauty of Common Things," as the Eameses called it?

Be that as it may, all of Michele De Lucchi's work prompts close reflection on the forms of the "culture of design," whether for industry or other fields, and on the education of designers. In particular, it raises questions about the recent institution of specialist university courses in design, paralleling the schools of architecture, and compels us to ponder a fundamental question. Is it indispensable for the courses to be autonomous and specialized, structured and specific but not segregated? Or, in this part of the world, is it still true, or at least preferable, to deceive ourselves that the work of a designer is just a job in general?

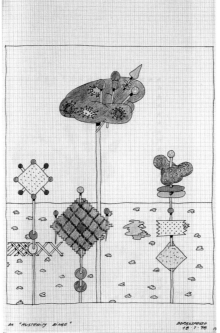
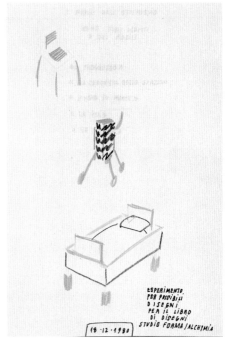

Austerity Binge, drawings
of lamps, Via Borgospesso,
January 18, 1978.
*Experiment for possible
drawings for the book
of drawings Studio
Forma/Alchymia,*
December 18, 1980.
Drawings for Oceanic lamp,
Memphis, 1981.
Drawings for Phoenix
bookstore, Memphis, Milan,
March 4, 1983.

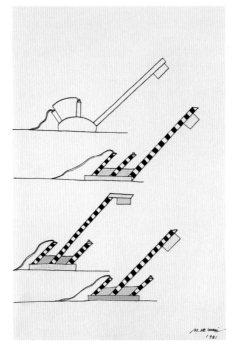
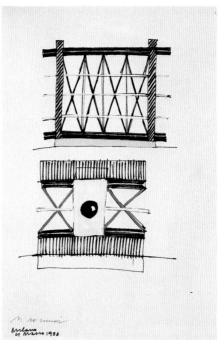

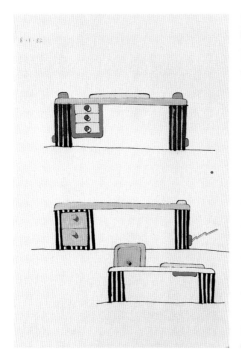

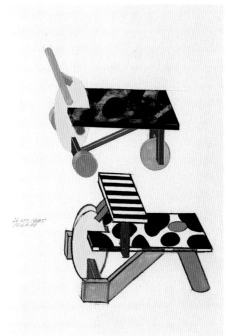

Drawings of a table,
January 8, 1982.
Drawing for Scarlet partition,
Memphis, March 30, 1985.
Drawings for a desk,
Memphis, October 26, 1985.
Drawing of lamp,
September 26, 1986.

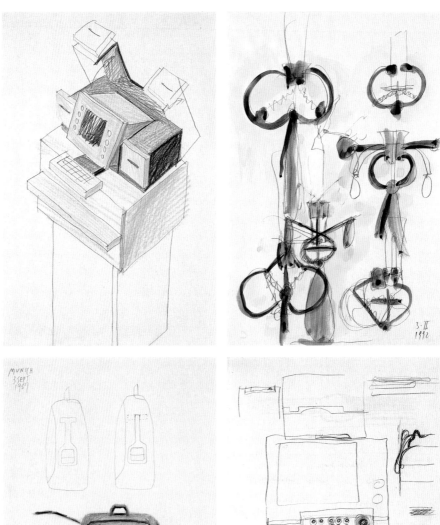

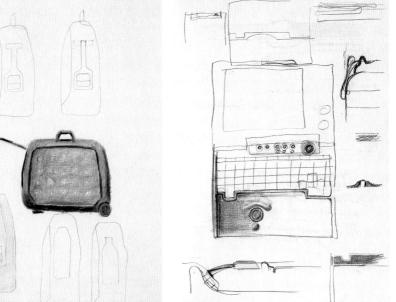

Drawing of automatic telling
machine, Olivetti, 1989.
Drawings for candlesticks,
Produzione Privata,
February 3, 1992.
Drawings for set of suitcases,
Mandarina Duck, Munich,
September 3, 1987.
Drawings of Echos 40 laptop,
Olivetti, June 16, 1993.

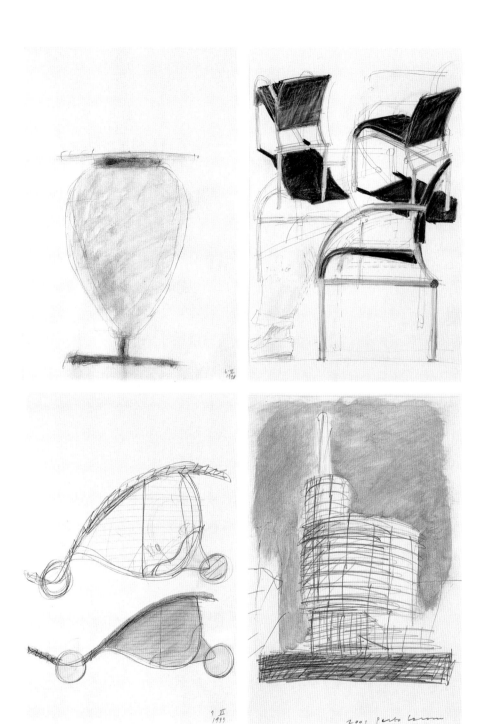

Drawing of vase for the
collection "A che cosa servono
i vasi da fiori?," Produzione
Privata, June 6, 1998.
Terrace, drawings for chair,
Bieffeplast, 1987.
Drawings for Trabiccolo
coach to navigate in Internet,
June 1, 1999.
Porto Corsini, drawing for Enel
power station, Porto Corsini
(Ravenna), 2001.

02

1973–77 radical architecture

Fiorella Bulegato

Radical architecture

1975–76
The Cavart seminars

On September 20, 1973, Michele De Lucchi made his public debut in the lobby of the 15th Milan Triennale: dressed in the uniform of a Napoleonic officer with a sign around his neck saying "Designer in General," he invoked the ethical responsibility of the designer, whose products and architecture partly define the behavior of the people who use them. He reasserted this interpretation of design as a discipline in a cyclostyled *Discorso del Designer in Generale*, document no. 8, Padua 1973, Cavart (Brombin, Checchi, De Lucchi, Tridenti): "I was interested," he declares today, "in raising questions about design as a discipline rather than political issues." This is how he was presented on the cover of *Domus* for January 1974.

When a student in Florence—one of the established centers of radical architecture in Italy—he formed a group in Padua that called itself Cavart ("quarry art"), together with Pierpaola Bortolami, Gian Pietro Brombin, Boris Pastrovicchio, Valerio Tridenti and, in the early days, Alessandro Checchi. From 1973 the group fueled lively cultural and political debate, choosing the local stone quarries as their favored venue. Their subjects ranged from ecology to the struggle against urban blight and academics in architecture, which they confronted in provocative documents, happenings, performances, films and competitions (meant as forms of democratic participation), in the quest for a more human approach to design.

"Essentially it was our way of trying to find a different kind of approach," De Lucchi explained in an interview with *Domus* for October 1999. "Cavart was closely bound up with the idea of the quarry. The group was set up to organize a competition, a competition to reclaim a trachyte quarry near Padua. We chose the name Cavart because we wanted to design, but not so much by adding one thing to another, houses to the houses, condominiums to condominiums, but by paring them away, so it

previous page
Michele De Lucchi, performance *Designer in General*, **15th Milan Triennale, September 20, 1973.**

Michele De Lucchi in the trachyte quarry in the Euganean Hills, 1973.

Cavart seminar *Designing on Yourself*, **railroad bridge at Colze (Vicenza), September 27, 1975. On the right, next to Michele De Lucchi, Gaetano Pesce and Ettore Sottsass.**

was like quarrying, the quarry was a sort of metaphor for removal. The quarry was like an extraordinary, wonderful stage, created simply by taking away the rock."

They held their first event on July 14, 1973 in the quarries of Mount Lonzina at Luvigliano (Padua) to deal with the question of how to protect and preserve the quarry as the form of a new landscape. The same concern with environmental issues turned up again, for example in the film *Design &cologico* (1973) and *Santa Ecologia Vergine Martire*, with which the group won the international competition organized by the Centro Psicografico at Maser (1975). These themes were interwoven with others, for example the freedom of the mind, which they expressed in the traveling show "Guernica: Prospect for the Twenty-First Century" (1974)—*Guernica* as the symbol of freedom violated—recreating the mural and taking it into the streets and squares. They attracted international interest by organizing the competition and seminar *Culturally Impossible Architecture* (July 7–12, 1975) in the abandoned trachyte

quarry at Santa Rosa on Mount Ricco, near Monselice (Padua). A hundred or so people took part—Italian and foreign students, artists and architects from the radical groups. "Numerous projects for housing and monuments were produced," wrote Alessandro Mendini in 1975, in an introduction to the volume *Architettura Impossibile*, republished in *Casa Vogue*. He went on: "They differed in form and intention, but all showed the same stubborn desire to dismantle the architectural models that imprison mankind within the standard patterns of everyday life." On this occasion De Lucchi, "the impresario of architecture and other pleasures" (so Adolfo Natalini described him in 1977) built a vertical house. In these years representatives of Cavart were also in contact with the Global Tool experiment, a series of teaching workshops organized by Mendini and culminating in two seminars in 1973 and 1975: De Lucchi took an active part in the second and it was there he first met Ettore Sottass. The experiments with seminars continued with *Progettarsi addosso* ("Designing on Yourself"),

held on September 27, 1975 on a derelict railroad bridge at Colze (Vicenza). Here each of the participants designed a paper shirt, reflecting (so *Domus* wrote) the fact that "I put on clothes, I will put on a house, I will want to put on a project." Sottsass also took part in this last experiment.

After a further workshop on the subject of "impossible" architecture at the Galleria Eremitani in Padua, from January 31 to February 6, 1976, this series of initiatives was brought to an end with an international get-together called *Homo Trahens*, held on June 29 on the top of Mount Morello (Florence), to which people brought dwellings that could be transported by human musclepower alone. Outstanding among these nomadic houses were a sedan chair and stilts designed by De Lucchi. Others who took part were Matteo Thun with the Kite (Free Human Flight), Marco Zanini with a Flying Carpet, Fried Rosenstock with the Ovalrotor, and Adolfo Natalini, Dodo Malagigi, Giuseppe Maggiori and Marco Zanuso Jr. They also expressed their critical attitude towards the architectural situation

in Italy with projects for the Stucky Mill in Venice at an event called *Ricordati di ricordare*, which showcased all the projects by the fathers of the Modern Movement that had failed to get built in the city, followed by the *Baleniale*, a provocative occupation of St. Mark's Square with a whale-shaped volume during the Biennale of the Visual Arts in 1976 directed by Piero Brombin.

In "Cavart continua," published in *Eco d'arte moderna* for 1976, Silvana Weiller Romanin Jacur wrote: "All this looks like gratuitous playfulness. At most it could be a fanciful game, artificially induced. But actually Cavart aimed to reawaken the vital elements in contemporary man that consumer civilization had numbed or even destroyed: the urge to rediscover ourselves and rebuild our world without taboos, without misgivings, in any way provided they are truer, traveling along untrodden paths, hyperbolic routes that will intersect the right road sooner or later, provided the eye is ready to recognize it. From the factual point of view, the man in the street gets little satisfaction out of

Cavart seminar-competition *Culturally Impossible Architecture*, Euganean Hills (Monselice, Padua), July 7–12, 1975. View inside vertical housing and of the area with installations.

this, but in ideological terms the initiative deserves careful attention because it responds to an urgent need, perhaps the only hope in the midst of the present breakdown, by appealing in good time to the ultimate forces of the creative imagination."

And in 1975, speaking of the students in Padua, Sottsass said: "If there are students, young people and others, who, apart from the mountain of laborious and unreal actions and counter-actions for homes for the homeless […], apart from the sad public conditions, sit in a field because they want to understand what is a house and what is a man in a house and what is a man with a woman in a house and what it means to work and then sleep and eat and go out and come back and get rained on and snowed on and stay out till dawn, and what it means to look at yourself aging and all for nothing […] and walking for interminable hours of your life amid monuments, buildings, banks, factories, offices and all these things, then it seems to me it's the right thing to do. […] By now architecture

no longer even means Le Corbusier or Duiker or Frank Lloyd Wright or Louis Kahn or whatever, but it means creating a wider awareness, in which the reality and the functions of the home are not just extracts or pieces or quotations of themselves […] but end up being identified with the idea of the home with a possible general design of life."

1975–76
Vertical Housing

The projects for vertical housing grew out of a dissertation titled *Vertical Architecture without Floors*, which De Lucchi presented for his degree at the school of architecture in Florence in 1975, with Adolfo Natalini as his supervisor. The ideas also drew on the seminar *Abitazione: oggetto d'uso semplice* organized by De Lucchi in December 1976 as part of the course in *Plastica Ornamentale* also held by Natalini.

"I was disturbed by the idea," De Lucchi wrote in 1978, returning to the events of two years earlier, "that there existed some rules that enabled designers belonging to the race of experts

[the reference is to an article in *Spazio e Società*, 3, 197, ed.], as specialists in improving the quality of people's lives, to present products designed exclusively to satisfy an esthetic formalism, when they were beautiful, or a scientific formalism, when they were functional […] I asked myself if there was really nothing else to be done or if it wasn't worth the trouble, before designing by these rules and unconsciously accepting them, to see if by any chance it was possible to design to different rules, new or at least more interesting and amusing.

One of the things I was most interested in understanding was what the real role of the designer ought to be […] I was terrified by the thought of the incredible power held by the people who, as institutionalized designers, planned and imposed products and so conditioned the behavior and lives of those who would use them."

Picking up on a debate that was simmering in those years, De Lucchi's approach dissolved the difference between architecture and design. He conceived the house as "an object for living in, […] one that needs to be studied, conceived and above all invented." So he suggested a new concept of inhabitability, "perhaps because inhabiting doesn't just mean living in a house […]; we inhabit our clothes, a chair, a table, a town, the world, the universe, etc." For example, he thought, we might explore original forms of behavior by devising dwellings for people compelled to live and move vertically. So he imagined nine "Tarzan houses," all variations on the prototype of the vertical house, the only one he actually built in the competition for "Culturally Impossible Architecture" organized by Cavart in July 1975 in the quarry in the Euganean Hills. Set in a tower, fitted with a single door and a window-roof giving light, the interiors were reduced to those considered necessary to survive in reasonable comfort (cooking, eating, thinking and sleeping) and assembled so as to be defined laterally but without floors. The occupant would live in it by climbing up and down and using the implements hanging from the walls—a stove, pots and pans, bathtub, table and lastly

Housing made of five stacked pyramids, 1975, model (Centre Georges Pompidou, Paris).
Housing made of tottering tower of stacked cubes, 1975, model (Centre Georges Pompidou, Paris).

Embedded housing, 1975, model (Centre Georges Pompidou, Paris).
Housing as a cube embedded by a corner, 1975, model.

a bed. By monkeying about with ropes, poles and slats, the occupant recovers the physicality of his body, "which is absent from man frustrated by Functionalism."

The version that De Lucchi constructed himself, designed for a single person, was made out of Innocenti piping; it measured 2 x 2 meters and was 10 meters high. He covered it with ordinary wire netting. "Removing the floors means disrupting not just space but the ways space is used." The other structures, left at the stage of models, made on a scale of 1:10, were superimposed pyramids, cubes stacked like a spinal column, parallelepipeds, convergent pyramids, concentric pyramids, or pyramids embedded by their summits directly in the ground or set one on top of the other, in all cases essentially vertical.

In 1980, writing in *Modo* Mendini commented: "Michele at any rate grasped the essential point: the fact that space is minimal does not mean that the quality of life has to be minimal." At present some models are preserved at the Centre Georges Pompidou in Paris.

1975–77
Mobile Architecture

De Lucchi presented two projects at the free international gathering called *Homo Trahens*, held on top of Mount Morello near Florence in June 1976: one was a set of fully furnished stilts and the other a sedan chair.

The event was announced with a program issued by the Cavart group for the design of forms of traveling dwellings, which were to be transported, lifted, dragged or propelled by systems of human traction. The designers were required to travel the last leg of the journey up the mountainside carrying their own living spaces, assembled or ready for assembly, using human musclepower alone. This was one of the responses to the topics of discussion fostered by Cavart, which included a critique of consumerism, the disquiet caused by the current spate of urban development and the responsibility of the designer, guilty of widening the gap between people and architecture: "Why don't people understand architecture or take an interest in it?" wrote De Lucchi

Vertical housing, 1975, model.

Drawings of housing in the form
of stacked and zig-zagging
cubes, 1975.
Interior of embedded housing,
1975, model.

in 1977. "Because there is nothing pleasant, fascinating or striking about architecture. [...] And then architecture is complicated nowadays, made up of a lot of different things: technology, space, culture, form, ideology, etc. and Cavart suggests making it 'simpler,' by 'simply' proposing its 'simplification.'"

As one way of redressing the balance and providing new stimuli for individual creativity and design, it was felt to be essential to experiment with original forms of architectural behavior, for example by reinventing archaic modes of life such as nomadism. The mobile home, which embodies the idea of a respectful relationship between the environment and the human construct, was seen by the "Cavartisti" as a vital part of the individual. They shaped them as small untraditional dwellings and the mountain was studded with numerous homes, self-built, made of different materials in different forms, based on different conceptions, with different uses and functioning in different ways.

Following out this line of thought, we can see De Lucchi's stilts as a home for someone who wants to live six feet above the ground. Made out of two poles with footrests, they were equipped with a trestle back, hooks, shelves, a sturdy canvas seat, and an umbrella to keep off sun and rain. The design meant the stilts were stable even when he stopped walking so he could sit down, eat or even snooze.

The sedan chair was "a small non-technological living cell," he stated in 1977, "an object of design that served as a dwelling." It measured 2 x 1 x 2.3 meters and contained all the most commonly used spaces of a house. It had a frame made out of eight vertical load-bearing wooden struts and two thicker horizontal poles, which rested on the shoulders of eight bearers when it was being carried. It was bolted together and braced for rigidity. It had a "ground floor" with a chair, set in the middle to balance the weight, with a table in front, hinged for easier access; this formed the study. Behind the chair was a second shelf, level with the backrest. The utensils for preparing food could be placed on this, though it was advisable to do the cooking outside. On the

Fully furnished stilts, Cavart international gathering *Homo Trahens*, summit of Mount Morello (Florence), June 29, 1976.

Sedan chair, Cavart
international gathering
Homo Trahens, summit
of Mount Morello (Florence),
June 29, 1976.

"upper floor," under the roof, there was a bed. The sedan chair had a pitched roof and was lined with dark-red curtains, arranged so as to allow the occupant to look outside in all directions. "There's an obvious analogy with Zanuso's 'emergency housing,' Joe Colombo's dwelling cell, or Alberto Rosselli's accordion house," De Lucchi wrote in 1977. "In these models, technology predominates; everything is devised in terms of hair-breadth solutions: the use of a container as a house for Zanuso and the Colombo's super-equipped cube. But this was a very different kettle of fish!"

Both the designs were built in collaboration with Sem.Pre, a seminar organized by De Lucchi as part of the course in *Plastica Ornamentale* held in Florence in 1976. The seminar was titled "Coercion by Project Premeditation–Seminar for the design, construction and documentation of coercive physical situations," later abbreviated to Seminar of Premeditation and then simply Sem.Pre, with the motto *L'architettura è sem.pre architettura* ("architecture is always architecture").

"In practice," commented the architect, writing in *L'Eco d'Arte Moderna* in 1977, "I replaced the word 'design' with the word 'premeditation,' in the sense that all our actions grow out of a process of pre-judging, pre-deciding, pre-seeing […] Living means choosing, means planning, and if life is a unique personal and absolutely individual thing, anyone who designs for others chooses for others, practically lives for others. And this absurd task is entrusted to architects."

The project called The Wall formed part of this same research into reductive housing: it was a folding screen-house, built by De Lucchi in 1977 as the subject of a film he made. It was likewise a wooden structure bolted together and lined with roll-up curtains. It had fold-out floors and chairs which opened out when it was placed on the ground. When it was closed again, it folded up into a thick wall.

Bibliography: Gruppo Cavart, "I designer in penitenza," in *Progettare In più*, II, 10, n.d., pp. 1–4; AA.VV., *Architettura impossibile*, Florence

1975; "Alla 'Cappella,'" in *Il Piccolo*, May 8, 1974; "Architetture impossibili," in *Domus*, 552, November, 1975, p. 47; "L'arte va in cava," in *Il Gazzettino*, July 8, 1975; A. Branzi, "Global Tools scuola di non-architettura," in *Casabella*, 397, 1975, pp. 17–18; "Cava trasformata in Galleria di 'architetture impossibili,'" in *Il Gazzettino*, July 13, 1975; "Una città: ipotesi durata una settimana," in *Casabella*, 406, 1975, p. 57; "Concorso e seminario di architetture culturalmente impossibili," in *Casabella*, 402, 1975, p. 59; A.d.A., "Architettura culturalmente impossibile," in *che*, 3–4, October, 1975, pp. 32–33; M. De Lucchi, *Storia continuata ad essere interpretata per evitare di rifiutare*, film, 1975; A. Galderisi, "Pochi padovani al seminario 'architetture impossibili,'" in *Il Gazzettino*, July 24, 1975; *Impossible Architecture*, in "Building Design," October 17, 1975, p. 17; "Itinerario di Guernica," in *Casabella*, 406, 1975, pp. 10–12; A. Mendini, "La settimana di una città utopia," in *Casa Vogue*, 51, November, 1975; "Una mostra delle 'architetture impossibili,'" in *Il Gazzettino*, 22 July 1975; "Il pretesto del Mulino Stucky," in *l'Unità*, September 23, 1975; E. Sottsass, "Gli studenti di Padova," in Spettacolo e Società, October 1975; "L'architettura impossibile," in *Paese Sera*, February 24, 1976; S.W., "L'esplorazione sul "territorio corpo" di Cavart alla 'Steven,'" in *Il Gazzettino*, June 3, 1975; S.W.R.J., "La ricerca di Cavart," in suppl. to *Eco d'arte moderna*, 6–7, June–July, 1975, pp. I, IV; S. Weiller R.J., "La ricerca di Cavart," in *Foglio Libero*, suppl. to *Eco d'arte moderna*, 6–7, June–July 1975, pp. I, IV; B. Zevi, "Un magnifico tugurio," in *L'Espresso*, September 7, 1975, pp. 66–67; "Architettura impossibile," in *Domus* 554, January, 1976, p. 54; "L'architettura 'radicale,'" in *7 giorni Veneto*, VI, 7, February 19, 1976, pp. 19–20; "La Baleniale di Cavart," in *Eco d'arte moderna*, 10–11, October–November, 1976, p. 7; "Cavart, Seminari 'Impossible Architecture,'" in *Japan Interior Design*, 203, February, 1976, pp. 61–65; P.C., "Forme abitative portatili," in *Casa Vogue*, 58, June, 1976; M. De Lucchi, *Homo Trahens*, film, 1976; M. De Lucchi, *La portantina, film*, 1976; M. De Lucchi, "Raduno internazionale 'Homo Trahens'/Cavart," in *Parametro*, 47, June, 1976; M. De Lucchi, *I trampoli*, film, 1976; "'Homo Trahens' ovvero un festival d'architettura," in *Casa Vogue*, 62, October, 1976, p. 151; Michele De Lucchi, "Homo Trahens," in *Japan Interior Design*, 213, December, 1976; "Il Mattone di Cenere. Cerchiamoci un riparo d'architettura," in *Eco d'arte moderna* 12, December, 1976, p. 27; F.D. Mondello, "Architetture impossibili. Risposte possibili," in *Casabella*, 411, 1976, pp. 8–9; "Raduno internazionale 'Homo Trahens,'" in *Casabella*, 412, 1976, p. 51; S. Weiller R.J., "Cavart continua," in *Eco d'arte moderna*, 6, June, 1976, pp. 6–7; S. Weiller R.J., "Padova: l'azione di Cavart," in *Eco d'arte moderna*, January, 1976, pp. 4–5; "Michele De Lucchi," in *Space Design*, 7912, pp. 43–58; M. De Lucchi (for the Cavart Group), "Homo Trahens," in *fascicolo n. 4*, II, September, 1977, p. 20; M. De Lucchi, *Il muro*, film, 1977; "Michele De Lucchi," in *SD*, 12, December 1977, p. 58; B. Orlandoni and G. Vallino, *Dalla città al cucchiaio*, Turin 1977; "La portantina abitabile di Michele De Lucchi," in *Modo*, 3, September–October, 1977, p. 72; "Raduno internazionale 'Homo Trahens.'" *Cavart*, Florence 1977; M. De Lucchi, *Progetti di abitazioni verticali. Nuovi comportamenti all'interno della casa*, P. Bulletti (ed.) 1978; A. Mendini, "Abitazioni verticali," in *Modo*, 31, July–August, 1980, p. 13; P. Pavan, "Cavart: per una pratica dell'effimero," in *Galileo*, 87, January, 1997, pp. 24–27; "Laboratorio Aperto (Offenes Laboratorium)," in *Radical Architecture*, Museum für Angewandte Kunst, Cologne, 2000, p. 15; AA.VV., *Architettura radicale*, exhibition catalogue, Institut d'art contemporain, Villeurbanne 2001, esp. pp. 230–31.

The wall, hinged screen-house for the film by Michele De Lucchi, *The Wall*, 1977.

03

1978–89 the Memphis years

Fiorella Bulegato

domus

MONTHLY MAGAZINE OF ARCHITECTURE, DESIGN, ART

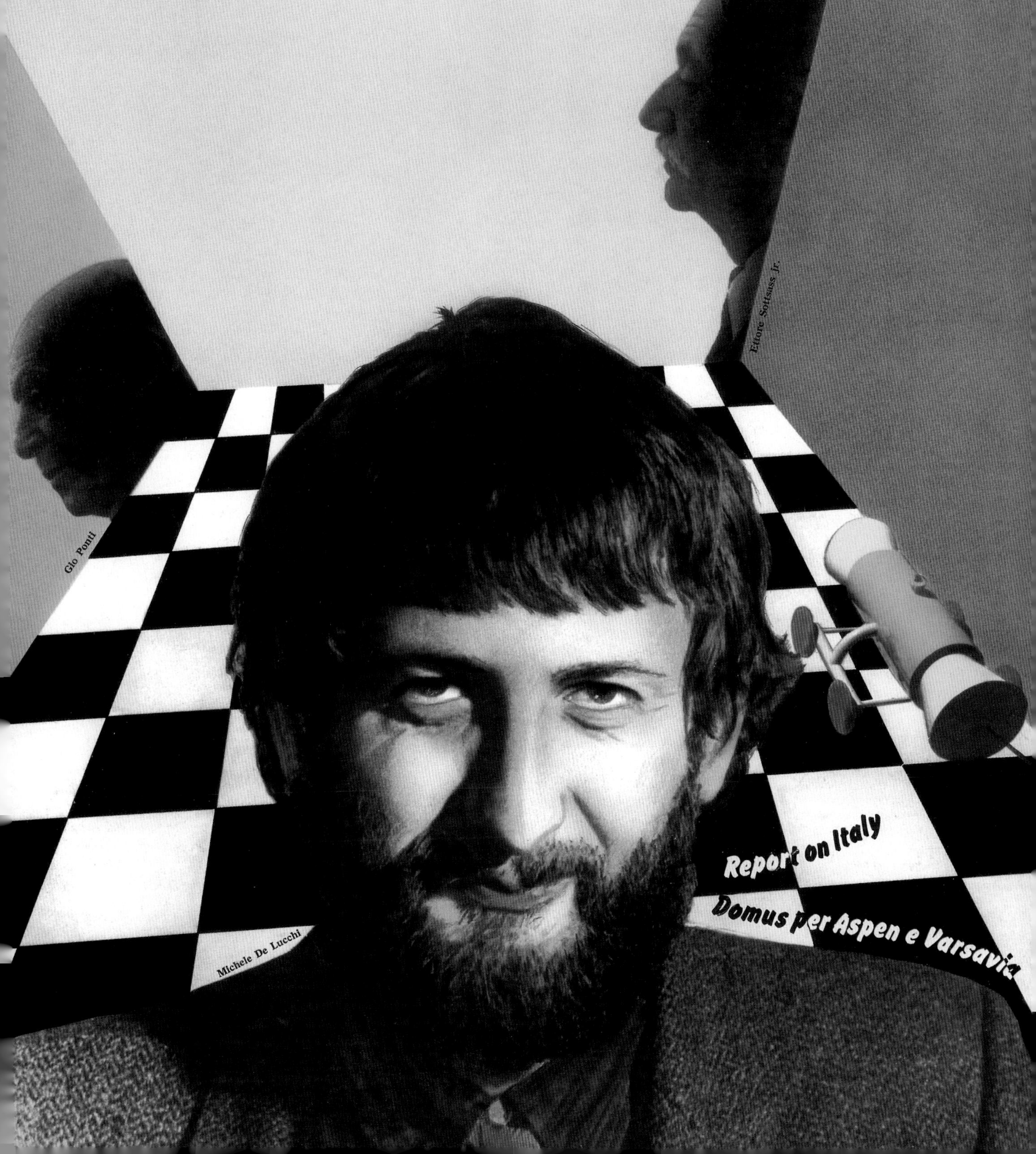

Ettore Sottsass, Jr.

Gio Ponti

Michele De Lucchi

Report on Italy

Domus per Aspen e Varsavia

Alchymia

1978
lamp
La Spaziale
production: 1980

1978
lamp
Sinerpica
production: 1979
(Alchymia, until 1992;
Belux, until 2000;
Vitra Design Museum)

1979
wall tiles
I Peli
prototype

1979
lamp
Sinvola
production: 1979

1979
rug
Sputnik
prototype

De Lucchi joined the Alchymia group in 1977, when he moved from Florence to Milan and began to work in product design. Earlier, in 1976, while he was still commuting between the two cities, he had been involved by Andrea Branzi and Paola Navone in working for Centrokappa. He designed a section of the exhibition on "Italian Design in the 50s," which ran from September 26 to October 30 at Noviglio (Milan) on Centrokappa's own premises. The same premises also housed the magazine *Modo*, founded the year before. Edited by Alessandro Mendini, it began to publish articles by De Lucchi in its January–February 1978 issue. De Lucchi was attracted to the Studio Alchymia by its cultural creativity and the experimental-laboratory approach typical of all its projects in this period. In 1978, for example, he coordinated the catalogue for the 1976 exhibition and an encounter with the same title. Founded by Sandro Guerriero in 1976 as a graphic design firm and a "laboratory of decoration," it immediately attracted the interest of Ettore Sottsass, Alessandro Mendini and Andrea Branzi. De Lucchi followed in the footsteps of these designers, his friends and "masters," driven by an urge to pass

from inventing utopias to designing concrete objects. Alchymia was set up as an experimental laboratory for one-off objects, hand-made or produced in small runs, a sort of manufacturing workshop: but it was enough to enable him to make the "leap between things only thought about or drawn, and these things that we actually made and could eventually even be bought," as De Lucchi later recalled. Underlying all this there was always an anti-rationalist impulse: industrial production failed to provide the right soil for research into design, because high technology, mass production and the dictates of the market denied freedom of thought and the scope to transform things as individuals. Nothing should ever seem too difficult: this conviction could enable design to break out of the impasse it had gotten into. Alchymia relied on color, decoration, the creation of new images and significances, but also, provocatively, on the revival of the banal, of objects not designed but omnipresent. It embraced the style of comic books, toys, animated cartoons, pop art. The new ideas developed by the broad and very mixed group of young designers (with Paola Navone, Ufo, Trix and Robert Haussmann, Daniela Puppa and Franco Raggi all arriving in the following months) were presented in annual "collections," like the creations of fashion houses: two were produced, titled "Bau.haus I" (1979) and "Bau.haus II" (1980).

For these two presentations De Lucchi designed five objects: the Sinerpica, Sinvola and La Spaziale lamps, the Sputnik rug and I Peli wall tiles. Only the first of them actually went into production (with the Swiss firm Belux in 1985); a few copies were produced of the other lamps, while the rug and the tiles were one-off pieces. All the same, these objects revealed De Lucchi's gifts as a designer to critics and the press, and they caused something of a stir. The phrase "gentle design" was used, because—to paraphrase Sibylle Kicherer—they evoke a placid, serene world, because they combat the idea of violent and aggressive objects, because they recount stories and dreams. Sinerpica (1978) is a plant growing in a pot: the bulb blooms on a stem made from a colored metal tube coiled around a support, both embedded in a cylindrical base. Sinvola (1979) is a captive cloud: the stem of the lamp (designed in both floor and table versions) rises through a cushion made of tartan fabric and stuck all over with pins. La Spaziale (1978) plays with mirrors: a half-sphere of gleaming metal supports the conical lampshade and a

mirror on an adjustable arm, ready to pursue and reflect the light. The surfaces of the Sputnik rug (1979) and I Peli tiles (1979) are studded with presences: small space ships on the former, while the latter have short colored, wavy lines that suggest hairs (peli in Italian), or worms, or the tails of mice. With their cheerful, evocative images, simple primary forms and pastel colors, they are already examples of that quest for friendly technology typical of all De Lucchi's later work as a designer.

His work for Alchymia lasted about three years. In 1980, after the important exhibition presented at the Design Forum in Linz (Austria), De Lucchi and Sottsass decided to leave and set up Memphis. But those were very busy, creative years: while he was at Alchymia he began to design Girmi electrical appliances and the hi-fi sets published in Domus, made contact with Olivetti (1979, again through Sottsass), where he was responsible for Synthesis systems furniture, frequented the newly formed firm of Sottsass Associati (set up in 1980), and opened his own firm next door, in Via Borgonuovo 9.

Bibliography: "Studio Alchymia salone del mobile," in La Repubblica, September 23, 1978, p. 13, insert; "Luce & colore," in Brava, October, 1979, p. 175; "Ornamento come delitto," in Casa Vogue, 93, April, 1979; D. Puppa and L. Prandi (eds.), "Scheda prodotto," in Modo, 18, April, 1979, p. 63; B. Radice and F. Raggi, "Avant-garde furniture: activities of Studio Alchymia," in Japan Interior Design, 249, December, 1979, pp. 19–41; F. Alinovi, "Casa di bambola," in Bolaffi, 95, February, 1980, pp. 16–18; "Il bagno: spugna e plastica arcobaleno," in Grazia, September 7, 1980, p. 76; R. Barilli, "Arredo alchemico," in Domus, 607, June, 1980, pp. 33–35, esp. p. 33; C. Donà, "Un designer gentile," in Zoom, 1980, 2, pp. 10–11; J. Kron, "Furniture and Anarchy," in Home Life, suppl. to The Washington Star, January 20, 1980, pp. 10–13; "Pezzi facili, pezzi insoliti," in Donna, 8, November, 1980, pp. 162–63; "La lampada," in Quaderni di Domus, 1, Milan 1984, scheda 37; K. Sato, Alchimia, Japan 1985, p. 24; "Lampe Sinerpica," in La collection de design du Centre Georges Pompidou, Paris 2001, p. 144.

Sketch for a poster of the exhibition, drawing for the exhibition of the Alchymia Bau.haus I collection, June 20, 1979.

La Spaziale lamp, Alchymia, 1978.
Sinerpica lamp, Alchymia, 1978.
I Peli tiles, Alchymia, 1979, prototype.
Sputnik carpet, Alchymia, 1979, prototype.

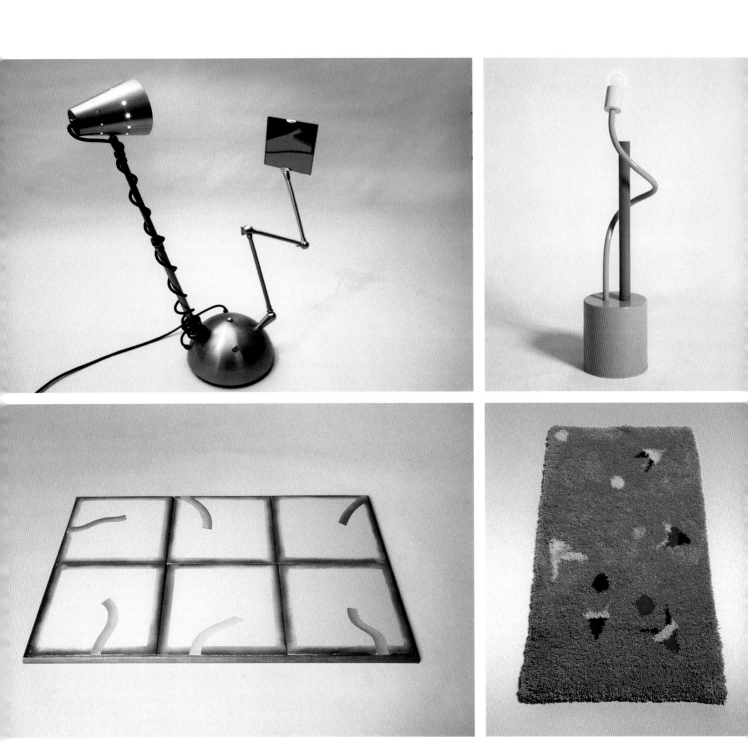

Models of Girmi electrical appliances and designs of hi-fi sets

As part of his studies of "classic" furnishings, which he was conducting with the rest of the team at Alchymia, in 1979 De Lucchi explored electrical appliances, using the same expressive language and with the same conceptual energy. "All utilitarian objects, down to household goods," he stated in *Zoom* in 1980, "now have a high-tech image [...] Everything is designed to bring out the technical qualities of an industrial product. The more ventilation grids, switches, flashing lights, and rounded corners a product has, the more 'attractive' it is said to be. So a gentle, refined woman is forced to dry her hair using an object that looks more like a laser gun than a hairdryer." The dominance of technology imposed opaque and dreary functional objects, largely the result of Japanese- or German-style design. De Lucchi wanted at least to make a dent in this image. "The idea was to confer a cheerful, human and relaxed image on technology and the result

was the use of certain shapes and colors for these objects," he told Giampiero Bosoni in 1988. "And I wanted to eliminate the fear, the awe, that often accompanies technology [...] I wanted to show that it is possible to create technologically perfect objects using forms that are quite different from the usual kind. I wanted to show they had other faces."

The chance to design and exhibit these inventions to a wider public came in 1980, when he was invited to participate, together with other architects under thirty-five, in the section *The Decorated Home* at the 16th Triennale in Milan. The subject was paralleled by an international competition announced at the same time by the Triennale and similarly open to designers under thirty-five, titled *The Interior after the Form of the Useful*. Construction of the painted wooded models was financed by Girmi, a firm based in Omegna (Novara), which specialized in making small electric appliances, but never put De Lucchi's designs into production. De Lucchi exhibited a wide range of appliances (hair-dryer, vacuum-cleaner, kettle, iron, coffee

Portable radio cassettes and *Radio cassettes*, drawings of hi-fi sets, February 1, 1981.

Image for Domus with kitchen in elevations. Proposal 2 Domus, February 26, 1980.
Room with home appliances, Milan, June 7, 1979.

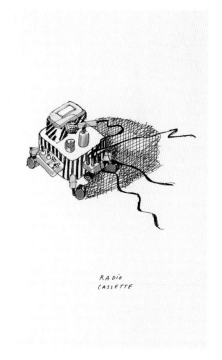

grinder, gas lighter, blender, insecticide vaporizer, stove, toaster and fan), created by combining a few geometrically simple pieces colored pink, blue, yellow, green and red. He chose delicate color schemes for highly innovative objects, playful as toys, designed to be "friendly" to the user.

The same effort to make technology look fresh and reassuring, making the relationship between people and machines more human, has been a feature of all his work, especially his long partnership, begun in 1979, with Olivetti, where he was brought in by Ettore Sottsass. His designs for Girmi were widely covered in the press, and not just specialist magazines. They boosted his reputation also because of the professional contacts that followed. One of them was the interest in his projects expressed by Ernesto Gismondi, owner of Artemide, which led to a collaboration that was to prove long-lived. The interest shown by the press—in 1978 De Lucchi began to contribute to *Modo* and two years later *Casa Vogue*—enabled him to publish other ideas on the subject that increased

the pool of objects, going beyond home appliances. For example, in 1980 he imagined a whole kitchen interior (*Domus*, May), a car designed for women (*Donna*, November), office interiors and above all, in 1981, he designed a series of hi-fi sets (again in *Domus*, May).

In the article that accompanied his designs, Francesca Alinovi commented: "Portable or tabletop cassette players, radios, stereo headphones and TV sets for lovely music, and lovely images designed for a lovely life of pleasure, made up of little, everyday domestic pleasures: this is Michele De Lucchi's latest technological fantasy [...] An extraordinary example of technological tailoring, providing physical garments for the invisible electronic soul." These designs explored a field that paralleled the beginnings of Memphis adventure, in which De Lucchi explored the value of decoration, in this case applied to the surfaces of dynamic and functional products. At a time when the working parts of machines were rapidly being miniaturized, designers had to find ways to enhance the products' perceptual-sensory qualities for the user. "It seems to me

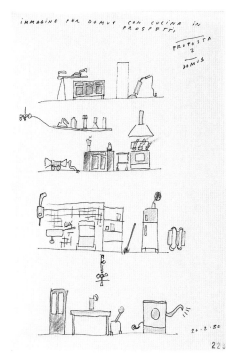

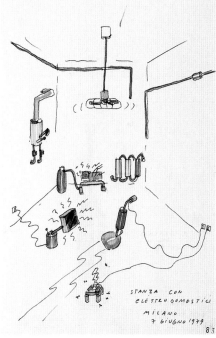

that the image of the object can now be open to a broader range of influences," the designer stated at a conference in Palermo in 1983. "This means it should allow itself to be more widely affected by behavior, fashion, ideas and culture." The main bodies of these audio-visual devices were all covered with a black-and-white pattern, to which soft volumes and stems were attached, all of different colors, forming buttons, control panels, microphones, aerials, feet, and so forth. A similar figurative vocabulary reappeared in the series of projects for Fiorucci stores designed in partnership with Sottsass from 1981 to 1983.

Bibliography: "The Possibilities of Michele De Lucchi," in *Manhattan Catalogue*, 16, September, n.d.; *L'ambiente cucina*, 16, May–June, 1980, p. 79; R. Barilli, "Triennale fantasy," in *L'Espresso*, 3, January 20, 1980, p. 99; A. Branzi, "Triennale anno zero," in *Domus*, 604, March, 1980, pp. 36–38; G. Contessi, "L'istituzione negata," in *Modo*, 27, March, 1980, pp. 28–32, esp. p. 29; C. Donà, "Un designer gentile," in *Zoom*, 2, 1980, pp. 10–11; M. De Lucchi, "Il corpo del televisore," in *Donna*, 6, September, 1980; "La Girmi alla Triennale," in *Articoli casalinghi*, Janaury–February, 1980, pp. 58, 65; "Girmi alla Triennale di Milano," in *Eva Express*, 28 February 1980; "Girmi alla Triennale di Milano," in *Gioia*, March 10, 1980, p. 202; "Interni alla XVI Triennale," in *Interni*, 298, March, 1980, pp. 64–66; "Italien: Michele De Lucchi-Futuristich," in *Vogue Deutsch*, 12, December, 1980, pp. 106–07; "Michele De Lucchi, 0000 Le nuove cucine," in *Domus*, 606, May, 1980, p. 55; B. Radice, "L'auto per la donna: sogno e realtà," in *Donna*, 8, November, 1980, pp. 170–71, and "Una Triennale-laboratorio," in *Casa Vogue*, 104, March, 1980, pp. 182–87, esp. pp. 186–87; F. Alinovi, "Hi-Fi secondo Michele De Lucchi," in *Domus*, 617, May, 1981, pp. 38–39; "Haushaltsgerate," in *md*, 12, December, 1981, p. 80; G. Riccio, "Quelli dopo i santoni," in *Scena*, VI, 6–7, June–July, 1981, pp. 58–59; P. Sparke, "De Lucchi designs: toys for adults," in *Industrial Design*, November–December 1981, pp. 15, 57; Michele De Lucchi. "Die freundlichen Haushaltsgeräte," in *Provokationen Design aus Italien*, exhibition catalogue, Deutscher Werkbund Niedersachsen und Bremen, Hanover 1982, pp. 209–17; M. Ghermandi, "Michele De Lucchi," in *Juliette*, 12, June–October, 1983, p. 31; P. Sparke, *Electrical Appliances*, Unwin Hyman, London 1987, p. 57; G. Bosoni, F.G. Confalonieri, *Paesaggio del design italiano 1972–1988*, Milan 1988, pp. 109–11; M. De Lucchi, "Nuovi elementi nel progetto dell'oggetto. Design primario," in A. Cannella (ed.), *ADS. Design per lo sviluppo. Atti del corso di conferenze per studenti di architettura*, Palermo, December 13, 1982–May 31, 1983, Florence 1988, pp. 44–55; R.-P. Baacke, U. Brandes, M. Erlhoff, *Design als Gegenstand*, Berlin 1993, pp. 118–19.

Home appliances, Girmi, 1979, models exhibited in *The Decorated House* section, 16th Milan Triennale, 1980. Toaster, vacuum cleaner, iron, electric heater.

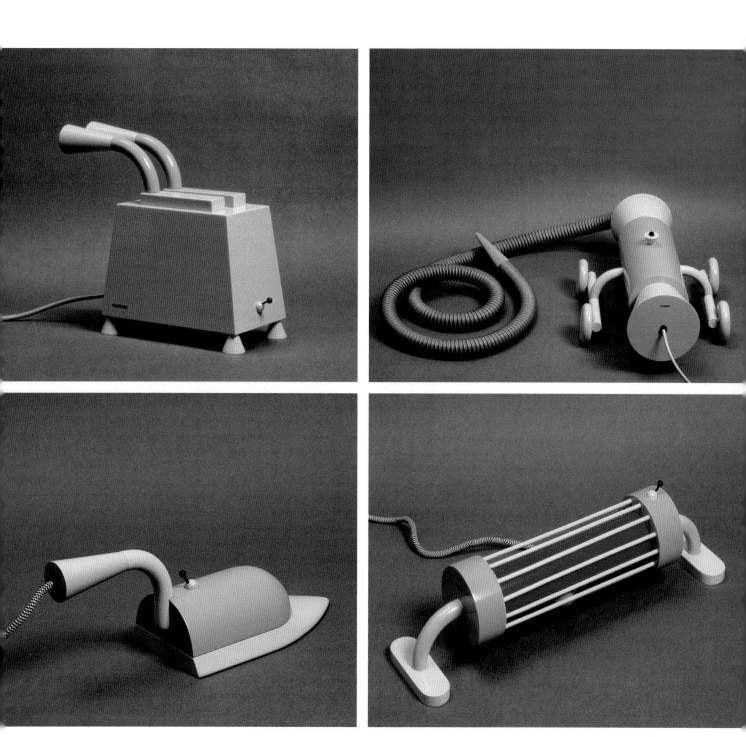

Memphis

"It is as, if after the ten years of stories, metaphors, theories and conceptualizations of the radical period," said De Lucchi in a recent interview, "all at once architects felt the urge to draw, color, decorate, in short to design concretely." In this transition from the abstract to the tangible, in the late seventies and all through the eighties, product design gave many radical architects scope for exploring their ideas. The result was the New Design. De Lucchi, who had arrived in Milan in 1977, conducted his first concrete experiments in the pieces he designed for the Alchymia exhibitions, his prototypes of home appliances for Girmi, his ideas for hi-fi sets and the Tarkin chair, a prototype realized in 1979 by Thema in Padua (a firm owned by Gastone Rinaldi). In 1980 the Forum Design in Linz (Austria), an international exhibition that ran from June to October, organized by the local faculty of arts and design, "was the event that revealed," so he recalls, "that the roads between Mendini and Sottsass were diversifying,

especially when it came to banal design, which was launched here, and the interpretation of the significance of decoration."
In June 1980 Sottsass summed up his work in the two years with Alchymia: "I designed some furniture—in the *Catalogue for Decorative Furniture in Modern Style*—which [...] represented the final moment (to date) of thoughts and actions, solitary or shared with friends, that had been fermenting for at least ten years (perhaps fifteen). For the sake of a name, we used to call it radical design or sometimes 'counter-design,' or other things like that. Of course the furniture I designed represented an attempt to get out of or rather an attempt to get back into the center of the problem [...] carrying forward everything that had happened and even everything that had failed to happen. I again tried to draw products, things, furniture and have them constructed. I made them big and heavy, set on plinths and bases [...] They didn't fit in anywhere and didn't match anything [...] They just stood alone like a monument in a town square [...] They were also decorated."

**Page of diary
October 11–22, 1982.
Page of diary September
5–11, 1983.**

The Memphis group in the Ring of Masanori Umeda, 1981. From the left: Aldo Cibic, Andrea Branzi, Michele De Lucchi, Marco Zanini, Nathalie Du Pasquier, George Sowden, Matteo Thun, Martine Bedin and Ettore Sottsass.

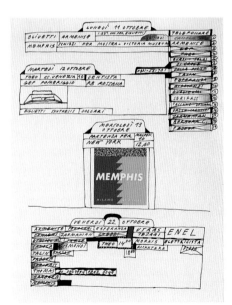 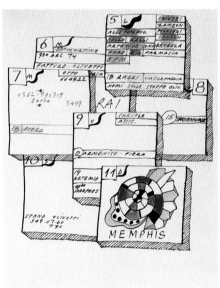

Ettore Sottsass left Alchymia in the autumn of that year; De Lucchi followed him and almost immediately they begin to create Memphis.

The name Memphis appeared for the first time at the top of a page in one of De Lucchi's notebooks dated November 12, 1980. Also present at the meetings that gave birth to the movement were Barbara Radice, Marco Zanini, Aldo Cibic, Matteo Thun and Martine Bedin; a few months later they were joined by George Sowden and Nathalie Du Pasquier. "Memphis was born in the winter of '80–'81 in the heads of a group of architects and Milanese designers," recalls Barbara Radice in *Memphis* (1984). "They felt an urgent need to invent a new way of designing, conceiving other interiors, imagining other lives. The idea didn't come all at once. They were projects the designers had been nursing for some time." Fueling the legend about the inspiration for the name, she states: "It was at Sottsass's. The music on the record-player was Bob Dylan singing *Stuck inside of Mobile with the Memphis Blues Again* and since no one bothered to change the disk, Dylan continued to yell, 'the Memphis blues again' until Sottsass said 'OK, let's call it Memphis.'"

The group's first exhibition was held in Milan (timed to coincide with the Furniture Show) on September 18, 1981 at the Arc '74 showroom run by Mario and Brunella Godani. The display presented fifty-seven objects with the exhibit designed by De Lucchi, who went on to design all the other exhibitions held by the group.

The other exhibitors—apart from the youngsters working in Sottsass's bottega—included architects and well-known designers from all parts of the world, among them Andrea Branzi, Hans Hollein, Arata Isozaki, Michael Graves, Javier Mariscal, Masanori Umeda, Shiro Kuramata. They named their pieces after hotels around the world to underscore the idea that Memphis was meant to be an international and multicultural experience, rather like finding yourself in a hotel in some part of the world with the same name. Apart from Mario and Brunella Giordani, the partners in the firm founded in June 1981 were Renzo Brugola, the owner of a sawmill with which Sottsass had worked when he was with Poltronova, Fausto Celati, another craftsman and small manufacturer, and Ernesto Gismondi, the owner of Artemide.

"Memphis […] was a real breakthrough," stated Gismondi in the late eighties, in an interview on a TV program called *Lezioni di Design*, "a new departure, because we moved from a panorama of uniform, grey, rectangular furniture, very Germanic, say, hence from austere design that had actually become rather obsessive, to completely new ideas. The Memphis team […] broke the mold. They said color was an essential part of life, that whatever we see in the different countries we visit […], whatever is attractive, we can bring it home, provided we use our discernment and make sure a product is worth becoming part of our world. Then add the revolution in form. Forget about the traditional table with four legs: they invented tables with three impossible legs […] At the wonderful opening in September 1981, in Corso Europa, the whole street was thronged, the police came, over two thousand young people were blocking the traffic to see the show."

This new approach to design revealed the widespread expectancy and the desire for change, the urge to create a new expressive language, cutting free from the Functionalist matrix and also the radical esthetic that had earlier sought to smash that tradition.

The innovations affected the functions of objects as well as materials, patterns and colors. Furniture, ceramics, glassware, textiles, laminates and lamps all formed part of the Memphis collections down to 1987, when the last show was held. They focused on aspects of composition, the visual and figurative impact. Designed for specific functions, these items were conceived as isolated pieces, not coordinated but versatile and multifunctional, suited to any setting. They embodied Sottsass's theory that when it comes to furniture, sculptural and figurative qualities are more important than functional ones, their presence in an interior counts for more than their actual functions.

With few exceptions, such as Karl Lagerfeld's house in Monte Carlo, the products were not intended to create a "Memphis home," though De Lucchi today confesses: "We liked to think that, like the Wiener Werkstätte and other early-twentieth century movements, we might succeed in identifying a style to represent the world at this precise historical point and design everything 'from the spoon to the city,' but we failed to achieve this because we were never guided by a coherent, analytic set of ideas, our approach was emotional, provocative, more against than for anything."

When it came to production, Memphis was a group of designers and businesses and it established a special relationship with industry. Aware of the Italian situation, made up of small industries, overgrown craft workshops, it initially looked for a cultured craftsman who wanted a role in the production of contemporary designer objects. When Gismondi stepped in, becoming the firm's president and major shareholder, it almost immediately acquired a different scale in production, marketing and communication. Yet its products all had an up-market image, and prices and production runs were always tiny. The firm's working relationship with Abet Print proved important. It gravitated around Francesco Comoglio and Guido Jannon, and had begun with designs for Alchymia. New ideas were produced for laminates; various patterns used for furniture often went into series production, until "at a certain point the design of the pattern," explained De Lucchi, "became independent of the object and we used to design a new series every year."

Laminates lent themselves to the group's provocations. "I chose textures from those cultural zones [...] that had been abandoned by kitsch [...], a sort of no man's land," wrote Sottsass of his patterns for laminates and more generally the choice of materials. "I chose textures like the grit floors in the lavatories of subways in the world's big city's or like the stripes on wire fencing in outer-city suburbs, or like the blotting paper in ministerial and police ledgers, and then I chose colors like those of the chairs in the milk-shop near my home [...] and then I chose corrugated iron from the municipal tram depots [...] I chose layers of rubber from airport floors [...] I also chose the galvanized metal used for electrics that are normally concealed." The design of fabrics occupied De Lucchi during his whole period with Memphis: "Besides doing the working drawings from Sottsass's sketches," he says, I drew geometrical patterns inspired by punk imagery and contrasted 'hard' black-and-white patterns with 'winsome' pastel colors. We did similar operations on fabrics, ties, linen."

Color and decoration thus acquired a purposeful function in studies of the role of the surface, as well as in "collages and unusual combinations of different materials, both elegant and simple," explained Barbara Radice in 1981, "such as wood, plastic, lacquers, brass, mirrors, aluminum, fabrics and the layering of rough and smooth, soft textures and sharp edges, plain and patterned surfaces, acid colors and pastel colors: these were all so many tiny electric shocks that stung, teased and soothed the numbed cells of our senses."

The success with the international press, not just specialist magazines, was almost immediate. Memphis products were rapidly acquired by museums like the Philadelphia Museum of Art and London's Victoria & Albert—which also hosted one of their exhibitions in 1982—as well as dealers and collectors. Their exhibitions toured the most important cities. In September 1985, for example, Bloomingdales in New York presented an exhibition ("Here's Italy"), and in 1983 the *Chicago Tribune* described Memphis like this: "It has been called vibrant, bold, funny, provocative, antimodernist, fantastic, crazy, kinky, vital, insulting, radical, surreal, pop, punk, funk, new wave, eccentric and bizarre. But Memphis [...] is perhaps best described, in a word, by stating what it is not. It is not boring."

The pieces De Lucchi designed for Memphis, about thirty of those produced, testify precisely to this urge "to create plastic representations, directly perceptible to the senses," as he told *La Mia Casa* in 1985, "images with which you can establish an intense, loving relationship, sometimes ironic, often playful. I'd like my objects to give people pleasure. My ideal was to be the Spielberg of design, someone who can communicate with big and little, young and old, scholars and dunces, progressives and conservatives, and make everyone happy, quite simply, without over-intellectual complications. I'd like to work so that design becomes a driving force, instead of having to dawdle along behind the figurative arts [...] I'd like to make the message of Memphis popular. I'd like to enable everyone to know about it."

Starting from earlier studies on the relationships between forms, colors and types—as clearly shown by his sketchbooks—he had five exhibits in the 1981 show, inaugurating forms of expression that recur in the subsequent collections. The Oceanic table lamp, in stove-enameled metal, has a slanting black-and-white stem and looks like some restless sea creature. The Grand floor lamp of 1983 is vaguely anthropomorphic, while the black-and-white patterns of the laminates reappeared in the Kristall side table, Atlantic dresser and Pacific closet of 1981 (less transgressive in their general approach). He used the same pattern later in the Burgundy dining table of 1985: the broad edge of the tabletop is covered with a geometrical pattern while the surface has a spotted pattern, which he had already used the year before for the support of the plastic Continental side table. In particular, in Kristall he provocatively skewed the axis of the composition in an experiment that combined metal and wood to create a rectangular body set on four colored metal legs from which sprouts a sort of neck, also of metal, that supports the tabletop. Memphis's 1982 collection featured collaboration with various firms for the construction of objects in glass (Toso Vetri d'Arte, Murano), silver (Rossi & Arcandi, Vicenza), ceramics (Porcellane San Marco, Nove, Ceramica Flavia, Montelupo Fiorentino) and marble (Up & Up, Massa Carrara). De Lucchi explored the qualities of marble in the Sebastopole table, working in partnership with a company equipped with modern production techniques.

Though it looks unstable, the table relies on the weight of the material to achieve a solid balance. The different stones, which include *pietra serena* and red Bilbao stone, are inspired by the polychrome patterns of the façades of Tuscan churches. The Lido sofa was presented at the same event: here De Lucchi broke up the volumes and stratified them, evoking semantic and emotional values through bright colors.

While the Riviera chair of 1981 featured the geometrical orthogonality of the seat, in 1983 De Lucchi embodied his stylistic studies of circular figures in First, which became one of the most representative of Memphis products internationally. This was a chair made of metal and wood with a structure that was visually very light plus three minimal elements that merely gestured towards the back and armrests. The Antares vase, his first ironic experiment with blown glass, also looks unstable, with colored spheres and cylinders stacked uneasily on top of each other.

The following year the general style of Kristall returned in the paired Flamingo side table and Polar end table, the result of combining three elements in different ways: foot, stem and tabletop in plastic two-tone or varnished laminate. The Horizon double bed is a composition of orthogonal planes, where the black-and-white optical pattern is transferred to the lining of the mattress, as in the decoration of the rounded ceramic Celery and Tomato dishes of 1985. At the 1986 exhibition, the Cairo table and the Madrid corner cabinet had a three-dimensional pattern with a powerful visual impact which tended to eclipse their stripped-down structure.

The collections came to an end in 1987 with two new designs, for a carpet, never produced, and the Kim chair, which combined bent plywood—a material De Lucchi was experimenting with in those years in products for Mazzoli and Tisettanta—with a light metal frame. The vocabulary of these designs was very remote from that of their predecessors.

Memphis's original and most vital impulse seems now to have petered out. "From the point of view of the movement," commented De Lucchi twenty years later, in an interview with *Domus*, "Memphis is still a landmark, because to date there's never been anything with the same kind of provocative and purposeful force. What strikes me as its outstanding message was its power to free thinking about design from the ideas associated with Ulm and the good old Functionalist school. There had never been an alternative before. Memphis cleared the field of a monopoly that was very restrictive and inhibiting. And it did this with a charge of irreverence lacking today. It's lacking because no one knows how to go about being irreverent now. Or for the right reasons. Being irreverent just for the sake of protest is no big deal. Being irreverent as a way of digging deeper into things and not being satisfied is a far more rare attitude."

Bibliography: E. Sottsass, *Catalogue for Decorative Furniture in Modern Style 1978–1980*, Milan 1980; B. Radice, *Memphis. The New International Style*, Milan 1981, pp. 19–23; B. Radice, "I mutanti," in *Casa Vogue*, 123, October, 1981, pp. 234–41, esp. pp. 238–39; J. Rouzaud, "Trente papas pour le premier meuble planùte," in *Actuel*, 24, October, 1981, pp. 68–73; "Memphis: l'avant-garde du meuble sculpture," in *Vogue* (Paris), December–January, 1981–82, pp. 47–50; P. Bosson, "Furniture with a Future," in *The Connoisseur*, January, 1982, pp. 42–45; P. Carlsen, "A Style Called 'Memphis,'" in *GQ*, 16, November, 1982; P. Goldberger, "Furniture by Architects: Vitality and Verve," in *The New York Times*, 16, October 14, 1982; "Die Heraus-Forderung von Mailand," in *Schöner Wohnen*, 3, March, 1982, pp. 244–50; "L'oggetto reinventato," in *Casa Vogue*, 134, October, 1982, pp. 288–91; M.P., "Getting & Spending Things to Buy," in *The Village Voice*, October 26, 1982; M. Sisto, "Faremo impazzire le vostre case," in *Panorama mese*, 3, November, 1982, pp. 158–81, esp. 158–66; D. Sudjic, "The Memphis Mafia," in *The World of Interiors*, December–January, 1982–83, pp. 47–50; N. Adams, "Memphis, snap, crackle, eyepopping stuff from a who's who of designers," in *The Chicago Tribune*, June 26, 1983; E. Chiggio, E. Francalanci (ed.), *Memphis*, Padua 1983; G. Cutolo, Michele De Lucchi and Gigi Lanaro, in *Gap casa*, May–June, 1983, pp. 94–97; M. De Lucchi, "La rivoluzione degli accostamenti cromatici," in *Interni*, 330, May, 1983, pp. 16–17; M.-C. Dumoulin, "Memphis dans ses meubles. L'imagination au pouvoir," in *Elle*, 1944, April, 1983; A. Friedman, "Direct from Memphis, 'shocking' design," in *Toronto Globe and Mail*, November 25, 1983; "Memphis," in *Abitare*, 217, September, 1983, pp. 88–89; S. Slesin, "Milan's Magic," in *The New York Times Magazine*, September 11, 1983, pp. 138–40; M.V. Carloni, "Entriamo nella fabbrica dei sogni," in *Epoca*, 5, October, 1984, p. 120; G. Carrari, "Memphis, sfida del design per riprogettare la vita," in *La Repubblica*, March 23, 1984; N. Chaves, "El caos controlado del diseño Memphis," in *El Pais*, June 30, 1984; K.F., "La casa camaleonte," in *Anna bella*, 5, October, 1984, p. 120; P. Martegani, A. Mazzoli and R. Montenegro (ed.), *Memphis una questione di stile*, exhibition catalogue, Rome 1984; *Memphis Design*, exhibition catalogue, Kruithuis-Hertogenbosch, April 20–May 27, 1984; *Memphis in Memphis*, catalogue of the exhibition at the Memphis Brooks Museum of Art, November 18, 1984–February 4, 1985; M. Mestiri, "La robe-objet," in *Jardin des Modes*, January, 1984; L. Moix, "La colección de mobilario vanguardista Memphis fue presentada ayer a Barcelona," in *La Vanguardia*, 148, June 8, 1984; P. Sparke, "The Man from Memphis," in *Blueprint*, March 5, 1984; B. Radice, *Memphis. Ricerche, esperienze, risultati, fallimenti e successi del nuovo design*, Milan 1984; "Stuck on Memphis," in *Playboy*, October, 1984, pp. 124–25; R. Cohen, "Italian Firm Turns the Table on Design, Replaces the Functional With the Playful," in *The Wall Street Journal*, December 19, 1985; M. De Lucchi, *De Lucchi, Michele*, in *Contemporary Landscape From the Horizon of Postmodern Design*, exhibition catalogue, National Museum of Modern Art, Kyoto 1985, pp. 50–51; "Michele De Lucchi," in *La mia casa*, 182, November, 1985, pp. 80–81; A. Freedman, "Keeping the oomph in

Memphis," in *The Globe and Mail*, March 8, 1985, p. E10; R. Horm, *Memphis. Objects, Furniture and Patterns*, Philadelphia (Pennsylvania), 1985, pp. 15, 19, 33, 36, 40, 59, 62, 117; "Memphis," in *The New York Times*, September 29, 1985, p. 19; G. Sambonet (ed.), Ettore Sottsass, *Mobili e qualche arredamento*, exhibition catalogue, Milan 1985, pp. 80–81; M. Slavin, "The New Design Hits Texas," in *Interiors*, February, 1985, pp. 102–07; E. Ambasz (ed.), *The International Design Yearbook 1986/87*, London 1986, pp. 80, 84–85, 272; "Michele De Lucchi," in *Memphis*, Neehan Paper, 1986, pp. 15–20, 52; L. Sannazzaro, "Il ritratto di un secolo a New York," in *Arredorama*, 157, April, 1986, pp. 12–13; R.A.M. Stern (ed.), *The International Design Yearbook 1985/86*, New York 1986, pp. 54–61, esp. pp. 56, 58–60, 220; "We're Going to Memphis," in *Michigan Home & Garden*, Autumn/Winter, 1986; J. Capella, Q. Larrea, *Architekten Designer. Der Achtziger Jahre*, exhibition catalogue, Barcelona 1987, pp. 62–65; S. Kicherer, "Michele De Lucchi, auf neuen Wegen nach Memphis," in *Idee*, January, 1987; G. Bosoni, F.G. Confalonieri, *Paesaggio del design italiano 1972–1988*, Milan 1988, pp. 120, 124; M. De Lucchi, "Nuovi elementi nel progetto dell'oggetto. Design primario," in Alfonsa Can-

nella (ed.), *ADS. Design per lo sviluppo, Atti del corso di conferenze per studenti di architettura e di ingegneria, architetti, ingegneri e operatori del settore della progettazione industriale*, Palermo, December 13, 1982–May 31, 1983, Florence 1988, pp. 44–55; B. Kristjánsdóttir, "Memphis," in *Hús & Híbyli*, 49, 1988, pp. 43–47, esp. pp. 46–47; A.-M. Thibault, "L'histoire du design peut se lire à travers la production du groupe Memphis," in *Le Devoir*, 81, April 8, 1988; G. Albera, N. Monti, *Italian Modern*, New York 1989, p. 85; L. Benaim, "Derniers feux de 'Memphis,'" in *Le Monde*, February 28, 1990, p. 9; *Memphis 1981–1988*, exhibition catalogue, Groninger Museum, Groningen 1990; P. Stirling, "Outrageous Memphis," in *Listener*, May 7–13, 1990, pp. 4–5; *Mostra Sitz. Avantgarde*, Design Zentrum Nordrhein Westfalen, Essen, April 4–May 4, 1991; C. Reinewald, "Michele De Lucchi. A Long Way from Memphis," in *Man*, 23, November, 1995, pp. 110–15; U. Dietz, "Memphis 20 Jahre danach," in *Häuser*, 2, 2000, pp. 128–39, esp. pp. 134–35; Stefano Casciani, "Vent'anni dopo," in *Domus*, October, 2001, pp. 108–19; S. Annicchiarico (ed.), *Il mondo in una stanza*, exhibition catalogue, Milan 2002, p. 98; A. Bassi, *Italian Lighting Design 1945– 2000*, Milan 2003, pp. 146–59.

Antares vase, Memphis
(produced by Toso Vetri d'arte),
1982.
Atlantic dresser, Memphis,
1980.
Oceanic lamp , Memphis, 1980.
Pacific closet, Memphis, 1980.

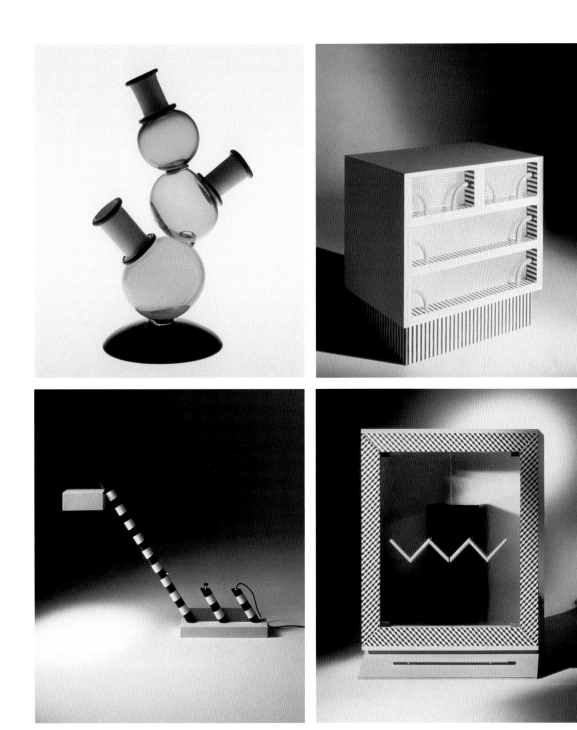

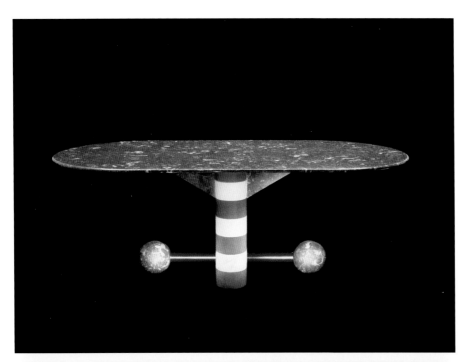

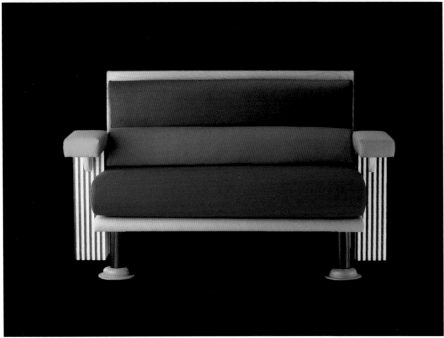

Kristall side table,
Memphis, 1980.
Flamingo side table,
Memphis, 1983.
Continental side table,
Memphis, 1983.
Polar end table, Memphis,
1983.

Sebastopole table, Memphis
(produced by Up&Up,
subsequently UpGroup), 1981.
Lido sofa, Memphis, 1981.

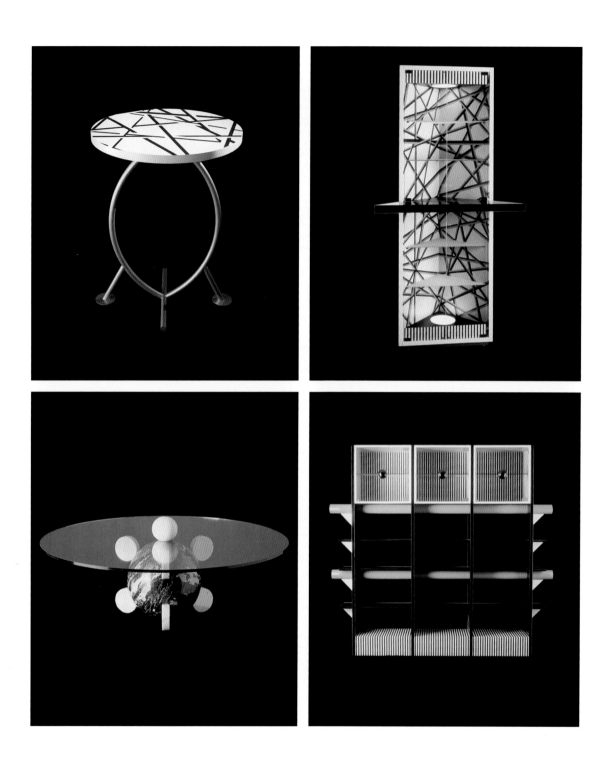

Cairo table, Memphis, 1985.
Madrid corner cabinet,
Memphis, 1985.
President table, Memphis,
1982.
Phoenix bookcase, Memphis,
1983.

Scarlet partition, Memphis,
1984.

First chair, Memphis, 1982.

Composition of First chairs.
The chair became an icon
of Italian design in the period.

Patterns for plastic laminates and fabrics, Abet Print, 1980–87.

Dress made from a material by Michele De Lucchi for *Ornamentalism*, Hamano Institute, Tokyo, 1985.

Olivetti 1979–2002

Olivetti has left its mark on the history of Italian industry and Italian capitalism, influencing design, architecture and communications but even politics and culture. Italy's first typewriter factory, it was founded in Ivrea in 1908. From 1932 to 1960 it was headed by Adriano Olivetti, who transformed it into a model for all European firms. Adriano Olivetti's outlook left a profound imprint on the company's history. Over the years it gradually diversified, passing from mechanical office technology to electronic machines and so to information technology and office systems. As early as the thirties Adriano had worked with various artists and architects, not only on architectural projects and urban planning but also designs of the firm's products and its corporate identity. Olivetti produced some of the outstanding examples of industrial design in Italy, like the Lettera 22 typewriter (1950) by Marcello Nizzoli, Elea 9003 calculating machine (1959), Valentine typewriter (1969) by Ettore Sottsass and Quaderno laptop (1992) by Mario Bellini.

Michele De Lucchi began designing for Olivetti in December 1979. At that time Sottsass was the director of the firm's product design and office furniture department; he delegated De Lucchi to oversee the design and industrial development of products at Olivetti Synthesis, the branch of the firm producing filing cabinets and related products. It was set up in 1930 with the first horizontal filing cabinet, designed by Aldo Magnelli. Among its products, in 1961 it realized the famous Spazio office line by the BBPR firm, and in 1978 became a joint-stock company. Sottsass decided to take on De Lucchi at a time when the "master," with a group of other designers, had just founded Sottsass Associati and De Lucchi had opened his first office next door. The long partnership with Olivetti provides a record of the development of De Lucchi's work in both office furniture and the design of technological artifacts. His work was deeply influenced by the the ideal legacy of Adriano Olivetti, the achievements of the great designers with whom he worked or who had preceded him, and by the firm's model of management of human resources and design. The experience was also fundamental because of what he was to describe in the mid-nineties as "service design." At Olivetti, he now states, "I learned to design office interiors by first defining the space around the machines. I got the commissions for Deutsche Bank and the Italian Post Office because I knew just how a counter functions and hence a workplace."

At first De Lucchi was required to redesign existing products, updating the 45 series designed in 1973 by Sottsass, revising colors and materials and adapting product lines for contract orders. The company's executive and marketing headquarters were in Milan, its administrative headquarters in Ivrea (Piedmont); so meetings with the designer took place first in Ivrea and then Milan, while the factory and the design offices were in Massa Carrara (in Tuscany), where De Lucchi commuted every week. "The first time I arrived in Massa by train," he recalled, "and after a tour of the factory and the technical office, the head engineer asked me a question: a defective consignment of sheet metal was preventing him from making some perfectly smooth doors for an order in Libya. He needed to find a way to stretch the metal so as to make good the deficiency. I nonchalantly sketched a profile of a shutter ribbed down the middle so as to prevent the metal from buckling. The next morning I saw the sample and a few days later ten thousand pieces were ready for assembly. This was my baptism into mass production: those doors were still in production in 1998, the year Olivetti Synthesis closed down."

The first project by the two designers was the Icarus office system (with Theo Gonser), in production from 1982, created after a fertile international journey to study innovations in the sector. Three years later they designed Delphos (1985, with James Irvine). Both projects were conceived as adaptations of American open-plan designs to suit the Italian office, based on extensive research into modularity, comfort and the position of the cabling. Another important office-furniture project was Sangirolamo, developed in 1990 with Achille Castiglioni (the design team included Ferruccio Laviani and Angelo Micheli). This embodied the idea of the office as a serene and welcoming space; its novelty lay in the invention of a type rather than a display of technology. Eidos and Pegaso (1995, with Geert Koster) brought together desks, chairs and filing cabinets in a single system. In the eighties Olivetti expanded its office automation and telecommunications sectors. Sottsass then brought De Lucchi in on the design of personal computers, telephones, fax machines, photocopiers, printers, etc. George Sowden, another young designer Sottsass had brought to Olivetti, was already employed in the same field. De Lucchi's working relationship with Sowden now became closer (they had already worked together on the design of work stations for monitors and supports for personal computers).

In 1985 he designed his first video for a PC, retaining Sottsass's general arrangement of geometrical volumes but seeking to reduce the visual obstacle it created for the user. In 1988 Sottsass cut his work down to project coordinator, leaving the designs to De Lucchi, Sowden and Antonio Macchi Cassia. Four years later De Lucchi was appointed director of design at Olivetti. Ever since the time of Adriano Olivetti, the company had had its own technical office run by professional design firms independent of the company structures (in the seventies and eighties Sottsass and Bellini had been responsible for the design of Olivetti products). "The designers kept their own firms," said De Lucchi in 2001, "and Olivetti set up supporting offices staffed by technicians who ensured the liaison between Milan and Ivrea. Ivrea had a Design and Font Center that would pre-engineer or even engineer the casings of machines for the various project divisions, preparing the drawings that the mechanical and electronic engineers would develop as far as the working prototypes and then the production models. In both Milan and Ivrea the modeling phase had become all-important. Models were made out of blocks of polystyrene (the way I still do it today in my studio using the old machinery and the cutting benches that I bought when the workshops went out of use) [...] The old Design Center in Ivrea was based in an ordinary house opposite the main office block, on the other side of the intersection. Everyone called it 'the chicken house,' perhaps because it originally had a chicken house [...] Executives, even the most important ones, would often stroll across the road to geek at what those oddball architects were cooking up and they would linger and discuss the handling of details or the way the forms of automobiles, home appliances, or whatever was evolving around the world [...] The whole design team and its organization came under something called the

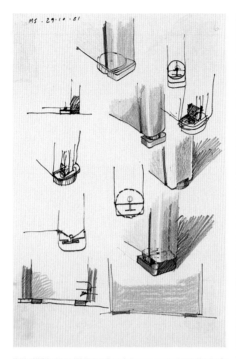

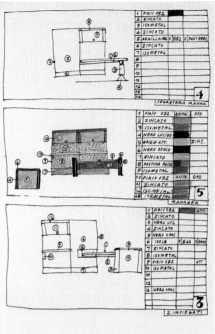

**Drawings for the leg
of the Icarus office system,
Olivetti Synthesis,
October 29, 1981.
Study of finishes for furniture
in the Icarus office system,
January 11, 1983.
Drawing for Olivetti cash
register, September 1993.
Drawing for automatic
telling machine, Olivetti,
July 16, 1990.**

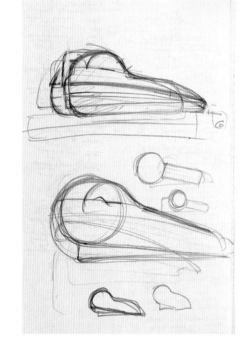

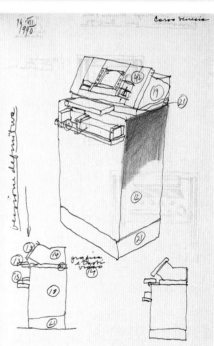

'Cultural Relations Management,' a name that suggests just about anything except design. In reality the head of this management was always [...] Renzo Zorzi, a unique and extraordinary character who went through the fifty years of life at Olivetti in all its phases, from euphoria to black despair. Renzo Zorzi is a scholar, writer, intellectual, very cultivated and curious, and he was unfailing in his commitment to defend the firm's cultural and social role."

From 1992 on De Lucchi designed and coordinated projects for all sorts of products (personal computers, laptops, cash registers, printers, fax machines, keyboards, videos, multimedia kiosks) as well as (in part) company communications, packaging and architecture, like the Olivetti System & Networks Research Center at Bari (1989–91, Michele De Lucchi/DEGW with Nicholas Bewick). He also directed cultural initiatives, like the joint workshop with Philips held at Ivrea and Eindhoven (The Netherlands) in 1993 (with Alessandro Chiarato, Torsten Fritze, Masahiko Kubo, Mario Trimarchi), or Domestic Chips (1996, with Torsten Fritze, Johannes Kiessler, Masahiko Kubo, Enrico Quell, Mario Trimarchi), and took part in numerous conferences, round tables and international seminars. De Lucchi summed up his contribution to design in 2001: "I took a more comprehensive approach to design than my predecessors," he wrote in *Il Mondo*. "I was busied with a lot of different sectors: from office products to computers and electronic systems and all the way down to systems furniture. I was faced with constraints dictated above all by the state of the technological potential, by the laws of commercial competition and the market, by the need for corporate coordination and, last but not least, by a concern for the environment and the natural resources available to mankind. In my first years on the job I sought to create a new vocabulary that would standardize all Olivetti products and give the company a distinctive identity on the market. With the smaller machines and portables, I sought to enhance their tactile qualities by chamfering the corners and lavishing my care on the textures of the bodies [Echos 40 laptop, 1993], I wanted to bring out their ergonomic qualities [NP9 prototype palmtop, 1994, with Alessandro Chiarato], and I scaled down the dimensions by working above all on their visual and emotional features [Echos 20 laptop, 1993–94].

In the case of machines for the home, I sought relationships and affinities with consumer products [Envision project, 1994–96, with Felipe Alarcao]. I tried to make the design express the technology in the products [Pronto mobile phone, 1994, with Enrico Quell] and I ran through geometrical and organic forms to make products commonly felt to be typical of offices more sensuous and attractive [Xana computer, 1996, with Felipe Alarcao and Masahiko Kubo]. I created a new image for desktops [M6 Supreme, 1993, with Mario Trimarchi] and laptops [Echos 40, 1993] by using images seen as more professional. In office products I devised surfaces that seemed to grow out of inner tensions [PR4 retail printer, 1995 with Johannes Kiessler], I simplified interfaces and control panels [JP 170 inkjet printer, 1995–96, with Alessandro Chiarato]. I integrated and scaled down forms [PR2 bank printer, 1994–95, with Johannes Kiessler], I worked so that the shadows they cast would be soft and delicate [OFX 1000 fax, 1994]. In products for public use I sought to visualize their functions in their form [cash dispenser, 1988, with Mario Trimarchi] and I introduced new and unexpected color combinations [multimedia kiosks, 1993–94, with Antonio Macchi Cassia and Enrico Quell]. Ultimately, I wanted to show that the reputation and history of Olivetti design were still vital assets, recognized internationally, and needed to be cultivated."

In 2001 De Lucchi explained his vision of technology: "My design work at Olivetti is based on the idea that all the electronics packed inside the innumerable machines we use every day is a great benefit and our task as designers is to make it widely accessible and bring these benefits and this quality into our lives as individuals and as a society. I don't in the least believe there's any difference between technology for the home and the office because I think that the need to do things well and in ways that don't waste time applies equally to both home and office."

The changes in the company's strategies and objectives in the course of the nineties, following various shake-ups, also led to changes in the methods of project management. Olivetti's last design office in Ivrea, in the "chicken house," closed down in 1990 and the Milanese one on Corso Venezia in 1994. Until 1998 De Lucchi gave a core group of technicians office space in his own firm, after which design was outsourced. His work for Olivetti, which has now merged with Telecom Italia, came to an end in 2002.

Bibliography: M. De Lucchi, "Gli uffici sono paesaggi e l'orizzonte è lontano," in *Abitare*, 199, November, 1981, pp. 48–56; G. Ricciardi, "Mezze maniche sprint," in *Il Mondo*, November 20, 1981, pp. 124–37, esp. p. 127; Ufficio Stile/Consul conference: "L'office automation e la progettazione e l'arredamento dei posti di lavoro nella realtà aziendale," in *Ufficio stile*, 4, June, 1982, pp. 14–16; M. De Lucchi, "L'era della scrivania elettronica," in *Domus*, 631, September, 1982, pp. 50–52; M. De Lucchi, "L'ufficio è elettronico e fa bip-bip," in *Ufficio stile*, 4, June, 1982, pp. 20–22; E. Sottsass (with M. De Lucchi), "Nuove 'figure' di Olivetti Synthesis," in *Gran Bazaar Documenta*, offprint of *Gran Bazaar*, 11, November, 1982; M. De Lucchi, "Il posto di lavoro attrezzato," in *Sumo*, 2, March–April, 1983, pp. 76–79; M. De Lucchi, "Il ruolo del design nell'arredo come strumento di lavoro," in *Mobili per ufficio (Olivetti Synthesis)*, 1983, pp. 38–39; M. De Lucchi, "Sottsass per Olivetti Synthesis," in G. Origlia (ed.), Album, *Progetto ufficio*, 2, Milan 1983, pp. 117–85; R. Zorzi, *Olivetti Synthesis: per una storia del design*, Milan 1983, pp. 15–35; M. De Lucchi, "Per un ufficio più comunicativo," in *Casa Vogue*, 148, January, 1984, pp. 114–17; "Olivetti Synthesis. Il progetto aperto," in *Gran Bazaar*, Olivetti Synthesis insert, suppl. to the February–March issue, 1985; *Italia diseño 1946/1986*, exhibition catalogue, Rufino Tamayo Museum, Oaxaca, Mexico 1986, p. 153; S. Carbonaro (ed.), "Silenzio. L'ufficio trasmette! Intervista con Michele De Lucchi," in *Ufficio stile*, 5, 1987, pp. 4–7; "Toimistokalusteiden, Huippumuotoilija, Uusia muotoja ja käytännönläheisyyttä," in *Uudistuva konttori*, 11, 1987, pp. 34–36; M. De Lucchi, "Nuovi elementi nel progetto dell'oggetto. Design primario," in A. Cannella (ed.), *ADS. Design per lo sviluppo, Atti del corso di conferenze per studenti di architettura...*, Palermo, December 13, 1982–May 31, 1983, Florence 1988, pp. 44–55; "De Lucchi Michele," in *Memphis & Transavanguardia*, exhibition catalogue, Fukuyama Museum of Art and Tokyo Museum of Contemporary Art, Aoyama, Fukuyama Museum of

Art, Aoyama 1989, pp. 30–33; A. Fanelli, "L'Edp muta la forma, lo spazio e l'ergonomia," in *Mondo economico*, May 6, 1989, pp. 102–03; S. Kircherer, Olivetti, London 1990; Michele De Lucchi and Mario Trimarchi, "Considerazioni preliminari," in *Annual Ufficio*, II, 1991–92, pp. 40–45; S. Carbonaro, "Safe, friendly or…lovely?," in *Ufficio stile*, 8, October, 1992, pp. 98–101; P. Catalano, "Office Tomorrow," in *Gap casa*, September, 1993, p. 83; M. De Lucchi, "Design: Style to Reflect a Personality," in *Dartamation*, 1, March, 1993, p. 17; M. De Lucchi, "Direzionali," in *OFX Guide 1993*, monographic issue, suppl. to *OFX Office International*, 9, September–October, 1992, pp. 32–33; "Design i menneskets tjeneste," in *Computer World*, 24, 9, 1993; "Et anderledes design for bærbare / A different design of Laptops," in *Erhvervsbladet*, 27, 9, 1993; G. Finizio, "Future Design," in *Ottagono*, 107, June, 1993, pp. 75–82; E. Grazzini, "Olivetti, il futuro è portatile," in *Corriere della Sera*, June 8, 1993, p. 25; "Grønne PC'er fra Olivetti/Green Pc from Olivetti," in *Datadit*, 29, 9, 1993; "Itaalia arvutitootja muudab strateegiat e Italiensk design!," in *Inside PC*, 9, 10, 1993; "Pelkkä muoto ei muutu rahaksi," in *Talouselama*, 30, 1993; K.I. Skeid, "Design og miljø skiller data-produsentene," in *Finansavisen*, September 22, 1993, p. 9; C. Steno, "Der farveløse får farve-engang / The colourloose gets colour sometime in the future," in *Berlingske Tidente*, 29, 9, 1993; E. Tamos, "Segreti scacciacrisi," in *Il Mondo*, March 15, 1993, pp. 74–76, esp. p. 76; S.C., "Michele De Lucchi, architetto e designer," in *OFX Office International*, 20, September–October, 1994, pp. 50–53; S. Carbonaro, "In the Midst of so much Noise…Silence," in *DBZ*, special issue, October, 1994, pp. 86–90; G. Di Matteo, "I piccoli Giugiaro che sbucano dal chip," in *Affari & Finanza*, insert in *La Repubblica*, July 8, 1994, p. 22; D. Grogna, "Et si l'informatique nous surprenait," in *L'Echo*, 29, 11, 1994, p. 9; Lott, "Anderledes PC-serie til fremtidens familie," in *Berlingske Tidende,* May 31, 1994; "Olivetti," in *Ascii*, January 18, 1994, pp. 321–25; A. Rawsthorn, "Talent Needs Intelligence Too," in *Financial Times*, June 13, 1994, p. 8; A. Tangvald-Pedersen, "Han Tegner Fremtiden," in *VG*, July 19, 1994, p. 22; S. Caullor (ed.), "L'ordinateur est l'outil le plus laid que je connaisse," in *La Tribune*, November 28, 1995, p. 26; "Michele De Lucchi: 'Los noventa están siendo la década del miedo,'" in *El País*, May 18, 1995, p. 46; *Olivetti Design*, Museum Scryption, Tilburg 1995, pp. 30ff; M. De Lucchi, "La tecnologia è già grigia," in *Ottagono*, 117, December–February, 1995–96, pp. 50–52; M. Beiter, "Kødet, blodet og elektronikken," in *Berlingske Tidende*, March 26, 1996, pp. 37–40; "Michele De Lucchi," in *Office Layout*, 69, August–October, 1996, pp. 31–32; E. Arosio, "Il '900 in punta di design," in *L'Espresso*, 43, October 29, 1998, pp. 213–15; M. De Lucchi, "Sui tasti della storia," in *Il Mondo*, 44, October 30, 1998, pp. 135–37; Direzione comunicazione e immagine Olivetti (ed.), *Olivetti 1908–1998*, 1998; R. Pasero, "Olivetti Un ticchettio lungo 90 anni," in *Il Giornale*, October 28, 1998, p. 27; H. Höger, "Olivetti. Storia di un'utopia italiana," in *Domus*, 813, March, 1999, pp. 86–95; L. Barberis (ed.), "I disegni di De Lucchi esposti all'archivio storico Olivetti," in *Il nostro tempo*, November 7, 1999; *Olivetti 1908–2000*, Associazione Archivio storico Olivetti, Ivrea (Turin) 2001; M. De Lucchi, "Il design in Olivetti. Una tradizione che non tramonta," in *La sentinella del Canevese*, April 19, 2001, pp. 25, 31.

office furniture system
Icarus
Olivetti Synthesis
production: 1982
with Ettore Sottsass
collaborator: Theo Gonser

In 1979 Ettore Sottsass brought in De Lucchi to work for Olivetti Synthesis. After revising the color ranges and materials of some products and adapting them for contract orders, Olivetti commissioned him to devise a new office furniture system. In the spring of 1980 De Lucchi set out on an international fact-finding tour to study advances in office design and technology and especially what was driving them. He visited Olivetti retailers and the major firms in the sector, including Steelcase and Herman Miller, made contacts with designers and architects, including Frank O. Gehry and Michael Graves, and visited Germany, The Netherlands, Canada, the United States, Australia, New Zealand and Japan. Out of the substantial store of information he collected—certainly also the antechamber of the Memphis experience—in 1981 he created Icarus. De Lucchi commuted every week to the Massa Carrara offices, which housed production and the firm's technical department, and here the project was slowly and concretely developed.

"In Italy we can actually say that offices for clerical workers had never been considered worth furnishing properly, they were just empty spaces to be filled with the cheapest furniture around," explained De Lucchi while interviewing Sottsass in 1983. "When we began work on the Icarus system things had changed out of all recognition. Many aspects of the work space had changed by the start of the decade, both with the development of electronics and office-automation and also because of a natural evolution in the concept of the office as a result of the increasing numbers of workers in the sector. So we had to think of a comfortable environment, more like the home, but also technology-rich, by relating furnishings to the machines.
In the same years the idea of a system—essentially American—was being questioned. The principle that a limited number of modular elements, a sort of 'Meccano,' could fulfill all the requirements in the planning of the office had produced confused and impersonal structures. Also the concept of modularity, an important theoretical argument for various famous products, had lost some of its shine because it failed to meet all the problems of practical use."

De Lucchi-Sottsass refined American open-plan design, which they had seen applied to large and small spaces, in more "Italian" terms, conceiving a functional system that could be adapted to different requirements (such as privacy or the need to have a number of people present together) and surface areas, particularly traditional Italian offices restructured.

To achieve this the two designers rejected the concept of an over-arching system, with everything laid out on a grid controlling the design of the spaces in plan and elevation (the system adopted, for example, in the 45 CR series of 1981). They produced separate units that complemented each other and consisted of two subsystems designed separately: a standard cubicle and a furniture unit. Their combination created a modular structure with a variable, multi-purpose plan that could be reconfigured to create open spaces or closed, to integrate or isolate functions, define private areas, lay out paths and equip secretarial offices, waiting rooms and receptions. The first unit contained the floors, ceilings and above all the screens separating the spaces, made from panels of various dimensions (with embedded wiring) that could be used to enclose the workers when they were seated or create a visually uncluttered interior. Its design was subordinated to the arrangement of the cables: the housing of the cables ran around the perimeter, attached to a metal frame. They could be enlarged subsequently to meet the needs of changes to the technical specifications. The panels were soundproofed, being lined with a thin interchangeable sheet of fabric, wood or laminate, or even glazing.

Icarus, designed with Ettore Sottsass, is an Italian adaptation of the American open plan, which can be adapted to smaller offices.

The furniture unit consisted essentially of workstations (desks and tables), conceived as independent sets, though compatible with the other elements of the system. Taking up a position in the debate then going on about the idea of integrating machines with furniture, De Lucchi and Sottsass were not interested in achieving formal integration in Icarus so much as in ways of relating equipment to furniture, combining the cables, position and ergonomics of the user with the need for modularity, flexibility, safety, status and comfort in the furniture. "The logic behind the development of office automation," noted De Lucchi, anticipating an issue that is still relevant, "is that office machines will have to be able to work in tandem, and as long as communications and energy are transmitted by cables, the problem for whoever designs office interiors will always be where to put all these complicated bundles of wiring."

They provided an original solution to the problem of where to put the cables by embedding them in the furniture itself, including the desks, the objects in an office with the greatest expressive force. The desks were fitted with a "smart leg," a large duct that contained the electric and telephone sockets and concealed a roomy cavity that housed the excess lengths of cable. This could be used to support the work surface at different heights, link two adjoining surfaces or be combined with ordinary legs. It also matched the ergonomic requirements both in relation to the anthropometric measurements of the user and the features of the machines resting on the desktop.

The walls were used as supports for various kinds of accessories like containers, shelves, whiteboards, lamps. Users' changing ideas of comfort were met above all by the color schemes. They ranged from the neutral, almost nonexistent, colors of the 45 series ("because back then we thought that the work environments should not have too much appeal"), to the muted tones of red, light blue, yellow and dark blue for Icarus. Back in 1983 he justified the color schemes by saying, "The prerog-

ative of this system is ... to be continually loaded with signals and visual messages rather than escape from them." But today De Lucchi recognizes that "the color system is the aspect of Icarus that has dated most quickly. The color scheme can be the strong point of a project but it reflects a period." And foreshadowing future developments in office interiors, in 1983 De Lucchi wrote in *Interni Annual*: "Icarus won't end here, [...] because the design of any industrial product should contain something more than just functional specifications [...] The design also seeks to transmit figurative, formal and chromatic significances [...] Through the rounded corners, the use of the stamped sheet metal, the thicknesses, the soft, tenuous colors, we wanted to transmit an idea of new comfort in the office because we felt that its evolution, to be synonymous with progress, has to seek to improve the quality of the relationship between man and the environment. Automation, today the principal driving force behind office development, continuously encroaches on the environment by introducing highly invasive machines. The forms of furniture should not seek to evade this massive invasion, becoming a mere support for the equipment. It should respond to sophistication with sophistication and be steadily updated to match its changing cultural and anthropological context."

In 1983 Renzo Zorzi commented: "Currently Sottsass is in one of his most fertile and significant phases [...] My impression is that the encounter between a period of such free creativity with the demanding conditions of industrial production, the need to curb spontaneity in industrial design, the transfer to the production line of the urge to 'change the landscape,' but without [...] the 'irresponsibility' of the one-off-piece, and incorporating the new technological data and formal structures, have currently made Icarus the most advanced achievement in this sector and also point the way ahead in a new direction."

Michele De Lucchi and Ettore Sottsass, Icarus office system, Olivetti Synthesis, 1981–86. The unit of the furniture and details of the work surface and cabling are housed in the "smart leg."

Bibliography: M. Bedin, "Icarus Design: E. Sottsass, M. De Lucchi," in *Architecture Intérieure*, 191, November–December, 1982, pp. 106–09; A. Branzi, "'Icarus,' gli uffici della 'Office Automation,'" in *Domus*, 633, November, 1982, pp. 61–69; "Icarus, linea d'arredo per l'ufficio del futuro," in *La Repubblica*, September 18, 1982; "Olivetti Synthesis: sistema Icarus per l'arredo dell'ufficio del futuro," in "*Corriere della Sera*, September 16, 1982, p. 29; E. Sottsass (with M. De Lucchi), "Nuove 'figure' di Olivetti Synthesis," in *Gran Bazaar Documenta*, offprint of *Gran Bazaar*, 11, November, 1982; "Casi d'ufficio," in *L'ufficio*, 5, May, 1983, p. 37; M. De Lucchi, "Il posto di lavoro attrezzato," in *Sumo*, 2, March–April, 1983, pp. 76–79; M. De Lucchi, "Il ruolo del design nell'arredo come strumento di lavoro," in *Mobili per ufficio*, 1983, pp. 38–39, pp. 60–61; M. De Lucchi, "Sofisticazione a sofisticazione," in *Interni Annual*, 1983, pp. 8–9; M. De Lucchi, "Sottsass per Olivetti Synthesis," in G. Origlia (ed.), *Album, Progetto ufficio, 2*, Milan 1983, pp. 117–85; A. Folli (ed.), "Linea Icarus. Un progetto di Ettore Sottsass e Michele De Lucchi per Olivetti Synthesis," in *Habitat Ufficio* (Olivetti Synthesis), 1983; "Icarus," in *Domus*, 645, December, 1983; M. Marabelli, "Verso l'ufficio del futuro," in *Casa Vogue*, 140, April, 1983, pp. 222–24; R. Zorzi, "Olivetti Synthesis: per una storia del design e Ettore Sottsass, Il progetto Icarus," in *Olivetti Synthesis 1930/1983*, Milan 1983, pp. 15–35, 36–37; "Icarus System," in J. Pile, *Open Office Space, Fact on File*, New York 1984, pp. 26–27; "Il nuovo comfort ambientale per l'ufficio," in *Domus*, 655, November, 1984, pp. 67–74; *Von der Mechanik zur Elektronik. Olivetti: Konzept und Form*, exhibition catalogue, Munich 1984, p. 58; "Comfort e flessibilità nell'ufficio. Sistema Icarus della Olivetti Synthesis," in *Management & Impresa*, 1, January, 1985.

office furniture system
Delphos
Olivetti Synthesis
production: 1985
with Ettore Sottsass
collaborator: James Irvine

Delphos, produced four years after Icarus, is again an attempt to find a solution to the system of office furnishings, particularly an efficiency arrangement of the cabling, set inside a more versatile, lighter and cheaper structure. Developed with Ettore Sottsass, it again developed the concept behind the 45 system, already revised by the two designers in the CR version of 1981 by elaborating on Sottsass's original project of 1973. The 45 system featured modular desk-tops and ducting for the electric and telephonic connections. Like Icarus, Delphos was adaptable to both open-plan layouts and small enclosed offices. The identity of the system was embodied in the semantic features of the individual components, each with a specific function: underpanel, cable channel, storage unit, separator panel and work surface, all produced in significant variants and easy to reconfigure.

The trough beam was the outstanding element of the system. Of solid dimensions, first of all it fulfilled the structural task of giving rigid support to the work surfaces, even when segmented, and could be connected to various types of vertical support (cylindrical legs with feet placed symmetrically, or off-axis or geometrical panel supports slightly raised off the floor on feet). Moreover it contained a large cable channel housing the connections, excess cable, and their horizontal development in series and parallel. In this way it freed the furniture system from the need to follow the course of the cables exactly, though with the drawback of making access more difficult if the system had to be modified. This constructional concept responded adequately to the need for compact workstations as a result of changes in the organization of the office due to automation, which tended to take up more of the desk surface. Delphos enabled between two and four desks to be joined to form a single island. This was a very serviceable feature because it could be extended with low screens and work surfaces of various shapes and sizes to favor interviews and equipment-sharing, making it far more functional while minimizing unused surfaces. Using planes and beams to build a rigid workdeck also made it possible to reduce the number of vertical supports, so making the space below more flexible and cutting the cost of the system. Simplicity and rational construction were also a feature of the panels that, besides separating the work stations, could house shelves, brackets and storage units. Produced in different finishes, they were defined by a base board in thermoplastic resin that housed the electrics safely. The color scheme of Delphos was designed by Trino Clini Castelli, who had recently finished working on Olivetti's office machines.

Bibliography: *Delphos*, vols. 1, 2, Olivetti Synthesis, Segrate 1985; G. Origlia, "Sistema Delphos, Olivetti Synthesis," in *Domus*, 670, March, 1986, pp. 66–69; U. Barbieri, "Olivetti, Olivetti Synthesis en Delphos," in *Car project-meubelen*, 1, 1988, pp. 4–7; "Beauty and the beastly hi-tech unit," in *Design Week*, March 25, 1988, p. 72; "Michele De Lucchi," in *Eciffo*, 3, winter 1988, pp. 4–5.

With Delphos, De Lucchi and Ettore Sottsass developed the Icarus system (1981) into a more flexible design that weighed and cost less.

Michele De Lucchi and Ettore
Sottsass (with Beppe Caturegli
and Giovannella Formica),
installation of the exhibit
"Research into an Office
Environment" using elements
in production for the Icarus
system, Milan Triennale,
October 1983.

Artemide 1980–present

De Lucchi began designing for Artemide in 1980. The firm, founded in 1959 by Ernesto Gismondi and Sergio Mazza, is one of the Italian leaders in the lighting field. One of the advocates of industrialization in the sector, above all with the coming of plastic, in the sixties and seventies Artemide produced lamps and furnishings that are now among design icons: from Polluce by Enzo Mari (1965) to Eclissi by Vico Magistretti (1967), Boalum by Livio Castiglioni and Gianfranco Frattini (1970) and the celebrated Tizio by Richard Sapper (1972). Gismondi—an aeronautical and missile engineer, entrepreneur and himself a designer—contacted De Lucchi in 1980 following the opening of the exhibition at the 16th Milan Triennale, where the designer had presented his lively models of home appliances for Girmi, and asked him to design lamps. In the first two years the architect produced numerous ideas, from which a dozen or so were chosen, the series ending with Cyclos in 1982: this was a wall and ceiling lamp, with a suspension model added later. "That was a period when I was into disks and balls," De Lucchi now comments. "It was the period of the First chair and the lamps I designed for Bieffeplast, when I decided to go in for curves, partly as a contrast to the things that Peter Shire or Ettore Sottsass, for example, were doing for Memphis, based largely on straight lines and pointed shapes. Just as First was an emblem of Memphis, a simple, functional object but with great visual resonance, so Cyclos was a novelty in those years because it was flat and had a quite distinct personality. The suspension version had just two cables to keep it parallel to the floor." In developing the products the company's technical and production skills were decisive. Today this side of its organization is embodied in a research and development center, which designs and engineers the products, and in its modeling workshops and test labs. "I just take along some sketches," said the architect, "and they discuss the preliminaries. If Gismondi finds the project convincing they go ahead with it."

His experience with Cyclos, a lamp still in the firm's catalogue, led the architect to reflect specially on the possibility of designing families of lamps starting from a single original model. This approach was applied very successfully in the Tolomeo series.

De Lucchi's and Artemide's paths crossed again in the same years—from 1981 to 1989—when Gismondi gave his backing to the Memphis adventure with Ettore Sottsass. "Memphis was the most impressive phenomenon of the eighties," declared Gismondi at the decade's end in an interview for the television series *Lezioni di Design*. "The Memphis team, led by Sottsass, […] broke with two dogmas: the dogma of no color and the dogma of form as function, within the bounds of possibility. Memphis meant 'let's be artists,' because that was the only time it's ever happened, I believe, in this world that the people who decided what a firm should produce were the designers and not a group of insiders, the people who controlled the business. It wasn't some CEO who said this is what we're going to do, but the designers, freely […] At the opening in 1981 […] some friends who were manufacturers came over and said: 'Ernesto, you're crazy, with this new kind of design you're killing your old design, you'll ruin Artemide.' I said: 'Don't worry, I know what I'm doing. I'm looking for a new path together with Sottsass and my friends at

Memphis [...] Let's move ahead and enter a more cheerful world, different, colorful. One where we're freer and less inhibited.'"

Diomede, the next suspension lamp De Lucchi designed (1983), remained a prototype. It was based on a mechanism for reversing the diffuser which he took up again a decade later with Sigira for Classicon. Meanwhile he concentrated on table lamps, with numerous designs. "Gismondi is also a designer and he doesn't like lamps that he could have designed himself," says De Lucchi. "They have to have some idea that he judges good or bad, to suit his personal outlook. This attitude gave me some trouble, and I don't deny that Produzione Privata was partly set up so I could produce the designs Artemide turned down. Friendship, affection, disappointment and frustration were, however, very formative in enabling me to understand the reasons behind his demands."

In 1986 De Lucchi presented the first idea for Tolomeo, an aluminum table lamp with a movable arm that was to become Artemide's biggest seller over the next twenty years. The prototype had severe teething troubles, but extensive modifications by Giancarlo Fassina, technical director of the research and development office, solved them and won him the role of co-designer. Conceived as a reinterpretation of Luxo, but with the springs concealed from sight, its shade is pierced on top, placed out of alignment with the bulb fitting, and can be swiveled to modify the quality of the light shed on the desktop. From 1987, the year it went into production, down to the present, De Lucchi has widened the Tolomeo range with numerous versions in different sizes, proving the design is extremely flexible and can adapt to complex spatial conditions and contexts. This is probably one of the reasons for its success and the interest it arouses in the media, besides the fact that "it is a highly practical lamp with a discreet yet distinctive design." He adds: "After Tolomeo I thought I would never make another lamp."

Tolomeo was the result of a conceptual path De Lucchi followed out all through the eighties and that led him to explore the relationship between man, products and technology. He embodied his ideas in experiments on "minimal machines": objects that looked mechanical and explored the relationship between performance and simplicity. In 1992, describing the "poetry of the machine," Sibylle Kicherer noted: "They are mostly lamps, because it is principally in the use of light that movement becomes performance."

In his Lighting Field experimental prototypes of 1994, again produced by Artemide (and then Private Production), De Lucchi mulled over bare light sources and electric wires, composing them into the forms of a dog, a puppet, a star and a face. By combining the warm light of incandescent bulbs and cold fluorescent light from compact tubes, he exploited the expressive potential of lamps even when they are switched off, wittily shifting the focus from the illuminating object to the object illuminated.

There followed some rather less successful products like Libera (1993), Aleppo (1997–98) and his experience with Telemachus (1996) for the Metamorfosi line (a series of lamps shedding polychrome light based on research into the psychological values of color by various international designers). Then in 1999 De Lucchi produced Dioscuri, subsequently developed into Castore (2003–04), a new family of lamps that, like Tolomeo, works well in very different spatial contexts. He reduced the form of the diffuser to an "archetype": the illuminated sphere here forms

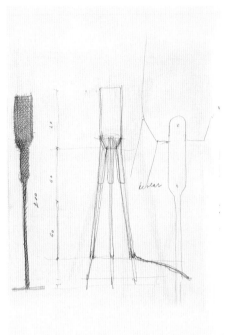

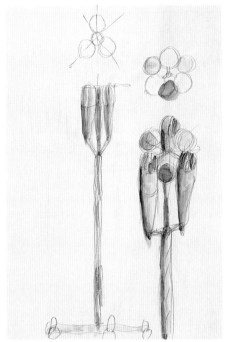

Drawings of lamps,
August 11, 1995.
Multicolor lamp for Artemide,
January 31, 1996.
Drawing for Diomede lamps,
Artemide, January 3, 1990.

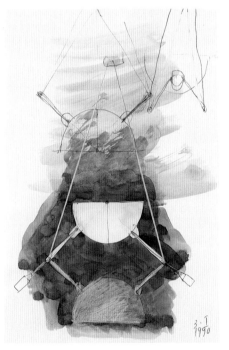

the central feature of the whole series, enhanced by the choice of an all-white color scheme and linear detailing.

De Lucchi then turned his attention to the expressive use of light in the Palme series of street lamps, designed in 1999–2000 for Dz Licht, one of the firms acquired by the Artemide group. In this lamp the light source is housed in a curving leaf-shaped form which directs the light downward onto the street surface, so adapting the lamp to its purpose. Then, in the Logico series (2000), he explored the possible qualities of diffused lighting, using blown glass with a silk finish and interlocking organic forms, the fruit of considerable skill in the definition of the working drawings as well as those for its assembly.

De Lucchi's most recent products reflect a strand of research in the sector that is being promoted by Artemide. This is an attempt to stimulate the senses by experimenting with lighting whose qualities are not just technical and functional but psychological and emotional. One example is Betelgeuse, a prototype presented in 2003: this is a lamp sculpted in organic shapes that varies the balance between light, sound and the quality of the air in an interior. He is also exploring the potential of digital technologies by experimenting with LEDs, as in the Sempronio table lamp of 2001, again still at the prototype stage.

"Artemide is Gismondi," concludes De Lucchi. "Working for Artemide means establishing a relationship with Gismondi. He respects ideas and considers their conversion into a product strictly dependent on his intervention and his firm. A simple outlook, true, but effective. I consider him a pioneer in his attitude towards design and much of my 'theory of ideas' actually derives from him. And then Carlotta De Bevilacqua is also playing a more important part. She is generally more willing to let herself be guided by market trends, which provide the reasons for new design ideas. For Ernesto, instead, the idea comes first, then the lamp." And he adds, extending these concepts to the present state of design in Italy and abroad: "The first thing I look for, too, are ideas, solid, not vacuous. A recurrent problem that I have with a lot of designers is that they aren't willing to understand the way the world develops, a tangled skein made up of economics, culture, technology, tensions, ambitions and defeats. They try to make design a form of personal expression. It's that, too, but it isn't enough. The point is to distinguish the market from the culture. Italian design owes a lot to the culture of design and it hasn't necessarily created market products. Italy is, in fact, a country where architects and designers work in terms of applying thought to reality, while generally in the rest of the world reality is analyzed for ideas. These approaches can be schematically presented as the difference between an analytic and rational approach and an eclectic and intuitive one. This mental lightness, however, creates room for experiment."

Bibliography: G. Bosoni, F.G. Confalonieri, *Paesaggio del design italiano 1972–1988*, Milan 1988, p. 112; S. Suardi, "Lampade minime," in *Domus*, 790, February, 1997, pp. 82–85; a.c., "Artemide," in *Modo*, April, 2002, pp. 76–79; M. De Lucchi, "Artemide et moi," in the exhibition brochure *Designer's Days*, Paris, May 30–June 2, 2002; I.s., "Parigi celebra 'Michele De Lucchi,'" in *Modo*, 221–22, August–September, 2002, p. 4; A. Bassi, *Italian Lighting Design 1945–2000*, Milan 2003.

lamps
Cyclos
Artemide
production: 1984–85

Cyclos was the first lamp to be designed by De Lucchi and produced by Artemide. In formal conception it reflects his contemporary projects for Memphis, where the designer rang the changes on circular figures, here embodied in a product with a strongly visual impact and a perfectly simple structure. Cyclos is made of two parts: a painted metal support with a pair of rounded studs that fix in place a circular glass shade. The center of the glass is sandblasted to screen the light source, dif-

fract the light and prevent dazzle. The distinctive feature of the suspension version, produced from 1985, is the fact that it is held level by just two wires. Juggling with this mechanism involved the Artemide's technical office in a careful study of ways to balance the weights of the different parts. Adjustable in height, it contains the light source in a shallow reflector and the quality of the light it sheds is similar to that of the previous version. The models are still in production.

Bibliography: "La lampada," in *Quaderni di Domus*, 1, Milan 1984, entry 96; "Michele De Lucchi," in *La mia casa*, 182, November, 1985, p. 81; *Arredorama*, 155, February, 1986, p. 24.

Chromatic versions and drawings for the Cyclos series, Milan, May 16, 1983 and January 14, 1984.

Cyclos lamps, Artemide, ceiling and wall version, 1982–83, and pendant, 1984.

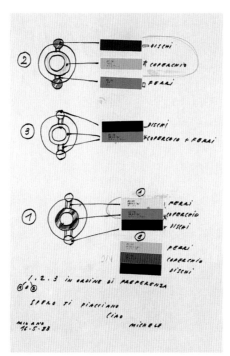

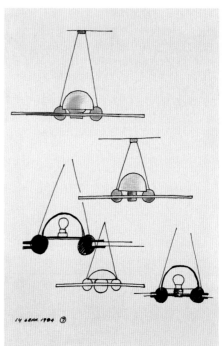

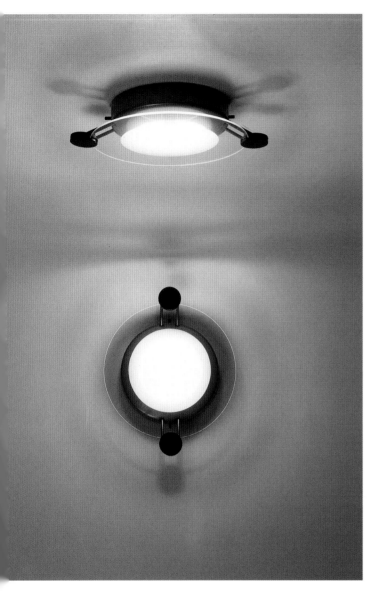

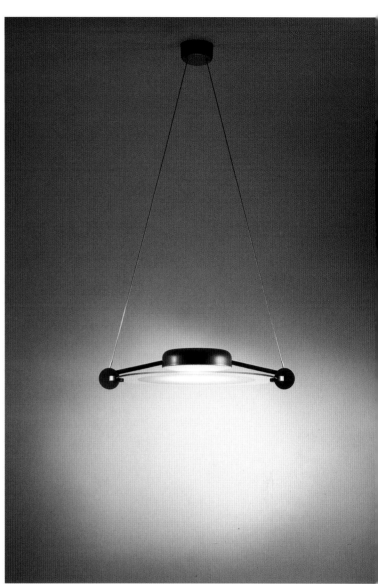

series of lamps
Tolomeo
Artemide
production: 1987
with Giancarlo Fassina

"I designed Tolomeo in 1986, or rather perhaps I should say I invented it in 1986," wrote De Lucchi in 2002, "because actually before the lamp itself I got the idea for a mechanism by looking at a fisherman hauling up a cross-net slung from a pole. To make the operation easier he had fixed the pole to the bank and was hoisting the net by pulling on a cord tied to the top of the pole with a pulley. It struck me as smart: using a small lever and a cable attached to a pole to hoist a weight. I had no idea as yet of applying the idea to a lamp. Everything fell into place a bit later when I undertook to design not a simple lamp but an updated version of the famous, best-selling, widely-used lamp marketed by Naska Loris, the so-called architects' lamp."
So De Lucchi began to study the mechanisms already in use for moving table lamps, and came to the conclusion there were three possibilities: the traditional friction joint, regulated by the pressure of a big joint on a large surface; the counterweight system, introduced by Edouard Wilfrid Buquet (patented in 1927), of which the best example is Richard Sapper's Tizio (1972, Artemide); a spring-balanced

cantilevered arm of the kind used by George Carwardine in the Anglepoise lamp of 1934, which later gave rise to Jacob Jacobsen's Luxo L-1 (1937), marketed in Italy by Naska Loris.
De Lucchi investigated the spring-balanced arm, trying to find a way (as he told Giampiero Bosoni in 1988) "to avoid emphasizing the mechanism, in fact concealing it as far as possible. […] This idea meant we could make it lighter and create an aura of mystery around the mechanism. Actually a lot of people can't make out how it works and wonder why there's that strange strand of wire running along the outside." The balance of Tolomeo is based on the tension that the thin steel wire outside imparts to the springs, each set inside the two arms, so they work not just for a small stretch but for the whole length of the arm to support the weight of the parts with a reaction equal and opposite to the movement.
After a first prototype assembled by the firm, Giancarlo Fassina, then technical director of research, realized the difficulties created by the mechanism and suggested replacing the aluminum pulleys with nylon: "That did the trick," says De Lucchi, "and I was so delighted that Tolomeo also bears Giancarlo's signature." Then followed the design of the actual lamp, again carried out in close collaboration with Artemide's technical office. They gradually solved the problem of threading the cable (it was built into a single metal profile together

Drawings and studies for lamps with a mobile arm, January 31, 1980 and January 10, 1980.

Drawings for the Tolomeo lamp, initial version with flanges on the diffuser and study of the tension system, 1986.

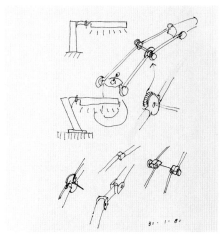

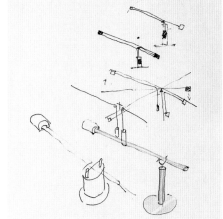

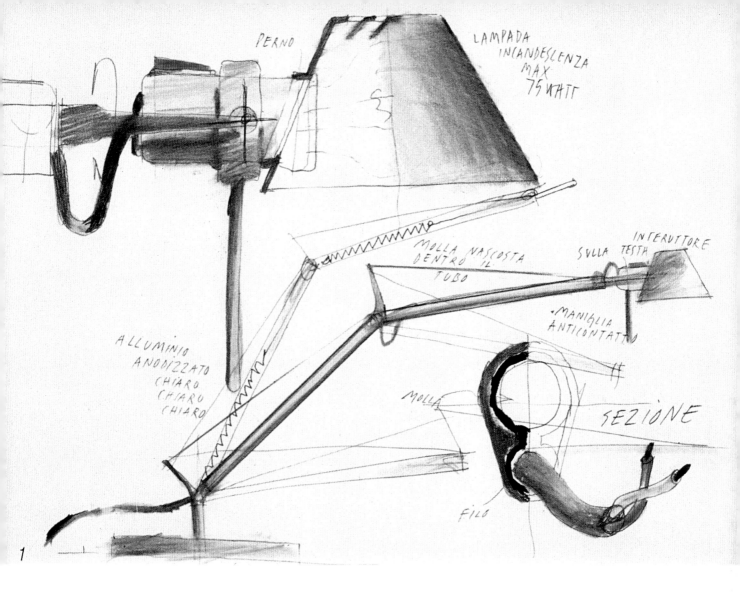

PERNO

LAMPADA
INCANDESCENZA
MAX
75 WATT

MOLLA NASCOSTA
DENTRO IL
TUBO

INTERUTTORE

SULLA TESTA

MANIGLIA
ANTICONTATTO

ALLUMINIO
ANODIZZATO
CHIARO
CHIARO
CHIARO

MOLLA

SEZIONE

FILO

1

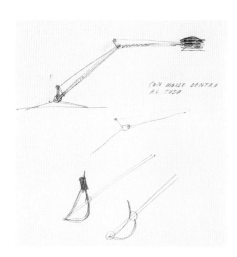

CON MOLLE DENTRO
AL TUBO

with the spring housing) and the form of the diffuser. The present "classic" design is a structure with a movable arm made of polished aluminum with a diffuser in the shape of a truncated cone, rotatable in all directions, made of opaque anodized aluminum. The lamp can be attached to the desktop by a clamp, a fixed pivot or a round base in polished aluminum. The position of the "hat," set off the axis of the bulb fitting and the bulb, is one of the distinctive features of Tolomeo as compared, for example, with Luxo. This feature freed the top of the diffuser, so allowing a hole to be made in it to let the air through and prevent overheating. This opening (originally flanged but later plain) focuses the light narrowly on the work surface when the head is rotated downwards.

First presented at the 1987 Euroluce exhibition in Milan while still a prototype, it was immediately a great commercial and critical success. In the first year of production, different colors, finishes and other variations were explored. In the second year a lever added to the arm joints enabled the lamp to fold in two, reducing its volume and simplifying packaging. Tolomeo's success certainly stemmed partly from its flexibility and adaptability to different kinds of spaces and settings in both the office or the home.

With its distinctive design, hi-tech yet graceful and self-effacing, after its debut it lent itself to numerous versions in a wide range of different sizes (from micro to mega). The first of these was a wall lamp followed by a floor lamp, reading lamp, spotlight, outside wall-lamp, clamp lamp, suspension lamp, off-center lamp, fluorescent lamp, and so down to a version in 2004 with a diffuser made out of parchment. With the arrival of new lighting technologies, other versions have been marketed with compact energy-saving halogen and fluorescent bulbs (and a special reflector designed for the fluorescent version). In this way Tolomeo spawned a family of lamps with a wide range of applications.

Tolomeo has won many awards, including the Compasso d'Oro-ADI in 1989. It is certainly an icon of Italian design. Present in the permanent collections of many museums, "it has also become in many ways a symbol of the modern object," De Lucchi stated in 2002. "It often turns up in photos presenting consumer products, fashions or furnishings. I sometimes see it in films and many of my architect colleagues use it instead of the old Naska Loris, though architects don't always find it easy to use a product designed by someone else. Naturally I'm proud of this." Showing that the reasons for the success of a product are not always conscious, he adds: "If I knew how I designed Tolomeo I would design others like it."

Bibliography: S. Anargyros, "Michele De Lucchi," in *Intramuros*, 10, 1987, pp. 17–18; G. Bosoni, F.G. Confalonieri, *Paesaggio del design italiano 1972–1988*, Milan 1988, pp. 112–15; K.M. Armer, A. Bangert, *Design anni ottanta*, Florence 1990, p. 108; "L'alogena degli anni '90," in *AxA*, 1, May, 1991, p. 64; M. Carrara, "Le lampade che inventano la luce," in *Casaviva*, 215, November, 1991; S. Kicherer, *Michele De Lucchi*, Milan 1992, pp. 171–83; M. De Lucchi and F. Clivio, "Licht ins Dunke," in *Design Report*, 10, 1995, pp. 70–73; C. Melograni, "Lezione su una lampada: introduzione alla funzionalità," in *Rassegna di architettura e urbanistica*, 92–93, May–December, 1997, pp. 54–66, esp. pp. 57–59; R. Rizzi, A. Steiner, F. Origoni (eds.), *Disegno italiano. Compasso d'oro ADI*, 1998, pp. 122–23; S. Suardi, *Michele De Lucchi. Dopotolomeo*, exhibition catalogue, Milan 2002; A. Bassi, *Italian Lighting Design 1945–2000*, Milan 2003, pp. 232–43, esp. pp. 237–39.

Tolomeo lamp, Artemide, 1986, table version.
Prototype of the Tolomeo lamp, Artemide, 1986 (Centre Georges Pompidou, Paris).
Prototype of a lamp with an alternative mechanism, 1992–93 (Centre Georges Pompidou, Paris).

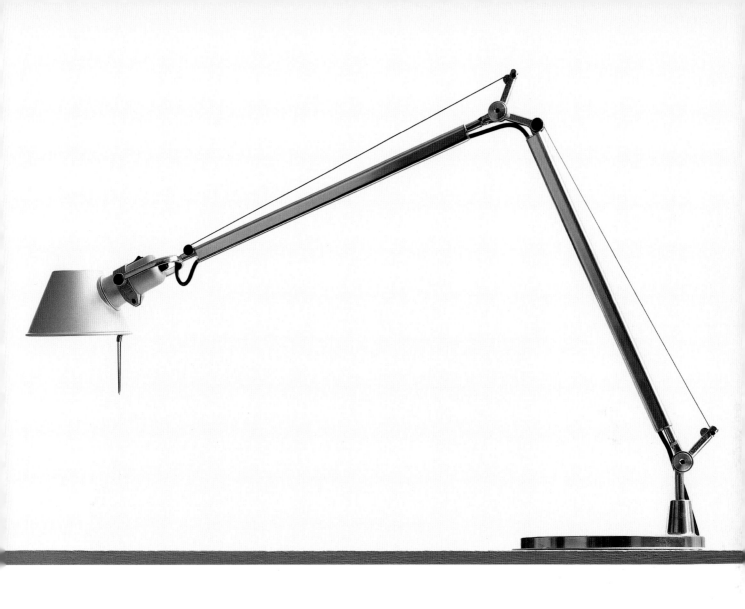

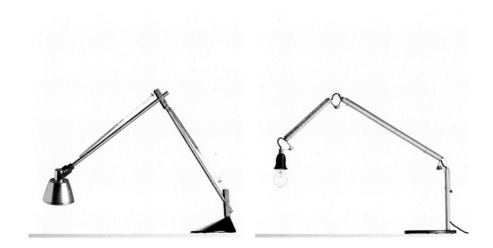

Tolomeo pendant lamp set
off center, Artemide, 1996.

Tolomeo clamp lamp, Artemide
1995.

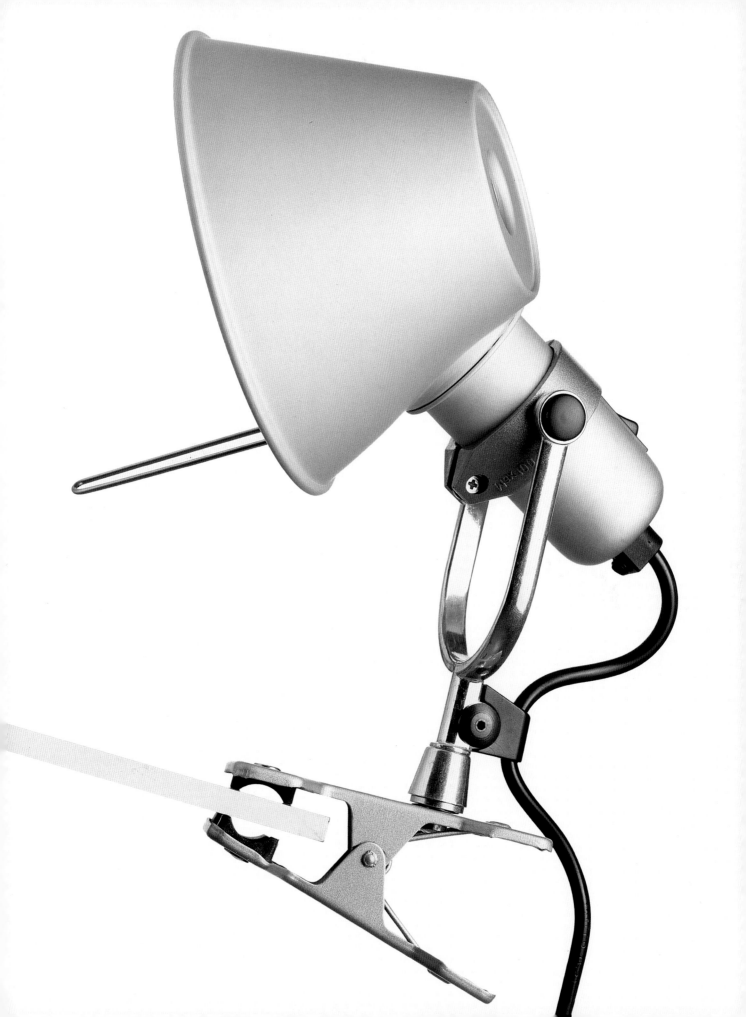

RB Rossana

1981–85
kitchen
214
production: 1985

1989–90
kitchen
La Fenice
production: 1991
collaborator: Mario Rossi Scola

The provocative display of colorful toylike home appliances for Girmi in 1980 led to De Lucchi's long working relationship with RB Rossana, a kitchen-manufacturer with a special interest in innovative design. (It eventually merged with the Febal group.) De Lucchi likes to experiment with the design of the kitchen because it is the focus of domestic life. His kitchen projects are complete systems; they can favor (or inhibit) basic anthropological values and forms of behavior that have an emotional side to them: eating, socializing, nostalgia, efficiency and so on. His first kitchen project was the 214, an upmarket kitchen that remained in favor for many years. The basic modular elements are reconfigurable; the wall and floor units create a single flat panel, a homogeneous surface with embedded electrics. The handles are recessed and the base forms a continuous plinth. As the designer explains, this model "transports the kitchen from the world of wall-hung units to the flush-fitted cupboard." It is "a composition made up of solids for storage and voids for operative functions" and allows for endless reconfigurations. One significant innovation was in the fully furnishable space below the wall units, which is usually disregarded and treated more as a cavity than a functional space. Here it is organized in niches for washing, cooking and storage, thanks to a special set of shelves (made for glassware, china, pan lids, etc.) and the fact that it can be fitted with doors.

The range of materials confirms that this is a quality product: beechwood, laminates, marble or stone for the work surfaces, with burnished copper—protected by transparent varnish—lining the niches, and shutters painted with polyester enamel in a basic range of eight colors. The qualities of the kitchen were captured in photos by the American Tom Vack. Invited to Europe by De Lucchi, after the RB Rossana campaign he became one of the leading design photographers of the nineties. The kitchen's overall image was refined and very sophisticated: it recreated the geometrical patterns and bright colors of Memphis, but it also expressed a hi-tech precision and an austere elegance. The kitchen accessories included items such as chairs and stools and notably the circular La Festa table (1984), which rested on a central pedestal supported by four disks.

The La Fenice kitchen was designed in 1989–90. One innovation was its clear distinction between the unit containing the work zones (washing and cooking) and the unit containing storage space (refrigerator-oven and pantry). The latter has a restrained, linear design, with small handles and a baseboard and ventilation grids in aluminum. The cooking unit evokes a traditional, almost nostalgic, image, and is dominated by a large metal cooker hood. This image signals the craving for safety, stability, and warmth typical of the nineties: in the most complete version, this "hearth" is a wooden counter on metal legs covered by a marble work surface that contains the recessed sinks and hob and is continued onto the back wall, which is also lined with marble.

Other projects for RB Rossana were the prototype Expo (1992, with Mario Rossi Scola), with a central island containing the sink and a work surface, and Mdl95 (produced from 1996, with Mario Rossi Scola), a kitchen designed for a wider public with the emphasis on functional, specialized storage units.

Finally, the support of RB Rossana (in the person of Fulvio Brembilla) led to the creation of the Solid research team in the mid-eighties. Headed by De Lucchi, it was staffed by eight young designers, both Italian and foreign, who spent two years designing products for the kitchen. Between 1983 and 1990 De Lucchi also designed all RB Rossana's exhibition stands and in 1988 its stores (with Ferruccio Laviani).

Bibliography: "La cucina '214 Rossana,'" in *La mia casa*, 173, December, 1984, pp. 56–57; "Michele De Lucchi," in *La mia casa*, 182, November, 1985, p. 81; S. Anargyros, "Michele De Lucchi," in *Intramuros*, 10, 1987, pp. 16–17; "Un programma diversificato," in *Interni*, June, 1987, pp. 30–31, 92–93; "Michele De Lucchi, Un nuovo rapporto tra uomo e tecnologia," in *L'ambiente cucina*, 94, May–June, 1993, pp. 30–31; L. Bocchi, "Una cucina ad alto contenuto di design," in *ddn*, 34, 1995, pp. 84–89; "Michele De Lucchi," in *Interni Annual*, issue dedicated to Italian International Kitchen Design, 1995, pp. 28–29.

214 kitchen, RB Rossana,
1981–85.
La Fenice kitchen, RB Rossana,
1989–90.
La Festa table, RB Rossana,
1984.

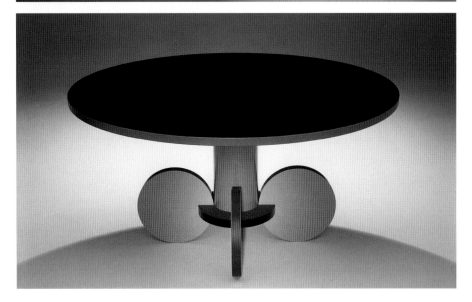

dispenser
Kleberoller
Pelikan
production: 1987
collaborators: Ferruccio Laviani,
Angelo Micheli

The Kleberoller dispenser was an innovative object: here De Lucchi invented a type of product that had never existed before. He had first contacted Pelikan with designs for highlighters and pens which never made it to production. However, the firm had invented this novel addition to its line of office materials as a way of spreading glue and whiting-out typing errors and asked De Lucchi to design a dispenser as it was preparing for mass production. This device, with its twin spools, became De Lucchi's most widespread product in the late eighties, probably, as he commented in a recent interview, "because the design intuitively solved all the practical problems."

In working on the design he examined all the crucial points, only superficially banal, and tried to make them clear to the user: the best way to hold the dispenser (between finger and thumb); how to spread the material on the paper and avoid malfunctioning (by pulling it towards you, not pushing it away); how to open it and insert the refill. The result is a unique object, apparently simple, with a vaguely trapezoidal profile, which evokes a toy car: the "business end" of the dispenser, the underside, is red; the body is dark blue or transparent and the rolls inside visible. The slanting edge is milled to indicate the correct grip and the direction of the gesture; the circle in the bottom corner indicates the position of the reel.
Seen as part of De Lucchi's broader quest to transform the office environment, even a small object like the dispenser is eloquent: its tactile and symbolic qualities reveal a light and playful approach to communication, making work more homely and rescuing it from the technocrats.

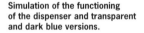

Simulation of the functioning of the dispenser and transparent and dark blue versions.

office accessories
Segmenti
Kartell
production: 1989–91
collaborator: Tadao Takaichi

This is a series of office accessories in thermopolymer. The design emphasizes their family likeness and is based on the formal principle of the free-standing slab. This was a feature of De Lucchi's architecture in the same period and it also turns up in some of his interiors, as he sought to create connections between the different scales of design, one of the basic principles behind his work. The pieces in the series (twelve in all between 1988 and 1991) include a pen rack, photo holder, correspondence trays, drawer pedestals, disk-racks and floor-based elements like umbrella stands, coat stands and waste baskets. Their forms all derive from the archetypes of the square and the rectangle.

De Lucchi chose a very distinctive formal vocabulary, completely detached from the sculptural qualities of resins, generally emphasized by die-casting. Instead he used forms based on strict geometries with orthogonals and diagonals, alternating smooth surfaces and ribbed (with the grooves carved obliquely into the slabs) and eliminating sealed edges as far as possible to emphasize the independence of each slab. This called for special care in designing the molds, as he sought the smallest thicknesses that would stand up to use and the need to conceal the points of injection.

Their dark coloring brings out the pieces' formal austerity, clean lines and technological qualities, while the rubber-like texture of some surfaces creates a more tactile and playful impression.

Bibliography: E. Morteo, "De Lucchi Associati: oggetti da tavolo per Kartell," in *Domus*, 715, April, 1990, pp. 4–6; AA.VV., *Design Future Philosophy*, exhibition catalogue, The Design Centre Singapore, 1992, p. 96.

Some items in the set of the twelve desktop accessories.

stores
Mandarina Duck
collaborators: Nicholas Bewick,
Paolo De Lucchi, Geert Koster, Angelo Micheli,
Silvia Suardi, Mario Trimarchi

De Lucchi has worked widely in retail design, from the first Fiorucci stores he designed in partnership with Ettore Sottsass (1981–83) to stores in Japan (1986–90) and the Pulloveria Americanino chain (1988, with Nicholas Bewick). In this field, his working relationship with Mandarina Duck (a brand created by Plastimoda in 1977) is noteworthy for its quality and continuity over a fair span of time. He first worked for the firm in 1984, designing a set of rigid suitcases (with Ferruccio Laviani and Angelo Micheli) that never went into production. Three years later he was commissioned to redesign the chain's sales points (franchises, specialist shops and counters in department stores). Because of the trend towards predefined "systems" then gaining ground in the sector, De Lucchi suggested an industrial approach to modeling the interiors of sales points to create a single, constant, reproducible image whose quality could be controlled all the way from the design phase. The result is a sort of "architecture set within the architecture" and it reflects De Lucchi's predilection for panels as a formal principle in the design of buildings. Here the panels are made from reconstituted marble and plaster and mounted on a metal frame anchored to the walls. There are spaces left between the edges of the panels, so revealing their texture and geometrical design. They have sockets set in them at regular intervals to hold stamped aluminum brackets and rods. They can also be cut out to form niches, closed and lined with plain glass shelves. All parts of the system are modular and designed to match the sizes of the products. This system deliberately showcases the products on sale like museum exhibits, displaying them individually against light-colored backgrounds and using spotlights to pick out their elegant textures and designs. For the sake of contrast, De Lucchi used natural materials

Exploded axonometric drawing of the system for the Mandarina Duck stores (first generation 1987–93).

Mandarina Duck store on Corso Europa, Milan. The system is based on composition panels made of marble and plaster fixed to the walls by a metallic framework (first generation 1987–93).

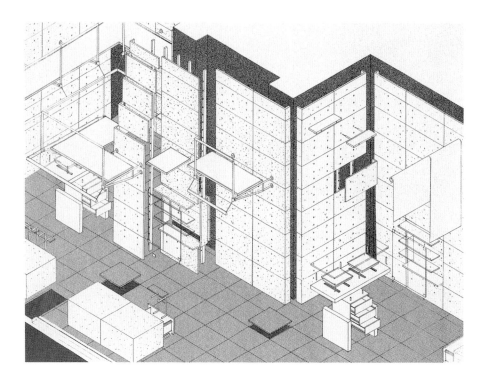

like dark basalt for the floors and teak for the sales counters. In 1994 the first of the stores was made over in response to the client's brief: to represent the brand worldwide as a standard-bearer of the excellence of Italian design. The modular system sheathing almost the whole surface of the interior was not essentially architectural, but consisted of display stands made of matt absorbent aluminum with built-in electrics. The lighting was again set in the ceiling so that its angled beams would enhance the products. A highly distinctive feature of the project was the use of macro images dominating the interiors: they were meant to be changed every three months as a way of continually renewing the appearance of the stores. After revamping the Milan showroom (1996–97, with Sezgin Aksu and Geert Koster), in 1998 a new design was proposed for the store in Milan's Via Montenapoleone to show off a line of clothing introduced the previous year. The idea of lining the walls with a smart "skin" remained essentially the same, but this particular design was never used again. The last generation of Mandarina Duck stores designed by De Lucchi in 2000 adopted a completely different approach to displaying products. Instead of being a system defining the architectural container, it set out the wares (handbags, suitcases, garments, etc.) on a series of stands, so creating a sort of "market" where shoppers could finally touch the products. "It completely redefined the function of the store and the way it was perceived," De Lucchi told *Interni* in 2000, "again in the essential effort to renew and enrich the shopping experience, so-called. We have gone from a shop window, where everything was displayed openly and publicly, to a store interior that encourages a sense of discovery."

The display units, seeming to evoke animal forms, mainly consist of thin shelves with rounded forms supported by curved legs. Arranged freely in the interior of the store, often in clusters to form islands, they create a fluid landscape studded with shelves and products bathed by the glow from suffused lighting that emphasizes the perimeter of the space and the bare walls. Particular care has been lavished on the design of the materials and finishes; for example different tones of white with varied textures and visual effects are used to color the walls, ceilings, shelves and supports. The mass-produced display units can also be used in small sales points, so cutting installation costs. The first store in the new series opened in Bologna.

Bibliography: m. am., "Mandarina Duck inaugura un negozio rivoluzionario," in *La Repubblica*, (Bologna), March 10, 2000; S. Suardi, "Il Dinosauro," in *Interni*, 502, June, 2000, pp. 110–13.

Mandarina Duck store on Corso Europa, Milan. General view and detail of the system of continuous shelving in opaque absorbent aluminum. Macro images, replaced every three months, are used to vary the interior (second generation 1994–97).

Mandarina Duck store, Bologna. The focus is no longer on the walls but on the display stands which create a "market" where the products can be touched (third generation 2000).

La Fenice

Osaka (Japan)
collaborator: Tadao Takaichi
client: Intergroup

La Fenice, a building in Osaka's "American Village," is the fullest representation of the theoretical principle that De Lucchi defined as "slab architecture." It is made out of flat, thin walls, with carefully calculated dimensions, an element that is both compositional and structural. The architectural project grows out of the way different slabs are combined and superimposed, an approach that is markedly different from the traditional method of composition by predefined volumes. The spaces they delimit are austere and simple, yet also rich and highly articulated; the elevations and plans eschew modularity as a way of avoiding the repetitive and impersonal aesthetic of industrialization. (Though De Lucchi sees industrial building as essential in modern architecture, he feels it should not be flaunted.) As is clear from the building's elevation, each slab is seen complete all the way to the edges and is not affected by decorations or apertures: doors and windows are fitted naturally into the spaces between slabs. The façade is never an abstract two-dimensional plane; it has its own thickness, its own depth. Here it is ranged along three successive alignments, with a large front slab concealing the entrance; two slabs at the sides covering the intermediate stories, leaving a central aperture to illuminate the stairwell, and two upper walls which are narrower, providing support for the upper landings and the square deck set in the middle; this anticipates the steep pitch of the roof, also made of slabs.

Evoking both the myth of the Phoenix and the famous La Fenice opera house in Venice, after which the building is named, De Lucchi notes that this façade is like a stage, open on the inside to the world, with the two slabs like the "flats" in a theatre or curtains, or "wings that glide down vertically." The audience are the people who stroll through the building. But the exterior is dominated by the wall of stone, "harsh and expressionless" rather like "one of the walls of a

Model of the building, rear elevation.

View of the zig-zagging staircases.

quarry" (as Junichi Simomura observed), giving the small building a severe, fortified appearance that contrasts with the lightness and vertical tensions of the interiors with their continuous spaces, sudden contrasts of level and gaps between floors and catwalks. The interiors are dominated by the zig-zagging flights of stairs—the designer likes to compare them to the vistas in Piranesi's prisons—and the two cylindrical pillars that traverse the whole space vertically.

The distribution of the interior is complex, being laid out on seven levels, two of them below ground. "A sort of skyscraper in miniature," De Lucchi calls it, since each floor has an area of just 60 square meters. The ground floor, slightly recessed, is an airy hallway free from partitions with a higher ceiling than the others. The two intermediate levels, with access also provided by an internal spiral staircase, contain reception and conference rooms; the brightly lit attic story houses an art gallery. In Japan there is a high tax on a building's shadow: this explains the decision to keep this one relatively low above ground. One feature of the project is the effort

to achieve an effect of permanence and durability, in contrast with the frenetic replacement of buildings typical of Japanese cities. As the client notes, the Vicenza stone used to face the building has a deep, opaque surface that absorbs bad weather and dries slowly, its color tones changing over time. Other details, carefully finished in every part of the building, are meant to weather naturally. Even the side walls are faced with stone, though they almost abut onto the neighboring buildings: they will be revealed when the others are demolished. The junctions between the panels are not filled with grouting, so the edges of the stones will gradually become rough and slightly corroded. The water stagnates and evaporates naturally in some small fissures, so accelerating this process of coloring and staining.

Bibliography: *La Fenice*, brochure, La Fenice Art Gallery, Osaka 1992; T. Kiriyama, "Michele De Lucchi: Standard-Bearer of Italian Design," in *Michele De Lucchi*, exhibition brochure, La Fenice Art Gallery, Osaka 1992.

View of the model of the building showing the three successive alignments of the façade.

View of the main elevation. The whole building is faced with Vicenza stone.

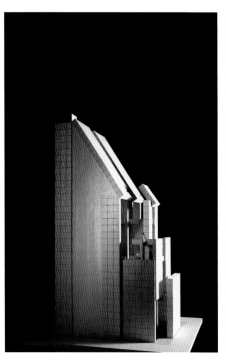 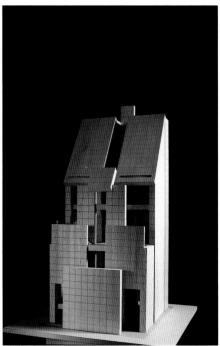

research center
Olivetti System & Networks
Bari
with DEGW
collaborator: Nicholas Bewick
client: Olivetti

The design of the Olivetti System & Networks research center in Bari is an extensive office complex, laid out essentially as two aligned and intersecting blocks that create an H-shaped footprint. At the points of intersection cylindrical towers house the stairwells. The pivot of the composition is a cylindrical structure that forms the head of a transverse block set in the middle.

Designed by De Lucchi in collaboration with DEGW, the building contains over 11,000 square meters of office space. The computer workstations are intensively arranged in spaces that combine comfort with flexibility. This will make it easier to update the technology, overhaul the company organization and introduce other changes as they become necessary, a possibility that needs to be borne in mind when designing large-scale projects.

The building includes executive conference and reception rooms, which converge on the cylindrical body, as well as a canteen and spaces for social activities laid out in the basement of the pivotal building. The offices are arranged in four three-story blocks, 18 meters wide and 36 deep. Architecturally the building is an example of the composition by slabs that De Lucchi began to apply in the late eighties, notably in some projects in Japan, such as the La Fenice building in Osaka and an apartment block in Kyoto. The slabs are abstract figurative elements, but at the same time quite distinctive. The slabs are always complete, nothing is allowed to encroach on them, and they are juxtaposed at contrasting perpendicular or oblique angles. They are ranged in a grid around the building, with uprights and sloping roofs forming a "second skin," set at a distance from the external walls to mediate the transition from interior to exterior, while they also provide protection from the harsh light and heat of southern Italy. This protection made it possible to scale down the air-conditioning plant in proportion to the volume of the interiors. The extensive strip windows of the circular block are likewise protected by curved sections of masonry carefully placed to provide the right amount of shade. The ends of the complex are also marked by vertical slabs set at 45-degree angles to mark the ends of the rectilinear route that crosses the building. As dynamic presences that enliven the setting, some of them open out like the "wings" of a stage in front of the inner courtyards, while others are closed like shutters to screen the fire escapes and secondary entrances.

Model of the complex. The two aligned blocks are united by a central building with cylindrical towers.

Sloping roof panels mediate the transition from interior to exterior.

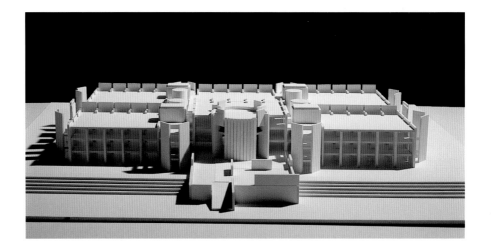

Vertical panels arranged
at an angle of 45 degrees
at the sides of the complex
and before the front elevation
screen the inner courtyards
and mask the secondary
entrances and fire escapes.

Sanpo House

Gumma (Japan)
collaborator: Tadao Takaichi

Built for an Italian marble-importer in Japan, this house was explicitly meant to advertise the material on the Japanese market, showcasing its beauty and other qualities. It is a "prefabricated marble house," the prototype of a building system consisting of three parts (entrance with veranda, living quarters and sleeping quarters), which can be reconfigured in different forms and sizes. In the development of De Lucchi's architectural language, the Sanpo House continues his research into the slab. It introduces walls with rounded edges and vaulted roofs with different radii of curvature. These elements are used to articulate the composition yet, like the slab, they retain their elementary shapes. The result is a richer architectural vocabulary with spaces that are highly articulated and less repetitive, more continuous. The forms contain traces of classical and Mediterranean architecture (the client wished to evoke a "popular Italian style"), but the design is still austere in a typically modern way. This appears in the volumes of the house: the central two-story block has a sloping roof with a barrel vault running down the middle, while the one-story wings at the sides are covered with lower vaults set parallel to the façade.

This threefold division is also reflected in the plan, with a large rectangular living room in the middle and two rooms with services at the sides. The entrances to the living room are concealed by two cylindrical walls that foreshadow the façade and are continued towards the ends of the building with pairs of square pillars supporting architraves. In the middle, clearly visible, is a large strip window, which opens out towards the fireplace.

On the inside, the living room is introduced by two walls arranged obliquely, which separate the kitchen zone from the anteroom and support the cantilevered staircase leading to the first floor. The upper level has just a single room which overlooks both sides of the house with large strip windows. All the windows are set in gaps in the geometry of the composition; even the frames, all consisting of a single

View of the front elevation showing the colonnade with a square section and the barrel vault that dominates the central block.

Model showing the tripartite division of the building with the higher central block and two one-story wings. The large windows in the rear elevation give a glimpse of the living room laid out in the central block.

panel, are concealed. The façade is preceded by two severe colonnaded portals ("propyla") with square cross-sections and dominated in the middle by a rectangular slab. This and the more conspicuous parts of the wall—the pillars and corners—are faced with two kinds of marble laid in horizontal bands that contrast with the red cladding of the other surfaces. Marble inlay also appears in the floors of the living room and the rear courtyard, which is enclosed by walls.

In 1990 and 1991, this phase of De Lucchi's work included other projects in Japan (a condominium block in Kyoto, the TK corner building in Tokyo, the 500 Forest Country Club in Mount Fuji) and the typological study of the Casa Tonda.

Bibliography: "Michele De Lucchi," in *Nikkei Architecture*, 9, 1991, pp. 97–99; E. Arosio, "Giappone Nostrum," in *L'Espresso*, 52, December 27, 1992, pp. 152–53; M. De Lucchi, "I designer si raccontano. Michele De Lucchi: confessioni di un architetto," in *Casa Vogue*, 239, March, 1992, pp. 88–95, esp. pp. 93–94.

Section of the Civic Museum
Groningen (The Netherlands)
collaborators: Geert Koster, Ferruccio Laviani,
Angelo Micheli (first project); Geert Koster,
Giovanna Latis (second project)
client: City of Groningen (first project),
Groninger Museum (second project)

As project coordinator for the design of the
Groningen Civic Museum, in 1988 Alessandro
Mendini invited a number of leading architects
and artists to each work on a section of this
heterogeneous complex. Opened in 1994, the
museum essentially consists of three blocks
projecting over the waters of a canal, with access provided by a footbridge. Mendini himself
designed the central entrance pavilion, service
block and storage spaces; and, on the east
side, the building housing the collections of contemporary art and temporary exhibitions, surmounted by the stunning de-constructivist
space by the Coop-Himmelb(l)au. The west pavilion is made up of two volumes: De Lucchi's low
fortified brick parallelepiped, originally intended
to house the local history and archaeology collections, and above it Philippe Starck's cylindrical construction containing the applied art collection. For a volume already defined by the
overall project, De Lucchi chose plain brick, a
traditional local material, inspired in part by
Berlage's architecture on the other side of the
river. He divided the interior into twelve sec-

tions, each representing a period of the city's
history, with forms inspired by the evolution of
local architectural languages. Here the handling
of light was all-important: the path from prehis-
tory to modern times was symbolically represented by the increasing brightness of the interi-
or together with clearer tones of color, inspired
by the hues of the brickwork, varying from the
dark red of past eras to the bright orange of
contemporary times. This scheme was radically
transformed after the floods in 1998, which
damaged the museum's historical and archaeo-
logical collections. When it reopened in 2001,
the pavilion housed a permanent collection of
works by the Ploeg, a group of Expressionist
painters active in Groningen in the early twentieth century, and exhibitions dealing with aspects of European Expressionism. The atmosphere of the central area, used for mounting
temporary displays, was produced by carefully
modulating the harmony of the lighting and materials, ranging from the warm floors to the patterns of colors and chiaroscuro created by over-
lapping panels set at a distance from the walls.

Bibliography: "Alessandro & Francesco Mendini, Philippe Starck, Michele De Lucchi, Coop
Himme(l)blau, In Groningen, Groninger Museum, Groningen 1994," in *Vogue*, April, 1991,
pp. 208–11; S. Dell'Orso, "È nato a Groningen
il museo degli anni Novanta," in *La voce*, November 1, 1994.

Plan of the first project,
**1989–90 (drawing by Geert
Koster) and view of an exhibition
area.**

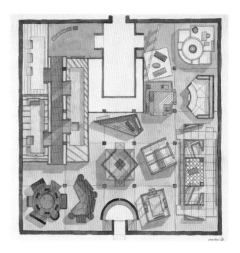

04

1990–99 Produzione Privata and the design of systems and services

Fiorella Bulegato

Produzione Privata

"It was New Year's Eve," De Lucchi told *Interni* in 1994, "marking the change from '89 to '90, and I was on my way back to Italy from Switzerland. I was on the approach road to the San Bernardino tunnel: when I drove in I was still assailed by misgivings, when I drove out my mind was made up." This was the beginning of Produzione Privata, an interesting experiment in the Italian panorama: a laboratory where the designer could experiment and think about quality products that would embody specific technologies and the skills of Italian craft workers, while avoiding the limitations and rigid restrictions of the market and industrial production.

In 1990 he described it as a sort of changing of the guard after the Memphis experience and the years with Sottsass spent coherently pursuing the sense of the project. "The idea grew up after the end of Memphis, a movement whose philosophy was to develop projects based on the needs of people, not industry.

But it was the shallower and more superficial side, the Memphis 'style,' that people caught at, and few of them grasped the deeper and more central concept, namely the research and experiment behind it. [...] And then, personally, I spend a lot of time thinking about the role of the architect in our period; I feel the urge to challenge and question the contribution made by my profession. Obviously there is no single practical result or concrete response, no one solution that suits all cases. But I also think the architect has a responsibility as an intellectual who is in a position to emphasize and make the most of the beautiful things we have, for example craft skills. That's why I and my wife Sibylle set up Produzione Privata together."

The firm launched a series of research projects, entrusting them to a number of small and medium-sized craft workshops that used traditional methods (in some cases quite ancient, practically extinct) as well as advanced and innovative technologies. The idea was that creating and developing design outside industry did

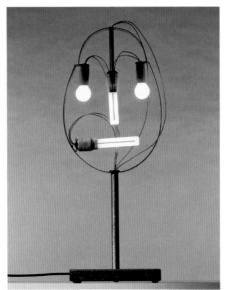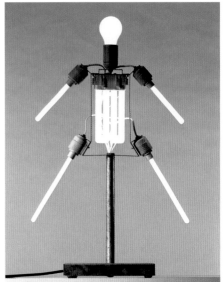

industry itself a service by finding new forms of figurative expression and making products new. "In Italy there is a rich subsoil of craft workers," De Lucchi told *Interni*, "people who are aware of their craft and have the sensibility to understand the cultural value of what they produce, who are happy to see their products presented at exhibitions and in the pages of magazines. This helps explain the worldwide success of Italian design and we are better able to comprehend phenomena such as Alchymia and Memphis (between 1980 and 1987 at Memphis we designed some 600 products, all produced using craft methods), and even the Milan Furniture Show. The Milan show is not a big business event, it's a showcase for craft furniture-makers, since many of the exhibits are not produced industrially. The success of Italian design is clearly made possible by the flair of the country's business class, but the craft workers are a seed bed for innovation and they can achieve manual qualities that industry tries to imitate without ever equaling." He saw craftsmanship as a field for ex-periment for designers, who could provide those "stimuli and human qualities that industry is no longer capable of creating. In the field of design the major companies are no longer capable of experiment. They try to create hot-house conditions for innovative research, with great labor and poor results." At the same time De Lucchi appealed to Italian craft workers, offering to work in partnership, to maintain and expand their culture while tenaciously safeguarding their spirit as people who "know how to get things done."

In this way Produzione Privata was like the *bottega* of a Renaissance artist, a place where mistakes were allowed. In fact they provided an opportunity for the designer to verify his ideas and turn out pieces systematically in small production runs and so at higher costs than in industrial production.

De Lucchi ran the firm at the same time as he continued with his normal work as an architect and designer. Various designers working in his office were also involved: Mario Rossi Scola, Elisa Gargan, Angelo Micheli, Ferruccio Laviani

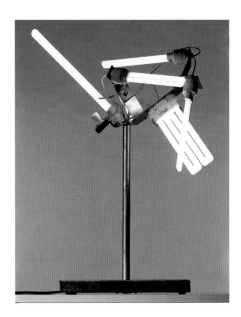

on page 113
Michele De Lucchi, 1992.

Viso and Burattino lamps, Produzione Privata, 2001.

Groviglio lamp, Produzione Privata, 2001.
These lamps developed ideas begun with the Lighting Field prototypes produced by Artemide in 1994.

Artemisia, Liriope, Giglio,
and Iris vases, in the collection
"A che cosa servono i vasi da
fiori?," Produzione Privata, 1999.

Phases of production of the Bianco vase, pottery workshop.

Bianco vase, Produzione Privata, 1990.
Vase in marble and stone, Produzione Privata, 1990.
Chair 2001, Produzione Privata, 2001.

and Daniela Danzi, who were active both in elaborating projects and organizing exhibitions at the office in Via Goito in Milan. Its first products were the Bianchi vases (1990, with Elisa Gargan) in ceramic, the series of Candlesticks in brass and silver (1990, with Elisa Gargan and Mario Rossi Scola), and a pearwood Bookcase (1990, with Elisa Gargan). These products expressed De Lucchi's changed attitude towards domestic interiors in the early nineties: he sought to achieve a feeling of reassuring intimacy, stressing the charm of natural colors and materials and creating archetypal forms. This perfect restraint, quite pronounced in some of his works, is found in all the products so far designed and produced by Produzione Privata.

In 1994, when the firm moved to Via Pallavicino, it was given a firmer business structure: Pio Barone Lumaga was put in charge of the technical office plus manufacturing, distribution and administration, Carlo Pintacuda of sales and Nora De Cicco of production and relations with the craft workshops. For some years the firm also became an area of experimentation for collaborators, as when it began production of Angelo Micheli's Rossa lamp in 1998. In 1995 it began to organize external exhibitions: the first was at Helen Van Ruiten and Peter Van Kester's Galerie Binnen in Amsterdam, followed by others in Belgium, Milan, Athens, Barcelona, Paris and various cities in Germany.

Its output can be analyzed by looking at the achievements of the nine workshops set up to date, distinguished by the materials worked, the technologies used in manufacturing or the principle of design. Over the years it has also created a number of special collections, produced in small production runs for connoisseurs and collectors. They include a set of twelve Murano blown-glass vases oddly named A che cosa servono i vasi da fiori? ("What's the use of flower vases?"), each a different shape, delicately colored and supported by a plain iron frame, produced in a numbered run of ten. Then there is a set of lamps called Pensando ai Poeti Sufi ("Thinking of the Sufi Poets"), de-

signed with Alberto Nason: nine lamps with low-consumption fluorescent bulbs on metal supports and with diffusers again made of Murano blown glass, some patterned by grinding or sandblasting, each produced in eighteen numbered copies.

The pottery workshop was the first to become operative. In 1987 De Lucchi had commissioned the ceramist Gisella Da Prà, owner of the Ceramiche San Marco firm at Nove (in Vicenza), to produce a series of vases and containers decorated in black and white patterns, similar in style to the laminates he designed in the Memphis period, and in 1990 he revived them for Produzione Privata. He designed three more vases (with Elisa Gargan; the Bianco vase is still in production): they had nicely rounded shapes and were all white. "It isn't just white, it's a color," he declared in 1999. "They have a distinctive, marvelous texture that varies with each batch of clay, with each firing." In the Caolina suspension lamp of 1996 (with Mario Rossi Scola) he explored the qualities of porcelain, designing a small white fluted diffuser with a texture that sheds a soft light.

The marble workshop began production in 1990. De Lucchi had long been familiar with the quarries at Massa Carrara, the principal source of marble and the center of the Italian market, visiting them regularly for Olivetti Synthesis. In 1982, for example, they had given him the idea for his Sholapur vase for Up&Up, made out of nine different kinds of marble. Now, however, he made three hand-polished vases (with Elisa Gargan, produced in nine copies each), where the three parts—the circular base of black Marquinia marble, stem of Dorata stone and container of veined white Carrara marble—are fitted together using a traditional technique and then glued.

The various objects built in the woodwork shop included furniture in 1991–92 for the designer's Milan home: its expressive language reflected the contemporary style of his Finenovecento collection for Design Gallery and Tokyo's Manager Restaurant NTT. Then there were two folding chairs for everyday use: the design sought to avoid the association between folding

chairs and cheap makeshift seating. In particular, Sedia 1993 (with Elisa Gargan and Mario Rossi Scola) was developed out of a piece made by Consonni International Masters in 1988. It consists essentially of three parts with profiles shaped in natural beech, finished without paint or wax, allowing the wood to develop the beauty of a natural patina over time. Sedia 2001 (with Gerhard Reichert) has a wooden cam mechanism that serves as both a comfortable armrest and a joint, allowing it to be folded despite its curved legs. The frame is dyed beechwood and the upholstery leather. The firm never set up a proper metalworking shop but it did produce metal parts for various products, ranging from the supports for its various collections of vases to candlesticks and the cast iron Pluvia plant pot (1997, with Mario Rossi Scola). "We wanted a sturdy plant pot that would be strong enough to stand up to violent storms and contain the luxuriant vegetation of the lake." For Pluvia, De Lucchi chose plain cast iron combined with a round glass base, so that the heavy, compact ogival

body seems "practically to rest on nothing." Craftsmen capable of casting it proved hard to find. Cast iron shrinks as it cools and tends to become misshapen. Although the mold was very precise, each piece differed considerably from the others and there were a large number of rejects in production.

The candlesticks designed in 1990 (with Elisa Gargan and Mario Rossi Scola; a series limited to ten copies for each model and material) came close to the idea of "minimalist machines" and De Lucchi developed them in a special laboratory. They grew out of his studies of simple mechanisms, being fitted with springs and balances to make it easy to replace the candles.

The various working parts transform the "classic" slender candlestick into a curious and elegant piece of gadgetry. Heavy, being made out of solid brass, either plain or silver-plated, with their different tactile qualities, each is made from a solid piece of metal. These "minimal machines" are the outcome of the designer's careful study of mechanisms capable of determining

Bayezid and Nizami lamps, Pensando ai Poeti Sufi collection, Produzione Privata, 1999.

the form, functioning and esthetics of a product: figuratively delicate objects with intricate mechanisms that could never be produced industrially and were often difficult to assemble by hand. Writing in *Domus* in 1992, Enrico Morteo pointed out: "This idea of simple gadgetry seems to be a more mature version of his old playfulness [the reference is to De Lucchi's early "radicalism"-*ed*.]. Objects that click open and shut, lamps with mobile screens to modulate and orient the light, candlesticks with obtrusive counterweights that are in equal measure superfluous and physically necessary. With the idea of the machine and movement, the irony that was originally a skin applied to his designs becomes an integral part of the design itself, making the product's form and functioning more flexible."

He explored this aspect of design most of all in his lamps, starting with the prototype Diomede (1983–84, Artemide), then clearly embodying it in Tolomeo (1986, with Giancarlo Fassina, Artemide) and the Sigira lamp (1991, with Mario Rossi Scola, ClassiCon). It crops up

again in the Tecnico table (1987, made for Cappellini International): this has a mechanism that keeps the tabletop horizontal as it moves up and down. The concept is clearly exemplified in Macchina Minima no. 7 (1991, with Mario Rossi Scola). This is a ceiling lamp that can be rotated and moved up and down by means of slender cables attached to a central counterweight in polished brass, and fixed in various positions by a painted metal rod with a twofold movement. Macchina Minima no. 8 (2001, with Alberto Nason) is an updated version with a similar lampshade made of parchment-finish paper.

In Trefili he experimented with a table lamp (1993, with Mario Rossi Scola). Here the design concentrates on the web created by three colored electric wires; at the same time it slips easily into a slim, specially designed flatpack. Still following in the wake of Munari, the Tre Forchette lamp, Petali centerpiece, Ovali serving dishes (1997, with Mario Rossi Scola) and other pieces, presented in April of the same year at the exhibition "Crudités," formed part

Artista lamp,
Produzione Privata, 2002.
Treforchette lamp,
Produzione Privata, 1997.

Macchina Minima no. 8
suspension lamp,
Produzione Privata, 2001.

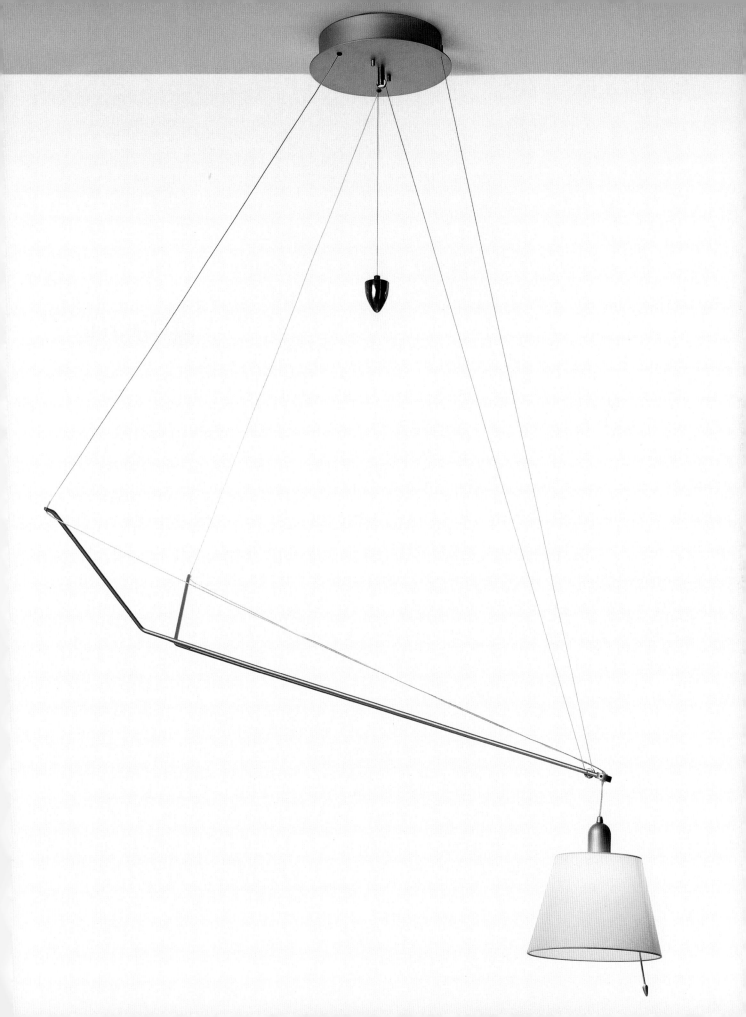

of De Lucchi's reflections on the ready-made. He drew on the exercises of the Dadaists, Duchamp, Achille Castiglioni and his experience at Olivetti in assembling components made by firms scattered across the world. De Lucchi explored this field in the light of the contemporary concern with the life cycles of products, recycling and reassembling existing pieces in the search for new esthetic qualities, an original formal and a figurative vocabulary. He continued this approach in the Bottiglia series of vases (1995, with Mario Rossi Scola), where he took some rather featureless glass food jars, sliced off the bottoms and set them inverted on metal supports. He repeated the trick in the Marionette series of lamps (2001, with Alberto Nason and Mario Rossi Scola, produced in a run of ten numbered copies of each model), a continuation of the work produced by Artemide in 1994 with the Lighting Field prototypes.

The glass workshops particularly distinguished themselves in blown-glass lamps and vases. "I feel today we no longer think of the beauty that flowers bring into the home and contemporary settings [...]," De Lucchi pointed out in 1999. "The most effective material is glass because it is transparent, it gives you a glimpse of the water."

De Lucchi's first work in blown Murano glass goes back to 1982, when he designed the Vega lamp (from 1986 Fontana Arte) for Luciano Vistosi, master glassblower and owner of the firm of the same name. This was a linear table lamp with the head in glass of various colors. His next works were the Antares vase for Memphis and other pieces for Cleto Munari, "But my real first designs in glass were the ones I did for Produzione Privata," he said in 1999, "because they grew out of a much deeper insight into the essence of glass and above all a fuller understanding of Murano's importance and its cultural history." The Acquatinta series (1996, with Mario Rossi Scola), with the variants Acquaparete (1998) and Acquamiki (1999, with Alberto Nason), are the essence of his work in this field. Blown in wooden molds, they have simple, continuous forms. The diffuser is a shallow cylinder with a roughly spherical protuberance on top that houses the bulb fitting. Its form shows off the various finishes of the glass, which may be crystal or etched, sandblasted, transparent, opaque, mirror-finished, and colored in a variety of hues (transparent green sandblasted; glossy white or black). Each model sheds a dif-

ferent kind of light. Also blown in a single piece, the Fata and Fatina table lamps (2001, with Alberto Nason) are like glowing mushrooms; made of satin-finish glass, they are mounted on circular bases made of painted metal. Among the vases, Basequadra (1997, with Alberto Nason and Mario Rossi Scola) combines the transparency and delicacy of raw blown glass, made mainly from siliceous sand containing iron oxide and chrome, with the rough of the natural metal. Its texture provides a sharp contrast to Pluvia, combining iron and glass with notable technical skill. In 2004 he also made a prototype of a floor version.

In 1999 the workshop that produced glass folded in sheets began turning out the Cubetta and Quattropieghe lamps, eventually leading in 2002–03 to the models La Grande (a large pendant lamp made of folded silkscreened glass) and Meteora, again with Alberto Nason. But his latest experiments are in Pyrex, a material produced chemically (glass containing borosilicate), transparent, tough and versatile, made by hand. The Ipy collection (2002–03, with Nora De Cicco and Aya Matsukaze) is made out of handcrafted blown glass using tubes of Pyrex glass. The hemispherical and conical shapes are obtained by the natural expansion of glass heated over a flame and controlled manually. In all the models, the housing of the bulb fitting, sheathed in porcelain, is transparent, while the diffuser comes in a range of different finishes.

Bibliography: "Licht-Flügel," in *md*, 3, March, 1992, pp. 68–69; E. Morteo, "Michele De Lucchi Macchina Minima n. 7," in *Domus*, 744, December, 1992, pp. 6–7; "Produzione Privata: Ein Designer realisiert ein individuelles Konzept der Produktion un Präsentation von Produktion," conference of Bremen Design-Innovation '92, 1992; A. Boisi, "Il nuovo laboratorio di Michele De Lucchi," in *Interni*, 446, December, 1994, pp. 178–85; "Michele De Lucchi, Ohne Titel. Without title," in *Gegenstände zur Zukunft*, exhibition catalogue, Stuttgart 1994, pp. 50–51; J. Huisman, "Saai speelkwartier van De Lucchi," in *de Volkskrant*, November 24, 1995, p. 30; "Michele De Lucchi van Memphis tot Produzione Privata en verder," in *Pi Projekt & Interieur*, 6, 1995, pp. 38–39; *Produzione Privata*, company catalogue, Geisenheim, 1995; J. van der Kris, "Alles wit en onbruikbaar. Rustigen wilde vormen van De Lucchi en Sottsass," in *Nrc Handelsblad*, November 23, 1995, p. 3; R. Bertugno,

"Accendere la notte," in *Io Donna*, suppl. to the *Corriere della Sera*, 36, 1996; "Produzione Privata," in *Design Report*, 9, 1996, p. 14; P. Scarzella, W. Schepers (eds.), *New Design in Glass*, exhibition catalogue, Düsseldorf 1996, p. 40; R. Sias, "Come un artista rinascimentale," in *Il cartolibrario*, 7, August–September, 1996, pp. 14–19; "Acquatinta Lamps and Eidos/Pegaso Furniture," in *I.D. The International Design Magazine*, July–August, 1997, p. 163; E. Melet, "Re-design van Michele De Lucchi," in *de Architect*, July–August, 1997, pp. 60–61; ua, "Rohkost aus privater Produktion," in *Design Report*, 8, 1997, p. 19; R. Cerulli, "Sperimentazioni private," in *Ville & Casali*, 5, May, 1998, p. 41; S. Kicherer, *Raccolta Completa della Produzione Privata di Michele De Lucchi*, Milan 1999; G. Maggioni, "Corpi leggeri," in *Elle Decor*, 6, June, 1999, pp. 31–32; C. Morozzi, "Création et artisanat," in *Intramuros*, 83, June–July, 1999, pp. 36–37, 77; M. Vercelloni (ed.), "Raccolta completa della Produzione Privata di Michele De Lucchi," in *Interni*, 494, October, 1999, p. 64; "Up to date. Design," in *Confort*, 42, 2000, pp. 6–7; "Genie mit Gefühl. Lucchi, Lucchi!," in *Mensch & Büro*, 5, 2001, pp. 94–100; M. De Lucchi, "La mia 'Produzione Privata,'" in *Artigianato*, 45, April–June, 2002, pp. 10–13; I. Forestier, "Objets sensibles," in *Maison Française*, September, 2002, p. 48; "Ipy, Ultim'ora," in *Abitare*, April 13, 2002, p. 18; S. Polano, "Produzione privata. Michele De Lucchi e i paradossi del design," in *Casabella*, 699, April, 2002, pp. 84–87; "Runde Sache," in *Vogue Deutsch*, May, 2002, p. 146; E. Ascheri, "Michele De Lucchi le souffle du verre," in *Coté sud*, 84, October–November, 2003, pp. 131–38; M. Di Bartolomeo, "Progettati senza fretta," in *Domus*, 859, May, 2003, pp. 116–23; "Michele De Lucchi Produzione Privata," in *Mug*, 4, 2003, pp. 31–33; E. Ascheri, "La magia del vetro," in *VilleGiardini*, April, 2004, pp. 110–14; B. Loyer, "Michele De Lucchi, Productions privées," in *Techniques & Architecture*, 469, 2004, pp. 121–25; "Michele De Lucchi/Milano," in *Brutus Casa*, 49, April, 2004, pp. 206–07.

Mold for Fata blown glass lamp, Produzione Privata, 2001.

Fata and Fatina lamps, Produzione Privata, 2001.

Candela lamp,
Produzione Privata, 1999.

Acquatinta lamps,
Produzione Privata, 1996.

office system
Sangirolamo
Olivetti Synthesis
production: 1991
with Achille Castiglioni
collaborators: Ferruccio Laviani,
Angelo Micheli

"Sangirolamo was the first work that I did with Achille Castiglioni, who was the second of my great masters after Ettore Sottsass," said De Lucchi in a recent interview. "Working alongside him provided an opportunity to observe Castiglioni's approach to design. He replaced drawing by a kind of dramatic verve. The experience was an eye-opener because I came from the school of Sottsass, where you would start drawing even before you began to think. Here I saw the other side of the genesis and development of design based on reflection and on a curious, ironic, irreverent attitude towards things, which carried you along in its wake." The far-ranging research into the basis of this office system by Castiglioni and De Lucchi involved studying numerous life-size wooden models. They started by analyzing the needs of the client, even surveying offices in literature, film and paintings. At a certain point they found themselves looking at Antonello da Messina's painting of *St. Jerome in his Study*, where the saint is withdrawn from his surroundings in a quiet raised corner. The saint and his attitude came so close to the spirit of the design that they named the system after him. "Achille Castiglioni and I," De Lucchi told *Interni*, "had an ideal image of the cultivated executive who has no need to emphasize his status or celebrate his position by surrounding himself with symbolic trappings." They designed not so much an office as a study: intimate, peaceful, welcoming, a place where he could keep his books, notes, projects and familiar objects. "The great innovation in Sangirolamo," De Lucchi told *Modo*, "strikes me as the fact that it's not the usual kind of system furniture. It's a set of individual pieces of furniture that form a movable scenario (the table and the cabinet in its various configurations),

Achille Castiglioni with the Olivetti Synthesis engineers studying the Sangirolamo office system, 1990.

Achille Castiglioni in front of the prototype of the table Sangirolamo system, 1990.

but at the same time they are a modular system. [...] There is no single overall arrangement. In fact these two items could well be sold separately. We spent a lot of time above all on the imagery of the design, trying to make sure it didn't look like standard-issue office furniture, big on technology [...] A sort of movable scenario within which the position of the user can be changed, either encouraging or avoiding intimacy and privacy. Sangirolamo embodies a double spatial model. The table represents the public side of the suite, open to dialogue, where you receive people, call a meeting or talk things over. The cabinet, especially the slide-out desk, is private, like the bookcase, which has a place for everything." The system consists of a table (so slender as to be practically two dimensional), cabinet and console. The tabletop is in cherry or rosewood and can be protected with a woolen cloth, the usual baize lining. It has four slender curving legs set at the sides, made of cast iron, finished in grey epoxy resin. Some commentators saw the soft curving line of

the legs as harking back to Art Nouveau, but it is actually meant to prevent them getting in the way of people gathered around the table. Cabinet and console (with the same legs as the table) also come in cherrywood and palisander with their surfaces treated with transparent closed-pore varnish. They form the floor-based and raised versions of the "private" part of the system. The wall cabinet is designed to house a video, printer, fax, hi-fi or TV set, with all their cables fed through the backboard. It can be turned into a fully equipped workstation by adding a slide-out desk and a set of compartments protected by a drop front. Semi-transparent glass doors (available on request) provide a view of the equipment inside.

So the duo worked, De Lucchi noted, "Innovating through the design and not the technology. [...] I believe that 'the aura' of Sangirolamo stems from a lot of different factors, like the visual choices, the materials, the chiaroscuro effect of the design of the cabinet, and more generally from a set of qualities that I would

describe as sensuous and relate directly to current sensibility." The strikingly original feature is the contrast between figurative lightness and structural weight in these two pieces of furniture. The table has a top 3 meters long but everything below 70 centimeters high forms a void (even the cabinet). And De Lucchi concludes: "The quest for innovation involves all the figurative aspects. [...] Studying technology is just one part of innovation. [...] Technology is not conspicuous in Sangirolamo, yet I feel that even technologically it rests on substantial research into engineering, so as to make it perfectly stable with a minimum of material structure."

Bibliography: "Achille Castiglioni, Michele De Lucchi, San Girolamo, stanza di studio," in *Sangirolamo, Olivetti Synthesis*, Milan 1991; L. Arduino, "I sempreverdi," in *Progetto ufficio*, 5, September–October, 1991, pp. 64–68; A. Bucci, "Uno spazio per pensare," in *Habitat Ufficio*, 50, June–July, 1991, pp. 90–93; F. Doveil, "La stanza di studio," in *Modo*, 132, 1991, pp. 52–54; P. Guidi, "Mobili speciali per il boss," in *Fortune*, July–August, 1991; "Idee per uno spazio, conversazione con Achille Castiglioni e Michele De Lucchi sulle nuove sfide della professione designer," in *Notizie Olivetti*, 4, December, 1991, pp. 24–26; L. Porta, "'Sangirolamo', stanza di studio. Il fascino di un progetto," in *Office Layout*, 39, May–June, 1991, pp. 30–34; D. Premoli (ed.), "Olivetti Synthesis: Sangirolamo, dal museo all'ufficio," in *Interni*, 410, May, 1991; *Un progetto di comunicazione Sangirolamo, stanza di studio*, Milan 1991; "Repräsentativ und operativ," in *md*, 6, June, 1991, pp. 98–99; "Sangirolamo: aristocrazia austerità per l'ufficio del manager colto," in *Ufficio stile*, 5, June, 1991, pp. 39–41; M. Zelinsky, R. Taker, "Do Olivetti's avant garde Italian contract furnishings have a future in the U.S.?," in *Interiors*, November, 1991, pp. 70–71; "Michele De Lucchi e Mario Trimarchi, Considerazioni preliminari," in *Annual Ufficio*, 1991–92, pp. 40–45; g.m., "Una nuova linea allo Spazio Olivetti," in *la Nuova Venezia*, February 29, 1992; "Nuova gamma di mobili per manager in mostra allo Spazio Olivetti," in *Il Gazzettino*, February 28, 1992; "Olivetti Synthesis il mondo dell'ufficio," in *Class*, 6, June, 1992; S. Polano, *Achille Castiglioni tutte le opere 1938–2000*, Milan 2001, pp. 400–01.

Michele De Lucchi and Achille Castiglioni, Sangirolamo office system, Olivetti Synthesis, 1990. Profile of the leg and model of another version of the frame.

The set of office furnishings; model of the square table; drawing of the bookcase, Massa, June 29, 1990.

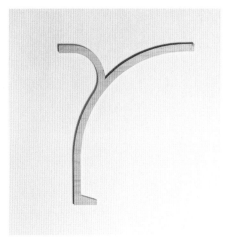

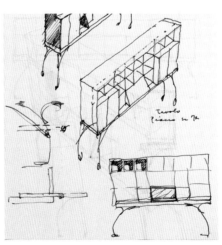

furnishings
Finenovecento
Design Gallery
production: 1991
collaborator: Mario Rossi Scola

In 1991, four years after the last exhibition with Memphis, De Lucchi first exhibited a new collection of furniture at Milan's Design Gallery. "The novelty of this show," Barbara Radice wrote in the catalogue, "lies in its intimate and personal quality, its detached meditation on manners and styles. It has a self-effacing quality that shuns striking and provocative images. As if to say: no, I'm not playing like that any more, because the game has changed, it has to change or is changing."

Here De Lucchi sought to move beyond the Memphis experience, partly because, compared with the earlier period, he no longer saw any stable figurative context, so there was no longer anything to fight against. He now worked with traditional forms and values, convinced that "just as Memphis tried to be provocative in the eighties," as the designer said recently, "so we were called on to be re-assuring in the nineties. For this reason I called this furniture Finenovecento ["late twentieth century"], because this sense of security should grow out of a sort of synthesis of all the figurative cultures of the twentieth century."

His search for "timeless values," evident in other projects of the same period—like the Joyce lounge suite for Moroso and the interiors of the Manager Restaurant in Tokyo—led him to make this set of sofas and armchairs very solid and to lavish special care on the details. They owe their distinctive character to the careful balancing of forms and compositions and the use of natural materials, colors and patterns. He combined solid cherrywood, a feature of the whole collection, with laminates made out of recycled paper in traditional textures and muted colors. Even their names are reassuring, each piece being called "Dedicata a" ["Dedicated to"] something: in this way the table's name means dedicated to generosity, the desk to elegance, the coat stand to hospitality, the cradle to happiness, the bookcase to literature, the chairs to courtesy, the sofas and armchairs to idleness and quiet, the desk to curiosity, the lamps to wonder, and so forth. Yet De Lucchi still adds touches of instability and disproportion to the designs. For example, the sofa has three massive legs that seem to push at it from behind and the bookcase rests on a single large wooden ball, as if to deny all a priori certainties or truths.

Bibliography: "Finenovecento Exhibition by Michele De Lucchi," in *FP*, 34, 1991, pp. 64–66; "Finenovecento Exhibition by Michele De Lucchi," in *Wind*, 13, winter 1991, p. 50; "Milan," in *Axis*, 38, winter 1991, p. 16; B. Radice, *Finenovecento*, exhibition catalogue, Design Gallery, Milan 1991.

Drawing of an armchair for the Finenovecento collection, January 6, 1990.

Dedicato alla Letteratura bookcase, Finenovecento collection, Design Gallery, 1991.

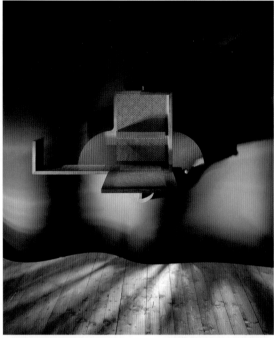

Finenovecento collection,
Design Gallery, 1991.
Dedicato all'Ospitalità
coat stand.
Dedicato alla Curiosità
drinks cabinet.
Dedicato all'Eleganza table.

Dedicato alla Cortesia chairs.

1991

sofas and armchairs
Joyce collection
Moroso
production: 1991
collaborator: Elisa Gargan

Conceived as characters in a literary café, this collection of sofas and armchairs designed by De Lucchi for Moroso in Udine was given Joycean names (Dublino, Dedalus, Ulisse and Plurabella). They clarify the way the designer was thinking in the late eighties and early nineties after Memphis, turning his sensibility towards what he thought of as "timeless values": a personal interpretation of the traces of the past as a way of coping with a period of worldwide economic, social and cultural confusion. Related to his parallel experiments in the Finenovecento collection and the furniture he designed for the NTT, Ulisse and Dublino in particular break up the traditional geometry of the sofa. In contrast with the usual arrangement, it is the back of Ulisse and not the seat that is supported by the two front feet made of solid wood. Slanting and longer than the two rear feet, which support the seat, they prop up the back and armrest which form a single continuous wrap-round form, calling attention to the separation between the two parts. Dublino is based on a similar structural concept but has squarer and more massive forms. It is also stuffed with foam polyurethane and upholstered in leather or fabric. It also makes a strict distinction between back, seat and armrests. Judged rather eccentric when they appeared in 1991, they were never a great commercial success.

**Drawings for Moroso armchairs,
January 7, 1991.
Drawings for armchair,
January 6, 1990.**

**Ulisse and Dublino sofas
and armchairs break
with the traditional structure.**

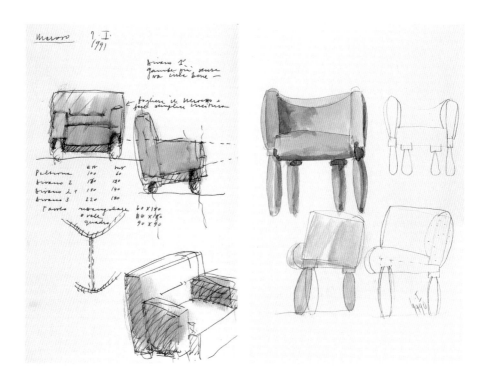

Manager Restaurant NTT
Tokyo (Japan)
collaborators: Angelo Micheli,
Tadao Takaichi
client: NTT Japan

Set at the top of the NTT skyscraper, the Manager Restaurant enjoys panoramic views over Tokyo. This project is based on material and stylistic contrasts between the treatment of the surfaces and the forms, especially in the furnishings. Playing up to the orthogonal geometry created by the building's pillared structural grid, the ceiling, floor and walls form a sort of rigid cage. The combination of steel and glass defines walls and ceiling in a linear design that includes the air conditioning vents and spotlights, while the floor is laid with two types of wood forming a precise square pattern. To offset the "coldness" of this setting, the furnishings, which are in closer contact with the patrons, are made gently enfolding and natural-looking by using materials such as leather

and giving them markedly softer shapes.
In the center, for example, to make the interior more intimate, the tables set on a chubby rounded pedestal are separated by wooden screens. Though based on a cruciform plan, the screens rise in high curving lines and culminate in a white flower vase. They reflect the same "decorative fervor" as the Memphis experiments: the chairs are specially designed in three different variants and their parts are made of different materials and colors, composed in complex curving forms.
This project, together with the almost contemporary Finenovecento collection for the Design Gallery and the Joyce lounge furniture for Moroso, clearly represented De Lucchi's attitude to the world at the start of the nineties. "I liked the idea of reusing and passing on forms, materials and patterns that had stood the test of time," he said recently. "For this very reason they are closer to our human sensibility and more reassuring, creating a sense of security, familiarity and warmth."

Table and chair and views of interiors. The rectangular geometry of the structure contrasts with the warm materials and soft forms of the furniture.

Olivetti computer monitors

1985–87
Computer monitor
production: 1987
collaborator: Eric Gottein

1994–96
Multimedia computer monitor
production: 1996
collaborator: Masahiko Kubo

The first electronic appliance that Ettore Sottsass—at that time Olivetti's design director—commissioned from De Lucchi in 1985 was a computer monitor, one of the first PC monitors based on cathode tube technology. Faithful to Sottsass's teachings, De Lucchi set the tube in a case in the form of a truncated pyramid, symmetrical on its horizontal axis. Separating the configuration of the slightly bulging screen from the casing, he rounded the edges and recessed the front so that a simple frame bordered the screen, reducing the visual obstacle to the user. The design of the ventilation intake called for careful study. The upper surface had a ridged cross-section that fell away sharply at the back: at Olivetti it was dubbed the "washboard." The monitor was a commercial success. It stayed in production for ten years, after which it was replaced by the one De Lucchi designed in 1994. In this the geometrical configuration, though as rigorous as before, was softened by applying what at the time the designer called "a system of soft shadows." The front was a square almost wholly lacking in chiaroscuro effects, while the box behind it was shaped by a subtly curving line. The upper surface was riddled with circular ventilation holes. The two computer monitors designed in 1985 and 1994 clearly document the evolution of De Lucchi's expressive language and the way he worked within the company.

Drawings of computer monitors, Olivetti, 1984.

Computer monitor, Olivetti, 1985–87, 14 inch version with control panel set below.

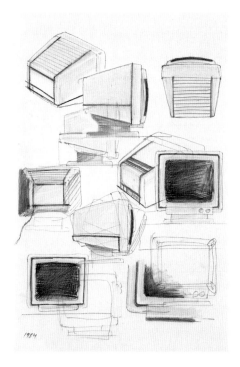

Multimedia computer monitor,
Olivetti, 1994–96,
general view, side and study
models in polystyrene showing
the development of the form.

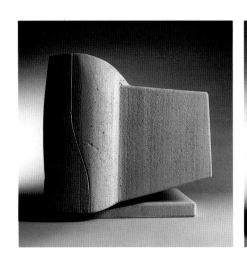 

Olivetti laptops

1992–93
Philos
production: 1993
collaborator: Hagai Shvadron

1993
Echos 40
production: 1994

1993–94
Echos 20
production: 1995

"Philos is the object that I was able to design in the fullest detail," De Lucchi commented recently, "because Olivetti practically asked me to devise a sort of continuation of the Quaderno, a multimedia portable designed by Mario Bellini in A5 format and hence almost pocket-sized, thinking of it as if it were a book but A4 in size. In April 1992 I took over from Bellini as director of design."

Philos was presented in 1993. Apart from the evocation of a printed book evident in the design of the side which, when closed, formed a series of flat lines, it contained two highly original innovations. The first was an interesting attempt to compromise between the usability of the mouse and the portability of the computer. In 1991 Apple had already replaced the external mouse with the trackball (sunk into the plane of the keyboard). Here the user simply pressed a key and the ball and housing folded out from the right-hand side of the laptop. Certainly better suited to right-handers, the ball was set in a sort of elastic cradle that rested on the worksurface below: it fitted neatly into the palm and responded easily to oscillations of the hand.

The second innovation was that the keyboard folded out, giving access to the batteries and the hard disk below. The disk could be extracted enabling the data to be transferred to another computer. The case was a pleasant grey color, as in other projects that De Lucchi was working on at the time, for example the casing

Philos laptop, Olivetti, 1992–93, with hinged keyboard, front and side views.

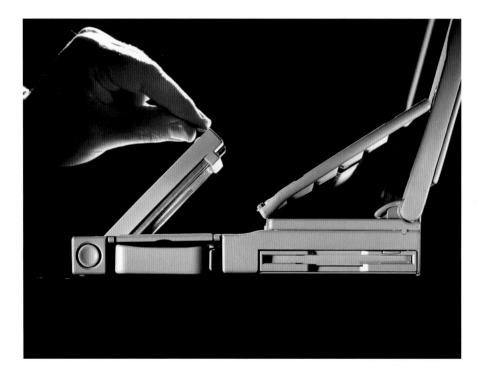

of desktop computers. Here he also used bulges and recesses to pick out the parts that responded to the user's touch, making it easier to identify the laptop's various functions.

Just a year later the model Echos 40 embodied the tactile and chromatic guidelines that emerged from research conducted by Clino Trini Castelli. It looked very much like a rubber brick. "To date, in electronics, the color of the material was in fact almost always syntactical," Clino Trini Castelli explained to *Interni* in 1995. "It corresponded to ergonomic requirements that set the product in an area of neutral identity. But I wanted to make up for this disembodied quality stemming from high technology with something more earthbound, something that would enhance its physical presence." De Lucchi amplified this new identity: color, tactility and "natural" perceptions were achieved by using a mixture of metal oxides applied to the thermoplastic rubber that covered the internal workings of the computer. He designed a flat, monolithic object, strictly geometrical but soft, with some fea-

tures—such as the buckle-shaped catch—that made it look more like an ordinary portable accessory. By setting the keyboard well back he was able to place the trackball in front in the middle, with a clear rubber-finish space all around it, on which the palms could rest comfortably when using the keyboard. The outside was in ABS oxide color plastic to ensure rigidity and durability and protect the workings. In 1994 it won the Smau award.

Olivetti's brief for Echos 20 was to design the smallest possible portable computer with the same performance as the most powerful desktop model. It was produced in dark blue to make it look familiar. The keyboard was shifted forward slightly, still leaving a strip to support the palm, while the trackball was restored to the top right-hand side. After experimenting with other configurations and ergonomics to provide the most comfortable grip and use, De Lucchi integrated the ball with a mechanism that raised it when the lid was lifted. The structure (lower casing, upper casing and lid) was further simplified and

Echos 40 laptop, Olivetti, 1993.
Details of the design of the side and buckle clasp.

General view.
Detail of the panel at the front with the trackball in the middle.
Side view.

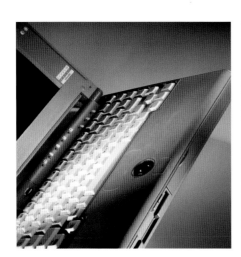

rounded off to enhance the computer's slenderness and tactile qualities. This was one of the last Olivetti laptops to have been designed, engineered and manufactured in Italy.

Bibliography: F. Carlini, "L'icona giusta nel tasto sbagliato," in *Il Manifesto*, June 10, 1993, p. 13; P. Catalano, "Office tomorrow," in *Gap Casa*, September, 1993; "Olivetti," in *Asch*, 18, January, 1994; "El diseño y el color de De Lucchi dan identidad propia a 'Echos' de Olivetti," in *Negocios*, 5, 1994; "Echos 44 color," in *PC*, 11, 1994, pp. 126–27; T. Edelmann, "High-Tech in Rosarot," in *Design Report*, 9, 1994, pp. 98–99; "Nueva estetica," in *El País*, May 25, 1994; A. Boisi, "Echos: il mattoncino informatico," in *Interni*, 450, May, 1995, pp. 140–43.

Echos 20 laptop, Olivetti, 1993–94, detail of the trackball and the side.

Olivetti computers

1993
M6 Suprema
production: 1993
collaborator: Mario Trimarchi

1994–96
Envision
production: 1994
collaborators: Felipe Alarcao,
Alessandro Chiarato

1996
Xana
production: (1996)
collaborators: Felipe Alarcao,
Masahiko Kubo

Between 1993 and 2000 De Lucchi designed the casing of various computers, particularly the front panel and air intakes. This essentially meant devising a shell to house functions such as the slot for the floppy disk, the control panel—including the power switch, lock, LEDs— and the ventilation grid, which is set vertically in the standard version and horizontally in the slim version. In the various versions of the M6 Suprema series of 1993 (some of which never went beyond the prototype stage), he housed the parts in a precise geometry of forms and created chiaroscuro and tactile effects to make the functions obvious and immediate.

By 1994 technical improvements had increased the lines of definition on TV screens and eliminated the problem of flutter in fixed images. This led Olivetti to commission De Lucchi to design the shell of a new multimedia tool that would use a TV set as a remote-control monitor. Called the Envision project, it was launched in September of the same year and development continued until March 1996, but it was never a commercial success. De Lucchi concentrated on the functional arrangement of the parts in the front panel—CD player, floppy disk drive, loudspeakers, the housing of connections and the labeling—and their design. First presented in red, it was then produced in dark grey and in 1995 won the Smau award.

The Xana series was presented in 1996, at a time when the company was presenting its first multimedia model, in an attempt to relaunch its personal computer sector. De Lucchi designed the metal casing, video and packaging. No longer required to setting the ventilation grille in the front panel, the designer grouped the components in a single console on the right, leaving the name standing clearly by itself on the opposite side.

Bibliography: P. Catalano, "Office tomorrow," in *Gap Casa*, September, 1993; "Heim-PC mit Büro-Potential," in *Mensch & Büro*, 1, 1996, p. 96.

M6 Suprema computer, Olivetti, 1993.

Xana computer, Olivetti, 1996, monitor, case and packaging. Models of the desktop and tower versions. Envision, Olivetti 1994.

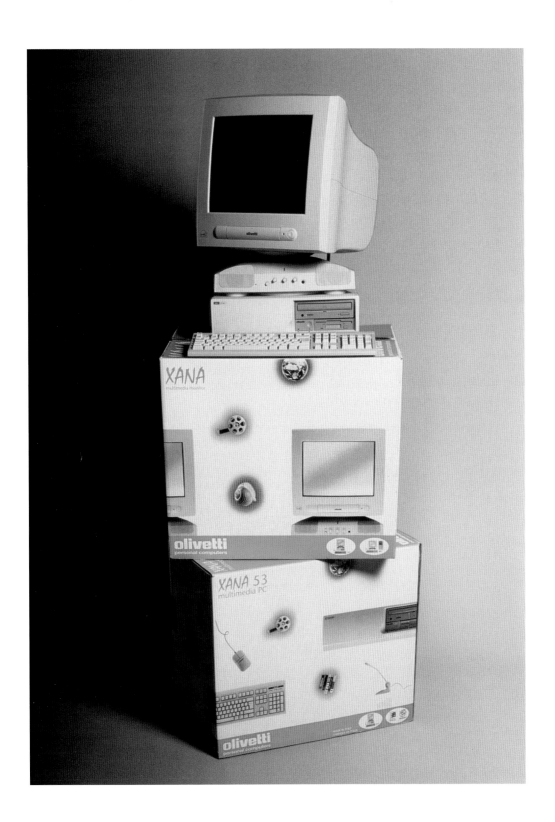

Multimedia kiosks
Olivetti-Mael Tecnost

production: 1995
collaborators: Antonio Macchi Cassia,
Enrico Quell

This multimedia kiosk was meant to meet the demand for automated equipment to replace staff in carrying out repetitive tasks or providing information to the public. They were designed at the start of the decade, essentially as self-service computers that bridge the gap between customer and suppliers of services in banks, sales points, car parks, railroad stations and so on. They were meant to be used by a wide public, sitting or standing, and above all they had to be proof against vandals. Compared with current models, which generally take the form of a box containing a screen and technical equipment, the kiosk designed by De Lucchi (in collaboration with Antonio Macchi Cassia, in those years a consultant at Olivetti for industrial design) had the general form of a personal computer and so could be easily recognized as an instrument capable of providing certain services. The shell housed four existing machines with integrated functions of different degrees of technical complexity. This made it easier to replace parts, simplified the software interfaces and made it generally more user-friendly. The models came in three different colors, each offering different services. They all had a "smart" top section which, depending on the version, housed a computer, monitor, loud-speakers, slot for a credit card or printer.

The basic model was red, came equipped with a touch screen or eight-function keypad, and was set on a plain column; the yellow one incorporated a laser printer to issue tickets and receipts, with a slot for the purpose in its lower section; the dark blue model could be used seated and, in addition to the printer, had a shelf for a keyboard and could be used for video-conferencing. It had a monolithic front but the side was more richly modeled, sharply recessed to underline the upper part and show that the slightly rounded front consisted entirely of the door providing access to the equipment inside. These singular objects, whose forms and colors recall De Lucchi's experiments with Memphis, proved particularly successful in Japan. The standard model was subsequently developed for certain firms such as the San Paolo bank in Turin.

Bibliography: "From left field to mainstream," *Blueprint*, April, 1994; "Olivetti," in *Asch*, 18, January, 1994; "Olivetti," in *Aschi Shimbun Weekly Aera*, May 29, 1995, p. 87; "Olivetti," in *Nikkei Business*, 4, 1995, pp. 50–51; "Olivetti," in *Nikkei Business*, 5, 15, 1995, pp. 112–13; "Olivetti," in *Nikkei Business*, 6, 19, 1995, pp. 84–85; "Olivetti," in *Nikkei Business*, 9, 11, 1995, pp. 44–45; "Michele De Lucchi, Olivetti," in *Nikkei Business*, 3, 25, 1996; R. Sias, "Chioschi multimediali non solo per la banca virtuale," in *Ufficio stile*, 1, January–February, 1997, pp. 28–32.

The three models of the multimedia kiosk: the yellow one includes a printer; the basic model is colored red; and a version colored dark blue can be used while seated.

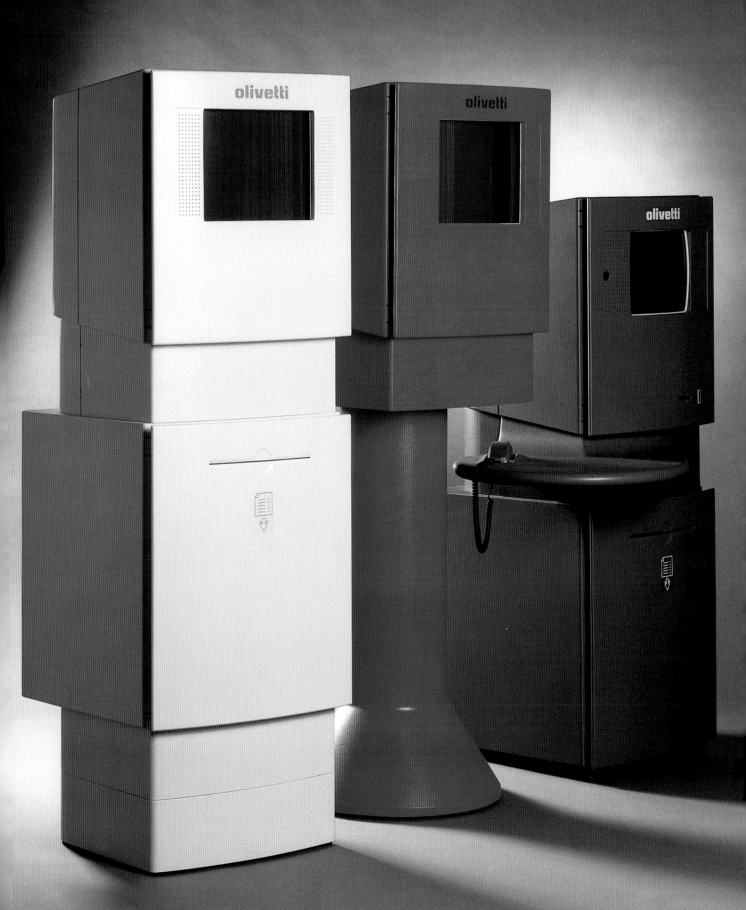

Olivetti faxes

1994
fax
OFX 1000
production: 1995

1996–97
fax
OFX 500
production: 1997
collaborators: Masahiko Kubo, Johannes Kiessler

1998–2000
multifunctional fax
OFX 300
production: 2000
collaborator: Masahiko Kubo

1999
multifunctional fax
Jet-Lab 600
production: 2000
collaborator: Masahiko Kubo

In a period when the fax was spreading from offices to homes, De Lucchi designed the OFX 1000, the first of a series of home fax machines designed for Olivetti from 1994 to 2000. This enabled the company to extend the range of its products, then largely confined to business machines, where sales were brisk.

The OFX 1000 used inkjet technology, eliminating the need for rolls of thermosensitive paper. It could print in thirty-two tones of grey on ten sheets of standard A4 paper at a time, making the reproduction and filing of documents much simpler. This was the second generation of Olivetti plain paper faxes, which made original-quality copies without any risk of their blurring, curling or fading. The print quality made them competitive with office photocopiers and they used solvent-free ink, reducing their environmental impact. They had an automatic tel/fax commutator so they could be used with a standard telephone line.

The design sought to keep the fax compact while using the same technology as the firm's office models. Production on the assembly line

OFX 1000 fax, Olivetti, 1994: front and side views and "vegetable" interpretation of the volumes.

consisted of fitting the working parts to a tray-shaped base and then adding a cover. At points where De Lucchi was unable to pare down the volume, he tried to ease its visual impact. The high base is slightly recessed to make it less conspicuous and raise the body of the fax, which is modeled as a series of superimposed volumes and rounded lines fitting snugly around the working parts. The sinuous design of the case and paper feed enhances the slim, dynamic profile, while the curved control panel in front looks friendly and simple to use with its clear display and soft colored keys.

As in other projects from the same period—such as the video for a multimedia computer (1994–96, with Masahiko Kubo)—the designer sought to model the forms to create soft chiaroscuro effects, embodying them in a general geometrical construct built up out of pure solids. Olivetti later used the same base to produce the OFX 1001, a version with squarer lines for Bosch and other distributors. Three years later Olivetti, for some years the leading manufacturer of inkjet faxes, needed to extend its product range for distributors eager to put their own names on fax machines. The result was the OFX 500, a machine that lent itself to customization while offering the maximum economy in technology, parts and costs. The base set a limit to the possible configurations so it was eliminated, though deeper analysis showed this actually made the fax heavier: at Olivetti it was dubbed the *panettone* ("Christmas cake"). "We had to try and make it slimmer and lower," De Lucchi recalls, "so the design would give the impression it was lighter than it actually was." The result was a cheap and solid instrument with outstanding technical specifications, which occupied only half as much desk space as the OFX 1000. It had two

OFX 500 fax, Olivetti, 1996–97: mechanism, general view and detail of the "mouth" that ejects the paper.

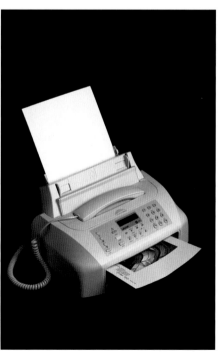

distinctive features: it was conceived as an evolved form of the fixed telephone and included an answering machine, so it had a slender receiver set above the control panel; and it had a large slot in front, shaped rather ironically like a smiling mouth, whose function was to support the paper as it came out curved. It expressed something of De Lucchi's approach to "technological" objects, his tendency to make them more domestic and "human," bringing a cheery touch to the humdrum.

The Jet Lab 600 designed in 1999 was a further evolution of these multi-purpose machines with the development of electronic technology. The configuration was dictated by the cylinder of the central block—visualized in the profile of the side—to which was attached the paper feed at the back and the control panel in front. "I again started to design machines as assemblages of parts instead of modeling them as single volumes," stated the designer. "It was partly a return to Mario Bellini's approach. This made it possible, for example, to devise small machines and then add a number of complex components, which would hardly have been feasible if the case had seamless edges." The subsequent OFX 300 of 1998–2000 was again an assemblage of parts, but concealed and given greater uniformity by a large curved instrument panel with rectangular outlines.

Bibliography: G. Fusari, "Ofx: I fax del futuro," in *Electronic Media Top*, 5, 1996, pp. 22–25; P. Palma, "Michele De Lucchi. Fax OFX 1000," in *Area*, July–August, 1996, pp. 74–77; *Mostra del XIX Premio Compasso d'Oro*, exhibition catalogue, Bologna 2001, p. 200.

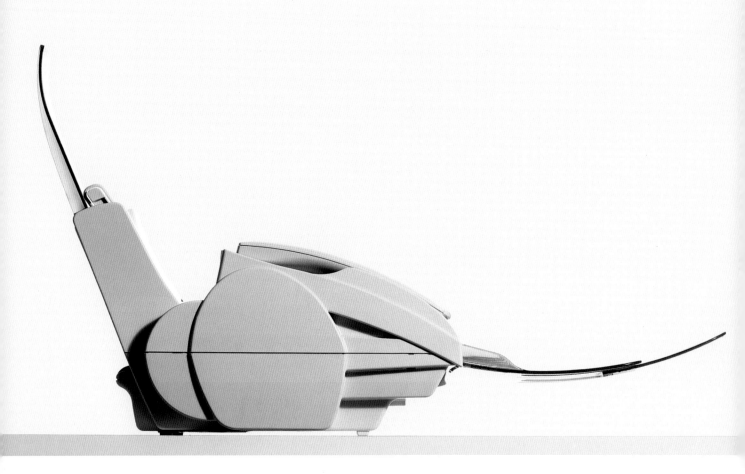

Jet-Lab 600 multifunction fax,
Olivetti, 1999,
side and general view.

OFX 300 multifunction fax,
Olivetti, 1998–2000,
side and general view
and wooden model.

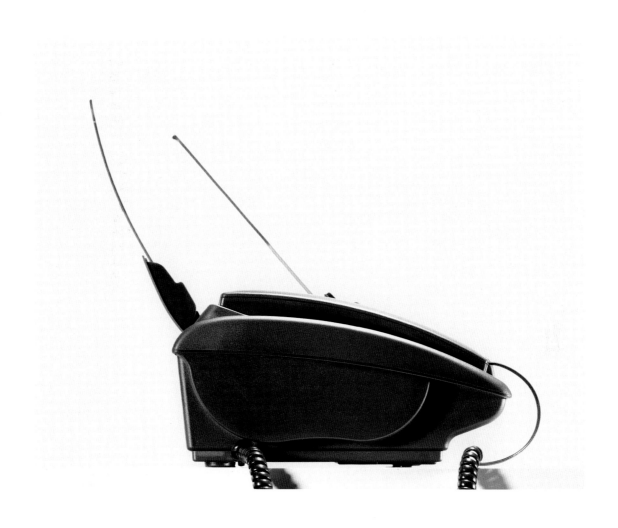

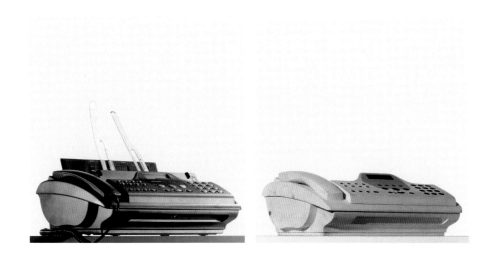

Olivetti printers

1994–95
bank printer
PR2
production: 1995
collaborator: Johannes Kiessler

1995
retail printer
PR4
production: 1996
collaborator: Johannes Kiessler

1997–98
printer
PR6
production: (1998)
collaborator: Johannes Kiessler

1998
printer
Artjet 10
production: 1999
collaborator: Masahiko Kubo

1998
printer
Artjet 20
production: 1998
collaborator: Masahiko Kubo

PR2 bank printer, Olivetti, 1994–95.

PR6 printer, Olivetti, 1997–98.

De Lucchi began to design printers for Olivetti in 1993, with a particular concern for two types: specialist versions and inkjet printers. As with the designs of other peripherals, De Lucchi devised configurations based on the functioning of the device, besides packing the machine and its electronics into the smallest possible volume. The letters PR designated printers designed for specific operations. These specialist printers were generally placed in front-office environments, so they had to be compact and sometimes integrated with the decor. The PR2 was designed for use in banks and received the Smau award in 1996. It was designed for Olivetti Lexikon, a company set up in 1996 to develop, produce and distribute faxes, inkjet printers, photocopiers, word processors, calculating machines and cash registers. It features a tray that juts out slightly from the base because paper loading and ejection are both frontal. Like the models PR4 and PR6, it was conceived in the years when De Lucchi was developing a vocabulary that he himself described as a "system of soft shadows," the fruit of his personal urge to tame technology. He tried to avoid the general effect of boxiness by going for rounded surfaces without gaps between the parts, which are here merged with the firmly perpendicular sides. The frontal tray for paper ejection and the compact volume reappear in the PR6 model,

designed three years later for the Italian Post Office (which commissioned De Lucchi to design its overall corporate identity in 1998). However, the upper part is different: it is set higher to make loading the paper easier and the front has an embossed surface to favor the flow of the sheet. The PR4 was conceived for sales points. It prints documents, tickets and receipts. The effort to reduce its volume is again behind the distinctive design of the cover, which encloses the roll of paper. To keep it compact, De Lucchi eliminated all the empty spaces inside it. The result is a machine in which the central section repeats the curve of the spool of paper, while the edges are chamfered to make it look smaller, as if the cover was actually shaped by pressing it against the top of the roll. The path of the receipts through the inside of the machine gave rise to the design of the large slot on both sides of the printer. The paper is guided by a transparent slide that also acts as a noise barrier.

Artjet 10 and 20 are inkjet printers designed by De Lucchi in 1998. Like the previous machines, their form derives from the technology they contain and the path taken by the sheet in printing. Both printers consist of a cylindrical volume that contains the moving print head, combined with a second block that keeps the device stable and contains the cylinders that spool the paper and the paper tray. A flattened cylinder then became an iconographic feature of the new Olivetti printers. A neutral light grey color (number 8 on the Munsell scale, made from a mixture of black and white) was chosen because it combined easily with the coloring of a personal computer. In Artjet 20 the paper is loaded and ejected in the same direction, with the paper fed in either from the front or the top. The result is it has two bases and the user can choose the arrangement on the work surface best suited to the space available.

Winner of the Compasso d'Oro-ADI award in 2001, Artjet 10's form reflects the shape of the cylinder, evoking the printer's inner workings. It is more highly integrated because the sheets are loaded at the top and ejected from the front.

Bibliography: *Olivetti 1908–1998*, edited by the Direzione Comunicazione e Immagine Olivetti, 1998; *Mostra del XIX Premio Compasso d'Oro*, exhibition catalogue, Bologna 2001, p. 69; M. Vitta, *Il progetto della bellezza*, Turin 2001, p. 352.

Artjet 10 printer, Olivetti, 1998.

Artjet 20 printer, Olivetti, 1998,
side and front view.

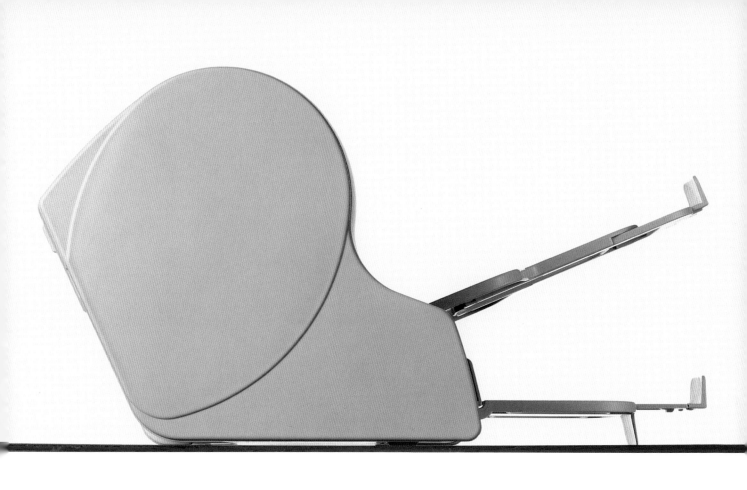

Workshop*
Olivetti-Philips
Ivrea (Turin); Eindhoven (The Netherlands)
collaborators: Alessandro Chiarato,
Torsten Fritze, Masahiko Kubo,
Mario Trimarchi

"Workshop"* was the name of a seminar held jointly in 1993 by Olivetti and Philips, in the persons of their respective design directors, De Lucchi and Stefano Marzano. They coordinated the team of designers who worked busily on inventing scenarios for the office environment. The work was divided into two phases: the first at Ivrea and the second at Eindhoven (The Netherlands). In particular, they sought to envision the future face and functioning of electronic devices. They started from people's real needs, with an approach that went well beyond technological advances.

"All too often technology tries to solve non-existent problems," commented De Lucchi, when he was interviewed in Milan at the presentation of the projects (the first stage in a traveling exhibition that was to visit Rotterdam, London, Vienna and Ivrea). "What we really need to do is interrogate our desires, ask what we want of the future, what we would really like electronics to do for us." This does not just mean being able to work easily in any place congenial to us, at home, in the subway, in a desert. Above all it means considering the office as a place that will foster encounters, encourage people to swap ideas, and where they can use highly sophisticated instruments. For this reason "Workshop"* produced a series of objects that steered well clear of the cold and aggressive esthetics of hi-tech, instead using soft or warm materials (wood, foam rubber) and gentle forms. Not science-fiction machines but products already feasible with the technologies that existed in 1993. The model that inspired the seminar was not the factory but the workshop, an example of harmony among the craftsmen working at their own pace. The seminar came up with three areas for innovation: the Tech Survival Kit, which included all the equipment needed for nomadic working; the Docking Office, which provided spaces where the users of electronic equipment could work together harmoniously; and the Empty Room, with walls that were together computer, hi-fi, TV and multimedia shelf for data, images, texts, and music. De Lucchi contributed to the second of these projects.

**Tool Panel project
at the exhibition presenting
the workshop and the model.**

Tool Panel is modeled on the side wall of a woodworking shop, with all the tools clearly in place. It is a panel where all the electronic devices likewise have a place of their own: PC, keyboard, screen, printer, telephone, fax and so on. They can be taken down and assembled as needed. Whenever they are hung up they recharge and are connected in a network so as to download and update their data. Their forms are attractive, more like toys or small kitchen appliances than computers, forming crescent moons, disks, boxes, frames. Above all, they are equipped with practical and very conspicuous handles, just like woodworking tools. All this contains a trace of satire on the rush to miniaturize everything, creating powerful but unmanageable computers.

Bibliography: S. Casciani, "Ufficio virtuale, ma tanto artigianale," in *Il Sole 24 Ore*, December 19, 1993, p. 34; S. Giacomoni, "L'ufficio del futuro come le antiche botteghe," in *La Repubblica*, December 11, 1993, p. 24; "Al posto della scrivania tappeti tecnologici e mobili intelligenti," and G. Francavilla, "Il nuovo ufficio è una casa laboriosa," in *Italia Oggi*, December 20, 1993, p. 41; S. Capra, "L'ufficio del 3° tipo? Lo tengo in mano, and re.cr., Designer all'Olivetti," in *La sentinella del Canevese*, May, 1994, p. 9; "Il futuro arriva domattina sul presto," in *P.G. Il mensile delle pagine gialle*, 4, May, 1994, pp. 22–25; "Philips & Olivetti develop advanced product concepts," in *Electronics Europe*, 72, May, 1994; K. Schmidt Lorenz, "Visionen zum Bürowerkzeug von übermorgen," in *Design Report*, 2, March–April, 1994, pp. 52–56; "Studio News," in *Design News*, 2, 1994, p. 7; F.V., "L'ufficio del futuro? Un 'tappeto' hi-tech," in *Il Sole 24 Ore*, May 24, 1994; S.T. Anargyros, "Michele De Lucchi: le matériau le plus précieux, la liberté, in Design. What's in store? Comment réfléchir le futur?," in *Intramuros*, 60, August–September, 1995, pp. 50–53; "Project Preparing for the Future / "Workshop,'" in *Design*, 4, 1995, pp. 102–07; L. Vachez, "Bureaux nomades," in *Libération*, Quaderno Multimédia, March 10 1995, pp. I–III; M. Vitta, *Il progetto della bellezza*, Turin 2001, p. 353.

exhibit design
"Citizen Office"
Vitra Design Museum,
Weil am Rhein (Germany);
Design Forum of Nänikon (Switzerland, 1995);
Istituto italiano di cultura, Moscow
(Russia, 1996)
collaborator: Geert Koster

This was a project devised by Vitra about furnishings and accessories for the new office. It was part of a research seminar coordinated by James Irvine and took the form of a traveling exhibition with contributions from De Lucchi, Andrea Branzi and Ettore Sottsass. The seminar explored new needs and forms of behavior for the workplace and touched on topics like temporary and "homely" spaces, splitting skills, ways to foster variety and cut waste. It reflected the fact that office systems, though highly functional and modular, lacked the flexibility needed to meet the challenge of the new ways work was being organized.

De Lucchi's project consisted of a set of simple units: L-shaped wooden screens that supported circular rotating work surfaces. Clustered in groups of four, these units formed a cruciform pattern. Because the work surfaces were round (they looked rather like café tables made of variously colored laminates), extra chairs could be drawn up around them and the monitor could be set in the corner formed by the wooden screen.

In the conference version, the table was fixed to the wall but a joint enabled it to tilt up and become a sort of decorative wall panel. The folding chairs set on wheels (Produzione Privata, 1993) helped define a familiar-looking and sociable kind of setting. This also appeared in the decision to abolish the traditional table lamps in favor of suspended elements and adjustable lighting, such as the Macchina Minima no. 7. The bookcase unit, integrated with the semi-transparent sliding doors, also made it possible to design a variety of different screens or openings and so reconfigure the interior.

Bibliography: J. Irvine, *Vitra Office Project, Branzi, De Lucchi, Sottsass, The Meetings*, abstract, April 3, 1991; J. Irvine, *Vitra Office Project, Branzi, De Lucchi, Sottsass, "The Research," "The Exhibition concept"…*, offprint, December 1991; S. Carlevaro, "Liberare, non occupare," in *Il Sole 24 Ore*, September 19, 1993, p. 28; "Changing the System from Within," in *Blueprint*, May, 1993, p. 31; "Citizen Office a project for Vitra. Ideas and Notes by Andrea Branzi, Michele De Lucchi, Ettore Sottsass," in *Terrazzo*, spring, 1993, pp. 81–104; "Willkommen in Klub," in *Der Spiegel*, 46, 1993, p. 144; A. Branzi, M. De Lucchi, E. Sottsass, *Citizen Office. Ideen und Notizien zu Einer Neuen Bürowelt*, Weil am Rhein 1994; A. Gonzáles, "Büro Visionen," in *Forbes*, 10, October, 1994, pp. 130–35.

Michele De Lucchi with Ettore Sottsass, Andrea Branzi and Rolf Fehlbaum at the "Citizen Office" seminar, 1992.
Drawing for the Citizen Office furniture system, April 26, 1992.

Interior by Michele De Lucchi
for the "Citizen Office"
exhibition, Vitra Design Museum
Weil am Rhein, 1993.

study for the
Festival Office
Domus Academy
with Nicholas Bewick, Torsten Fritze
collaborators: Eric Castets, Michael Corsar,
Paolo De Lucchi

The project was developed as part of a cycle of seminars at the Domus Academy titled "New Working Communities." It grew out of De Lucchi's reflections on changes in the office in the era of the data transmission and nomadic and delocated working, which tends to foster solitude. To exploit the potential to the full, it is necessary to remove the factors that breed routine, depersonalization and stress, while favoring festive and gregarious factors. Businesses need to create opportunities for staff to get together. They have to create points of social focus that allow the formation of temporary clusters where people can work in groups and swap experiences. De Lucchi felt that big boxy buildings with individual office cells were passé: what was needed were large versatile spaces equipped with sophisticated computing tools and flexible spaces for groups of different sizes, together with auditoriums, recreation areas, and services. These structures should not be permanent. They would have to be designed so they could be dismantled and moved elsewhere, above all to natural areas away from the towns—"a mountaintop or a glade in an impenetrable forest," De Lucchi claimed, "an oasis in the desert or a white sandy beach."

De Lucchi associated this idea of "festive businesses" with the image of large circus tents containing two or three floors and set on a plinth to house the technical infrastructures. The result was three standard marquees, differing in their plans and the truss frames supporting them, devised for groups of ten, twenty and thirty people.

The "Very Big Pavilion" has an oblong plan and a profile with slanting, vaguely trapezoidal, sides; the main floor is raised off the ground and houses a central auditorium surrounded by zones for multimedia projections onto a higher level. The Small Pavilion has a twelve-sided plan; the interior is laid out on two floors along the central axis, determined by the way the covering is arranged. The first level has a work zone with three areas for a multimedia theater flanked by services, storerooms and offices. This then leads to an auditorium set at the back, with big screens for projections on the upper floor.

A third pavilion has a faceted elliptical plan. It contains three walkways where the teamwork areas and the auditorium are connected by a system of staircases set parallel to the central axis. In 1972 Ettore Sottsass, in "The Planet as Festival," presented a project for small happy communities in close contact with nature. The Festival Office explicitly draws on this: it presents temporary working communities isolated in natural settings but linked to the web and accessible from all over the world. De Lucchi expresses the wish that such places might develop into *tòpoi*, symbols of the technological age, becoming what the perfect and self-sufficient monastic communities were for the Middle Ages. This project was given a concrete embodiment in the Conrad Creative Seminar House at Wemberg in 1996–98.

Note that the same design workshop also produced the idea for Market Offices, in many ways complementary to the Festival Office. These were permanent structures meant to be anchored at different points in the inner city, rather like street markets, but they offered stands in rotation for offices, to be installed on the large vacant lots created by brownfield sites.

Bibliography: M. De Lucchi, N. Bewick, T. Fritze with E. Castets, M. Corsar, P. De Lucchi, *L'ufficio senza ufficio*, in E. Manzini, M. Susani, *The Solid Side. Progetti e proposte*, 1995, pp. 78–89; M. De Lucchi, "Lavoro e Libertà," in *Interni. Il Contract*, 1996, pp. 3–11; "Michele De Lucchi, Büro und Freiheit," in *DBZ Deutsche Bauzeitschrift*, *Büro* issue, 96, 1996, pp. 60–63; G. Postiglione, "Nuove comunità di lavoro per il terzo millennio," in *Area*, 38, May–June, 1998, pp. 72–77.

Models of the Small Pavilion and a pavilion set on three levels (Centre Georges Pompidou, Paris).
Plan and section of the pavilion set on three levels.

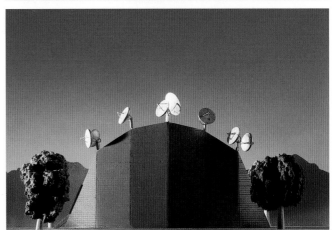
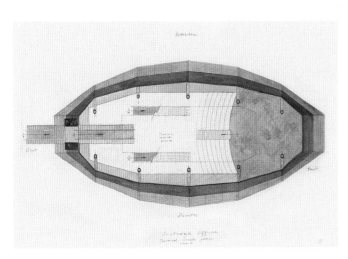
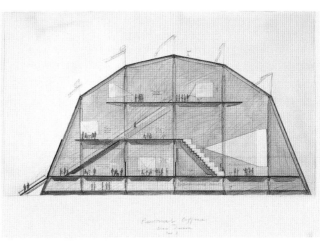

workshop
Domestic Chips
Olivetti

Ivrea (Turin)

collaborators: Torsten Fritze, Johannes Kiessler, Masahiko Kubo, Enrico Quell, Mario Trimarchi

The "Domestic Jobs" workshop, held at Cappellini in 1995, led to the parallel studies conducted by the design offices of Philips ("Vision of the Future," coordinated by Stefano Marzano) and Olivetti ("Domestic Chips," coordinated by De Lucchi). The latter was presented in 1996 in a videoclip by Studio Azzurro and at an exhibition held at De Lucchi's offices on Via Pallavicino in Milan.

Following the experience of the "Workshop"* design seminar organized by the two companies in 1993 to investigate the use of electronics in the office, "Domestic Chips" focused on the future of home appliances. It is important to ensure that the home—increasingly often also a workplace—never loses its intimate and informal character with the arrival of IT devices. At the same time it is necessary to rethink the cold, unfriendly esthetic of the latter. They look out of place in a domestic setting and all too often are shut away in a separate room. It is also important "to debunk the myth of the omnipotent computer." De Lucchi proposed to disintegrate it into a potentially endless series of small interesting-looking home appliances with simplified interfaces that could become everyday devices. He had in mind not a futuristic wired house but a family of new objects which could find a place in the ordinary rooms of the home or be carried from one to the other. Each would have its own function, coping with new needs, forms of behavior and little, everyday anxieties. Their esthetic is essentially low-tech, with the emphasis on conveying a sense of security associated with traditional forms.

In all there are six devices. Door PC, applied to the entrance or the doors of the different rooms, covers home security, recording entrances, taking messages and if necessary contacting suppliers. Mirror PC looks like an ordinary mirror but incorporates a processor that interprets the image and offers advice about health, diet and exercise. Memory PC is a computer that stores family memories. It is like a frame that can be hung up or placed on a bedside table and used to call up photos or videos, which otherwise would be put away in drawers or albums without ever being looked at. Diary PC is a light, pocket-sized electronic notebook that records and writes in personalized handwriting memories dictated by voice. It includes a facility for taking photos and inserting them in the text. The instrument called Collector PC is useful to collectors: it records, arranges and identifies all the relevant data about the items in the collection. Finally, Magic PC, perhaps the most provocative object, projects horoscopes and predictions of all kinds, downloaded from the web, onto the ceiling: a technological oracle that helps us cope with the irrational angst of today.

Bibliography: C. Coronelli, "Chips with everything nella casa telematica," in *Il Sole 24 Ore*, October 20, 1996, p. 35; R. Di Caro, "Lo scassa computer," in *L'Espresso*, 47, November 21, 1996, p. 147; L. Ferraiuolo, "Smau, è qui la festa," in *La Repubblica*, October 18, 1996, p. VIII; A. Reggiori, "A ogni cosa il suo chip," in *Virtual*, December, 1996, pp. 66–67; S. Carbonaro, "Domestic Chips," in *DBZ Deutsche Bauzeitschrift*, 3, March, 1997, pp. 87–90; S. Casciani, "Chips and chips," in *Abitare*, 361, April, 1997, pp. 168–70; "Case Study Studio De Lucchi," in *Axis*, 11–12, November–December, 1997, pp. 24–25; "Domestic Chips," in *I.D. The International Design Magazine*, July–August, 1997, pp. 190–91; "Domestic Chips," in *Mensch & Büro*, December, 1997, pp. 100–02; "Ideenschmiede für Hiemroboter," in *A.D. Architectural Digest*, February–March, 1997; kls, "Chips statt Kartoffeln," in *Design Report*, 5, 1997, p. 20; C. Morozzi, "Un pc per ogni desiderio," in *Casaviva*, 3, March, 1997, p. 192; M. Soppelsa, "Motorini e computer," in *PC World Italia*, January, 1997, p. 276.

Projects on the future of domestic electronics: Memory PC, Collector PC, Diary PC, Mirror PC, Door PC and Magic PC, "Domestic Chips" workshop, Olivetti, 1996.

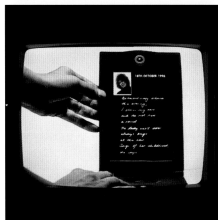
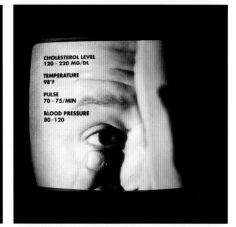

Conrad Creative Seminar House
Wernberg Koblitz (Germany)
collaborators: Nicholas Bewick
(project leader), Marco Della Torre,
Daniele Rossi
client: Conrad Family

As the owner of an ancient castle near Nuremberg, restored and converted to a hotel, the German Conrad electronics firm commissioned this building in the park as a place for seminars annexed to the hotel. De Lucchi considered it as a permanent version of his temporary structures called Festival Office, developed a few years before. The Seminar House reflects those principles by successfully combining high-tech and natural materials and plant to create an ambiance suited to business conferences.

Essentially it consists of two large rectangular spaces, laid out on two levels of a terraced hillside, connected on its longer side by a bridging flight of steps with a double ramp. The upper level has a spacious interior with access from the shorter side, defined by the stone retaining wall which forms a balcony running along its whole length. The stonework contrasts with the aluminum uprights and profiles, the three other walls completely faced with glass and with the curvilinear roof beams made of laminated wood, studded with skylights and projecting sharply beyond the profile of the room. It creates a large continuous surface with a warm, protective appearance, visually linked to the trees in the park through its all-glass walls. This room contains the community spaces, with a zone for exhibitions and cultural events, lounge bar, lounges and electronic library. It terminates in a spacious portico beside a reflection pool. The lower floor is also roofed with laminated beams that form a sinuous line, which, covered and with a false ceiling inside to house the technical plant, re-emerges to form a *brise-soleil* in the façade on the lower side of the hill. It is a space intended for conference chambers, reconfigurable as rooms of various sizes fitted with a large strip window. Finally, an underground level houses the services and the electronic control panel (engineering by Ove Arup): this is the pulsating heart of a sophisticated system of climate control that combines natural ventilation with panels for heating and air conditioning. On the outside the two rooms are also connected by a stone ramp, whose curving course recalls the sinuous lines of the roof.

Bibliography: G. Albretti, "Conrad Seminar House a Wernberg Koblitz in Germania," in *Abitare*, 389, November 1999, pp. 168–69; "Kommunikation am Hang," in *Büro '99*, special edition of *DBZ*, 10999, pp. 26–29; "Michele De Lucchi, Conrad Seminar House," in *OFX*, Annual 2000, suppl. to *OFX*, 4, 1999, pp. 98–109.

The two rectangular blocks of the Seminar House complex are linked outside by a stone ramp with curved and sinuous lines like the roofing.

View of the two blocks set on two levels because of the terraced site. View of the stairs connecting the two blocks. Interior of the upper block with the glass walls looking onto the park.

branch offices
Deutsche Bank
collaborators: Taku Arai, Jonathan Barnes,
Nicholas Bewick (project leader),
Hanno Giesler, Denise Houx, Angelo Micheli,
Michele Rossi, Christian Schneider
client: Deutsche Bank

In the autumn of 1989 Deutsche Bank announced a competition by invitation for the redesign of its branch offices. Four well-known European architectural firms were involved. De Lucchi was invited because of his experience with Olivetti and his submission was successful. The commission for the German bank was his first major project for a service facility. It marked a significant advance in retail bank design and the bank's overall image. In August 1991 the bank approved two prototypes of interior designs for its branches and embarked on the redevelopment of 1400 agencies, of which 350 have been completed. The first to be finished was in Frankfurt, the most important in Hanover. "Privacy and transparency"

were the key words in De Lucchi's competition submission. This neatly summed up the bank's objectives. It sought to convey to its customer base—expanded by the recent reunification of the country but subject to increasingly tough competition—a dynamic yet friendly image, as well as new and evolving technological services. It was felt the bank should not flaunt its opulence but express a sense of serenity and friendliness. The design of the system of furnishings also needed to be highly flexible, adapted to very different spaces while expressing a distinctive identity.

In this case the general layout begins with a large entrance area, a wired lobby with automated telling equipment, some free-standing units and others set in the walls. This space is separate from the bank's front office, which has a service counter and office spaces, with a line of "cabins" that house consultancy rooms. These form the true core of the project: the basic component is the self-supporting dividing wall, designed in an S shape so as to create two complementary spaces for workstations,

Branch office of the Deutsche Bank, Hanover, 1994–95. The entrance with the stairs linking the entrance to the customer service area.

Customer service area with the wooden counters: note the shelf running their whole length and the handrails of metal tubing.

wired panels or shelves. From outside the thicknesses of these "S walls" are visible. They alternate with the front walls of each individual room, entirely faced with glass and made of two panels, including sliding panels where requisite. Each has a silkscreened pattern forming a band across the central section to maintain the privacy of the rooms without diminishing the general effect of transparency. The interior of each unit contains space for a circular table for interviews: it also serves as a desk, with a jointed arm that makes it easier to consult the computer monitors ranged along the walls.

Suspended from the ceiling is a large vaulted element of micropierced metal that masks the air conditioning plant. It also acts as an acoustic screen and reflects light, while conferring an architectural quality on the interior and countering the tendency to coldness in systems furniture. The "cabins" are conceived as modular furnishings, independent from both floor and ceiling of the space they occupy and so making for a much greater variety of layouts. The commonest is to range them around a central space, a sort of indoor piazza. As Nicholas Bewick points out, this design draws on "the most significant symbol of urbanity: the square, an archetype of Western civilization, skilfully expressing the close relationship between business and walking." The counter, a central feature of this piazza/front office, provides for two formal treatments: one for the standing posture of both speakers and one raised on the inside to place seated tellers at the same height as clients. It is lined with wood and has a long shelf running along it. It also has tubular handrail that projects to divide the teller stations, enforcing respect for privacy. The care lavished on every detail helps to create a friendly atmosphere: from the choice of various kinds of wood and delicate colors to the spherical glass shades of the lighting, the large circular handles and the carpeting, specially designed with a wavy pattern and let into the floors. All of the elements have quite simple forms, making it possible to start producing them industrially. This enables the assembly and installation of the system to be carried out under the supervision of the bank's local technical offices. Finally, it is interesting to note that the completion of the project—combined with the design of automated bank kiosks for airports and shopping centers—was prefigured 1994 in virtual reality under the title *Three Possible Dreams*, produced in collaboration with the Fraunhofer Institute of Stuttgart.

Bibliography: E. Morteo, "Michele De Lucchi. Le nuove agenzie della Deutsche Bank," in *Domus*, 35, February, 1992, pp. 58–65; "Deutsche Bank," in *Office Age*, 27, 1994, pp. 46–51; L.J. Nasatir, "Studio De Lucchi," in *Interior Design*, March, 1994, pp. 106–10; B. Dacquino, "Banca da sogno," in *Virtual*, 20, May, 1995, pp. 18–20; T. Hoffhaus, "Disegno di Milano," in *Page*, 12, 1995, pp. 12–13; L. Matti, "I due volti della Deutsche Bank," in *Office Layout*, 63, 1995, pp. 30–36; DN, "Glückstreffer," in *Ait*, 6, June, 1995, pp. 16–17; "Deutsche Bank, varie installazioni in Germania dello Studio De Lucchi," in *Ufficio stile*, 2, 1996, p. 48; T. Edelmann, "Grosser Bahnhof für die Kunden," in *Design Report*, 4, 1996, pp. 36–44; "Übersichtlich, offen, diskret," in *Office Design*, 5, October, 1998, pp. 118–19; M. De Lucchi, "Privacy and Transparency per le filiali Deutsche Bank," in *Ottagono*, 136, 2000, pp. 52–55; E. Ratti (ed.), "Il Facility Management in banca," in *Ufficio stile*, 7, January–February, 2001, pp. 46–47.

Branch office of the Deutsche
Bank, Hanover, 1994–95.
At the far end are the "cabins"
of the consultancy rooms.
The self-supporting dividing
panels have an S-shaped plan.

Customer assistance counter.

Branch of the Deutsche Bank,
Hanover, 1994–95.
Data transmission area with
self-service equipment.
View of the "cabins."
Conceived as modular
elements, independent
of floor and ceiling, they
make for considerable freedom
in the layout of the interior.

The walls of the "cabins"
consist of two glass panels,
with a silk-screened pattern
across the central part
to secure privacy.

1995

ticket hall
Deutsche Bahn
Germany
collaborators: Nicholas Bewick (project leader),
Brigid Byrne, Michael Corsar,
Alessandra Dalloli, Gladys Escobar,
Torsten Fritze, Christian Hartmann,
Annelaure Lesquoy, Enrico Quell,
Daniele Rossi, Michele Rossi, Katia Scheika,
Steffen Schulz, Trond Sonnergren
client: Deutsche Bahn

In 1995 German railways embarked on a major overhaul of its stations to improve their structure and architectural quality and redefine the interiors. As part of this project they announced a competition for the redesign of its ticket halls and travel centers. The winner was the De Lucchi firm. The system designed for the ticket halls was flexible and modular. It gave the interiors clarity and a recognizable identity, while also being highly adaptable to the different architectural settings and specific configurations of space. It was eventually approved and extended to the whole network of over 1700 German stations.

Deutsche Bahn's first priority was to modernize its facilities. It also wanted to define a new image of efficiency, comfort and transparency for the railroad system as a whole, as well taking more incisive advantage of the commercial potential of its buildings and creating better working conditions for staff. The station was transformed from a place of hurried transit to a true center of integrated services. For this reason the ticket hall was linked to a Reisezentrum (travel center) that offered supplementary travel services retailed by Deutsche Bahn's commercial partners: the services include car rentals, organized tours and urban and intercity transport.

For the counter in the travel center, De Lucchi devised a system of modular furnishings based on clearly identifiable horizontal and vertical forms: the surfaces of the counters, the lines of the metal footrails and handrails, the constant height of the light columns, sign panels and dividing walls, and the further horizontal line of the walls and the shelving set against them, dominated by big blow-ups of trains.

The design emphasizes transparency and light, evident on a number of levels: as an integral part of the information system and furnishings, with the use of backlighted panels; as a way of ensuring optimal working conditions; as an architectural motif created by diffusing indirect light that distends the interior; and, above all, by using large sail-shaped lamps. Suspended above each transaction point, these lamps have a strong visual impact and focus attention on the service being offered. They also create a recurrent motif that identifies the Reisezentrum even at a distance. The materials used combines naturalness and technology:

**Deutsche Bahn ticket hall,
Frankfurt, 1996–97.
Backlit information panels
are surmounted by large
sail-shaped lamps.
The backlit counter with a metal
handrail and monitor platform.**

**The ticket hall with the modular
system of the ticket counters.**

sound-absorbing wood for the storage units at the back, synthetic stone for the floors, metal and glass for the counter. Each service point with its combination backrest and storage unit, base, information column and lamp form a single element. The soft, sinuous profile of the decks above confirm the urge to create a friendly atmosphere. Modularity and repeatability also appear in the plant. Since climate control is commonly poor in ticket halls because doors keep being opened and closed, part of the ducting was integrated in the counters, bringing the air conditioning to staff and public together with a system for sanitizing the air. This was particularly important for the staff after the elimination of the armored windows that separated them physically from travelers.

The most significant application of the system was in Frankfurt. Here De Lucchi was also responsible for refashioning the part of the station involved. The building suffered from serious security problems common, to stations in big cities. The usability and clarity of the principal services were also restricted by the piecemeal alterations made over the years, including the insertion of secondary commercial facilities. De Lucchi's project started by clearing them away. The result enhanced the façade and the great original arch with sail vaulting pierced by skylights. He then added a new structure forming a spacious, glass-roofed hall, in which the functional areas are arranged on several levels: public facilities, with the ticket counters and car rental points, at ground level; waiting rooms and recreation spaces (designed by the Zurich-based Trix Hausmann firm) on a mezzanine level, accessed by two transparent elevators and a staircase in translucent glass; offices and telephone services on the upper floor, arranged in a horseshoe layout and with access to the adjacent restaurant.

Bibliography: "Am PC planen Berater und Kunde die Reise gemeinsam," in *BahnZeit*, 10, 1995,

Deutsche Bahn ticket hall, Frankfurt, 1996–97.
The modular system of the ticket counters was also applied to the auxiliary services such as car rentals and urban and inter-city transport.

The constant height of the light columns is a strong vertical feature of the modular system.

p. 6; "Ein Arbeitsplatz mit Flair," in *BahnZeit*, 2, 1996; "De Lucchi's design goes on track," in *Blueprint*, February, 1996, p. 14; P.A. Tumminelli, "Nuovi concetti spaziali per le stazioni tedesche," in *Domus dossier*, 4, June, 1996, pp. 84–86; A. Borchardt, "Mit Komfort umwirbt die Bahn ihre Kunden," in *Darmstädter Echo*, 24, July, 1997; Frankfurt am Main, *Reisezentrum, Studio De Lucchi mit Stadler Projekt*, brochure, July, 1997; A. Wesemann, "Schöner warten," in *Design Report*, 10, October, 1997, p. 71; A. Dominioni, "Deutsche Bahn: il ridisegno delle stazioni ferroviarie tedesche," in *OFX*, 5, September–October, 1998, pp. 84–95; "Incontroluce iGuzzini. Neue Reisezentren für die Deutschen Bahn, Studio & Partner, Mailand," in *Lichtmagazin*, 10, 1998, pp. 6–11; "Die neuen Reisezentren der Deutschen Bahn AG," in *Details*, 2, March, 1999, pp. 274–75; P. Righetti, "Non solo treni," in *Modulo*, 254, September, 1999, pp. 742–44; J. Rosendaal, "Historisches Vorbild," in *High Light*, September–October, 1999, pp. 14–15.

Deutsche Bahn ticket hall,
Aschaffenburg, 1995–96.
Views of the area of the ticket
counter lined with glass walls
on both the sides.

The modular system
with sail-shaped lamps
at each transaction point.
The end wall features blow-ups
of Deutsche Bahn trains.

branch offices
Banca Popolare di Lodi
collaborators: Gladys Escobar, Angelo Micheli
(project leader), Silvia Suardi,
Claudio Venerucci
client: Banca Popolare di Lodi

The redesign of the premises of the Banca Popolare di Lodi was part of De Lucchi's research into the corporate identity of retail banks. His first concern was to remodel the layout of the branch office, where teller services were no longer the main activity but secondary to consulting and assistance. So the spaces needed to be welcoming, transparent and discreet. The route inside of the bank led first to a reception desk, a zone with consultancy rooms and then to the tellers' counters with the back office clearly visible. Developing a concept similar to that designed for Deutsche Bank, the offices consist of units set side by side, built using a flexible modular system, hence easy to apply to the different architectural settings of the various branch offices.
The leitmotiv of the interiors are broad surfaces marked by horizontal lines. They recur in the treatment of the extensive etched glass walls (including the one housing the telling machines, making the chamber look very light) and on the panels of reconstructed wood used for counters, tables and partitions. This conspicuously striped material embodies the overall image of dynamism, continuity and strict decorum. Metal is sparingly used: only the surface of the tellers' counter and the baseboards are lined with aluminum. The custom-built furniture includes an interesting table used in the consultancy rooms. It has an unusual "shark-fin" configuration which allows a staff member to talk comfortably with two people. A monitor sits on the broad part while the consultant and clients sit around the narrow part. This shortens the distance between them and makes talking easier.

Bibliography: S. Suardi, "Informalità e Innovazione," in *Ufficio stile*, 7, January–February, 2001, pp. 42–45; "Michele De Lucchi, Banca Popolare di Lodi," in S. San Pietro, A. Vasile, *New Office in Italy*, Milan 2003, pp. 20–27.

Branch office of the Banca Popolare di Lodi, Via Settembrini, Milan, 1998–99. View of the windows of the bank.

Detail of the panels in etched glass and reconstructed wood. Both surfaces feature the recurrent motif of horizontal lines.

Branch office of the Banca
Popolare di Lodi, Via
Settembrini, Milan, 1998–99.
The glass panels define the
arrangement of the interiors.
The "shark-fin" form of the table
in the consultancy room makes
it easier for the consultant
to converse with two people.

Branch office of the Banca
Popolare di Lodi, San
Colombano (Milan), 1998–99.
The motif of the horizontal lines
reappears in the wall behind
the automatic telling machine.

View of a consulting room.
The counter top and the base
board of the telling counter
are made of aluminum.

Mauser Office

1994
office system
Serie 4000
production: 1995
collaborators: Nicholas Bewick (project leader),
Hanno Giesler, Christian Schneider

1995–99
filing system
Sistemare
production: 1997
collaborators: Nicholas Bewick,
Gerhard Reichert

1999
office chairs
Allavoro and Attivo
production: 1999
collaborator: Gerhard Reichert

The partnership between De Lucchi and the German Waldeck company, specialists in office systems, began with the furnishings for Deutsche Bank's branch offices and developed with the design of various series of furniture between 1994 and 1999.

The first project was the Serie 4000, which aimed to provide an effective solution to the problem of incorporating wiring and connections without having to give up on flexible configurations for work surfaces. It is a knock-down kit made up of independent elements, so it can be shipped cheaply and assembled easily on the spot. This is a clear advantage over traditional systems, including those manufactured by Mauser, supplied ready assembled. Legs and crosspieces are made from mass-produced rectangular piping with a section measuring 50 x 100 millimeters. The work surfaces combine primary forms (rectangles, squares, triangles, circles) set on supports organized in modular blocks that can be superimposed (feet, drawer units, crosspieces). They slot together and can be adjusted at different heights, varying from 680 to 780 millimeters, at standard intervals of 20 millimeters. The cables are housed in horizontal and vertical grommets that fit together seamlessly using sections with modular angles. Extra elements can be added to expand the functions of the work surface: vertical panels, small raised semitransparent surfaces, drawer units, round terminal tables. "The project was about stripping away complexity on both the technological-constructional and semantic levels," states De Lucchi. "The aim was to create a set of minimal elements capable of designing and giving a soul to space and assigning a value to time [...], time measured by the freedom to use and rearrange durable modular objects." The system was completed in 1996 by a series of desktop accessories.

4000 series office system, Mauser Office, 1994, partition and accessory shelf.

Configuring the tables: the grommet for the cables set in the leg.

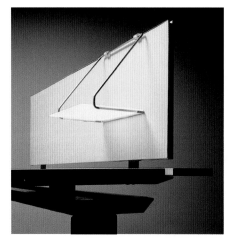
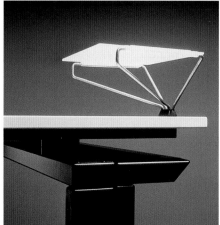

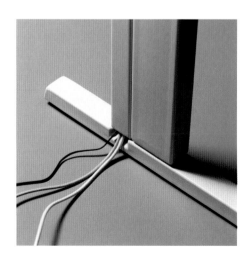

In 1995 he designed Sistemare. This is a system of all-metal modular and stackable office storage units, which went into production in 1997. Here, too, the stripped down forms produced simple ideas for combining the horizontal elements of the desk pedestals and storage units with the vertical elements of the cabinets, the two shades of grey and the various modules of different dimensions. The series was subsequently expanded with a system for distributing the writing desks; this was followed by a computer table with a drawer unit and tilt-up work-surface on wheels called Eccofatto.

In 1999, De Lucchi also began to work on two interesting projects for office chairs, Allavoro and Attivo. They were built out of separate components which could be assembled to create two quite different series of chairs. Both were produced in numerous variants, including a model on castors and another with a cantilevered tubular frame better suited to conference rooms. Allavoro had a bentwood back with flanges forming the armrests, while Attivo was higher, produced in both wood and stamped plastic, with upholstery of different kinds. The project included instruction manuals for assembling Allavoro and Profit.

Bibliography: S. Carbonaro, "In the Midst of so much Noise ... Silence," in *DBZ*, special edition, October, 1994, pp. 86–90; "'System 4000' ein Bausatz," in *md*, 12, 1994, pp. 48–51; "Architekt und Designer Michele De Lucchi: Der mit dem Bart," in *Mensch & Büro*, 1, 1996, pp. 37–40; "Trend per l'ufficio: che cosa ne pensano i designer," in *Ufficio stile*, 5, October, 1996, pp. 56–57; "Produkte schöner und intelligenter gestalten," in *Waldeckische Landeszeitung*, January 17, 1997, p. 14.

Sistemare office system, Mauser Office, 1995–99.

Allavoro and Attivo offices chairs: castor and cantilever versions, Mauser Office, 1999.

Poltrona Frau

1998
furniture system
Artù
production: 1998
collaborator: Silvia Suardi

2000
sofa and bed
Piazza di Spagna
production: 2000
collaborator: Silvia Suardi

2000–01
sofa
Orione
production: 2001
collaborator: Philippe Nigro

De Lucchi's first work for Poltrona Frau dates from 1981. It was the Long Beach sofa, which never went into production, he tells us today, "because I was dissatisfied with the result, and with the various subsequent designs, until after I had produced the Madrigale bed in 1987." After the experience with Luna in 1997–98, in his most recent projects he has concerned himself with designing home offices. But his most important contribution was definitely the Artù conference table system from 1998, later completed with a chair (project of 2001–02,

devised with Sezgin Aksu, never produced) and various storage units. The structure of the table is innovative: it is based on a thin, tough slab of aluminum which connects the legs and supports a splayed bracket that underpins the wooden table top. The table looks light and buoyant, its dynamic profile emphasized by the chamfered front edge lined with leather. The slab also houses the wiring and provides a base for the lighting; the leg, circular in cross-section, rests on a foot that tapers at the bottom, emphasizing the slenderness of the structure. The table top comes in various forms, making it possible to build tables with different configurations, using parts that are easy to assemble. The Artù system includes conference tables and executive desks, the latter fitted with a slender and elegant arching foot that increases the points of support, which can be set symmetrically or off-axis in relation to the leg.

The Piazza di Spagna and Orione sofas date from 2000–01. Though different projects, both reflect De Lucchi's urge to adapt the traditional forms of garden furniture, whether in wood or cast iron. Piazza di Spagna repeats the archetype of the park bench, which, as De Lucchi says, "is simply an outdoor sofa," mindful that the original meaning of *diwan*, in Arabic, was simply "a long bench." Here he combines it with leather upholstery, a feature of domestic interiors. The result is a plain sofa for

Artù furniture systems, Poltrona Frau, 1998. Details of the splayed supports of the table top.

The table with the slender arched foot and drawing of the profile, January 23, 1998.

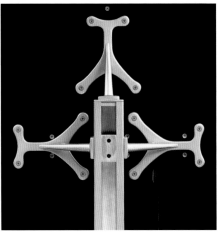

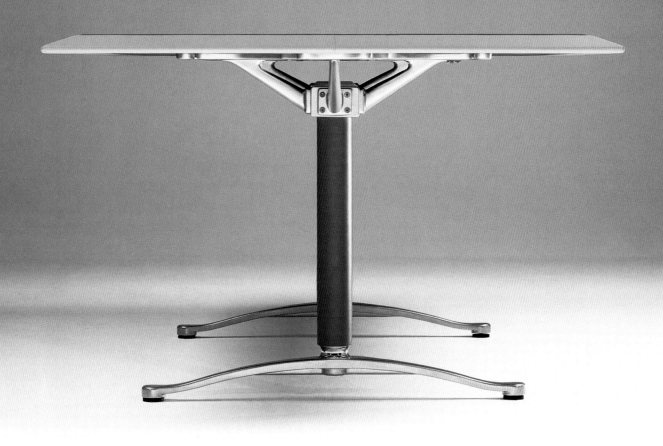

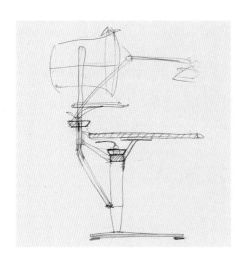

waiting rooms, offices and living rooms: light because it lacks the volumes of the upholstery but comfortable because of the slightly curving line of the back. The bed version repeats this configuration. Orione evokes Victorian cast-iron garden furniture: the frame is cast in aluminum, which is quite slender and has a certain charm because, like old cast iron furniture, it does away with sharp corners and joints. At the back, the metal frame is flanged and padded with leather to provide a comfortable support for the cushions. The cushions, which form the seat, back and armrests, have simple, compact volumes, so creating a light, airy image.

Bibliography: M. De Lucchi, *Artù*, Poltrona Frau, n.d.; R. Sias, "Sistema di tavoli conferenza Artù," in *Ufficio Annual Office*, suppl. to *Ufficio stile*, 1999, pp. 8–9; "Stabil und flexibel," in *Büro '99*, special edition of *DBZ*, 1999, p. 64; D.G.R. Carugati, *Poltrona Frau*, Milan 2000, pp. 169–77; "Komfort ist Programm," in *md*, 7, July, 2001, p. 84.

Piazza di Spagna sofa and table, Poltrona Frau, 2000.

Orion sofa, Poltrona Frau, 2000–01.

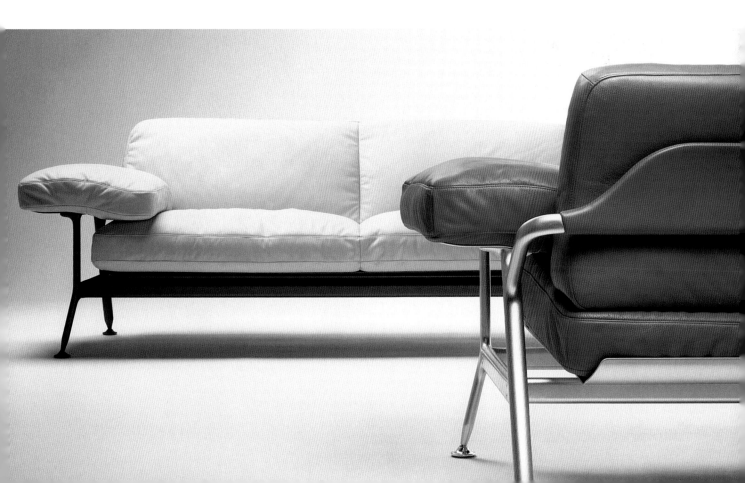

outdoor lamp
Palme
Artemide DZ Licht
production: 2001
collaborator: Gerhard Reichert

In the Palme series designed for DZ Licht, a German company acquired by Artemide in 1999, De Lucchi explores the subject of the urban lamp. This was treated as further opportunity to investigate the relationship between designer product and its setting. "Unlike indoor lamps," said the designer in a recent conversation, "lamps designed for outdoors are set in a void, they tend to disappear. And then the beam has to be projected onto the ground for the light to be efficient." Most other kinds of urban lamps deflect the light off a reflector, but Palme sheds a broadly diffused glow while concealing from view the light sources (metal vapor or high pressure sodium) and the tempered glass, sealed with silicon, used to protect and screen them.

The light is projected towards the ground by a reflector, shaped like a sort of sinuous leaf, white on the inside, sand-cast in hyperpure aluminum then ground and painted, set on a simple cylindrical steel stem. The reflector houses the light sources in the hollow on its lower side.

This eliminates all trace of dazzle, creating a soft glow, as if the light came welling up from the ground. The unity of the lamp is enhanced by making the stem and the outside of the reflector all the same color, a micaceous iron grey or white. "A kind of giant wrought-iron lamp," so Stefano Casciani described it to *Abitare* in 2000, "as an alternative to the eternal fascination with the constructivist machine." In 2004 the family of lamps was completed with Palme 330, a medium-height (335 centimeters) version fitted with a standard-diameter lamp attachment so it can be installed on any post.

For the same firm De Lucchi, again in collaboration with Gerhard Reichert, also designed the line of Milestone outdoor lamps in 1999–2000.

Bibliography: S.C., "Michele De Lucchi serie Palme DZ Licht," in *Abitare*, 394, April, 2000, p. 217; "Michele De Lucchi, Gerhard Reichert. Un'idea brillante ma non abbagliante," in *Domus*, 827, June, 2000, p. 62; AA.VV., *ADI Design Index 2000*, Bologna 2001, p. 195; "Diffuse Reflexe," in *md*, 7, July, 2001, pp. 26–27; *Mostra del XIX Premio Compasso d'Oro*, exhibition catalogue, Bologna 2001, p. 94; "Wegeleuchte," in *Designzentrum*, 2001, p. 28.

Ernesto Gismondi in the Artemide research office with models of the diffuser of the Palme lamp, 1999.

The characteristic folded
leaf form set on a cylindrical
steel stem.

05

2000–03 integrated corporate design

Fiorella Bulegato

Enel 1997–present

After his early work for Olivetti, Deutsche Bank and Deutsche Bahn, and while he was engaged on the first commissions for the Italian Postal Service, De Lucchi began to work with Enel (the Italian electricity company). This must have been one of the earliest examples, in Italy or abroad, of a designer's involvement in a comprehensive redesign project by a major power company. Enel had previously commissioned leading architects to design some of its facilities.

"With Enel we had a close, far-ranging relationship that lasted some five years," says De Lucchi. "We designed industrial products, buildings, interiors, exhibits, graphics. The company's interest in that short period was focused on communicating its identity through its routine activities as well as the usual advertising media." The experience enabled De Lucchi to express himself fully as an "architect in the service of industry." He explained this concept to *Modo* in 2003 in these terms: "Though involved in different disciplines, I do just one work. I interface with industry in all aspects of communication, but above all corporate identity and character. In all these years I have learned to understand industry, succeeding in relating appropriately to all aspects of business functions, conferring character and an identity on the various ways a firm expresses itself, regardless of whether they are products or showrooms, posters or buildings, offices or something else again."

The brief was therefore to provide a coherent image of Enel's technological legacy across the whole range of its activities, from power stations to office blocks, pylons and electricity meters. Over the years these projects were always accompanied by studies of their communicative impact, not just on landscape and the territory but also on people's lives.

Early projects included the design of a trade fair installation (at the Fiera del Levante in Bari, 1997, with Enrico Quell and Silvia Suardi), the "Virtual Basilica" exhibition in Assisi (1998, with Gladys Escobar and Enrico Quell) and the Aria lamp (1997, with Alberto Nason, Produzione Privata). Aria was a lamp that modulated its light with two diffusers made of blown Murano glass (one transparent, the other with a satin finish), the first product of a limited series titled I Regali di Natale.

Outstanding among these projects is the auditorium in Viale Regina Margherita, Rome, located inside an office block and corporate headquarters then being built. Having to work with a project already begun by another architect, De Lucchi sought to create a friendly, homely atmosphere in the auditorium through the architecture and color scheme, which is dominated by shades of grey subtly graduated with different degrees of gloss.

The most important opportunity came with a plan to upgrade Enel's power stations with a view to the privatization of the utility. Enel Produzione was founded in 1999 to modernize production facilities and shine up the company's image with the liberalization of the Italian energy market. "Completely different facilities," pointed out De Lucchi in *Modo* in 2003, "had to be somehow standardized under a single image. This enabled me to adopt an approach more characteristic of an industrial designer than an architect."

The only power station to have been completed to date is at Priolo Gargallo (Syracuse, in Sicily). Work is still under way at La Spezia, while at Porto Corsini (Ravenna), Castel San Giovanni (Piacenza) and Chivasso (Turin) the projects have been partly completed. Work has yet to begin at Civitavecchia.

This overhaul of plant began with the company's decision to renew the generators fueled by oil and/or coal used in most facilities dating from the sixties and seventies by converting them into combined-cycle gas turbine stations fueled by natural gas. The change would boost their energy output and at the same time reduce emissions in the atmosphere, so lessening their environmental impact.

It was also planned to mask the facilities with a well-designed architectural shell that would harmonize with their settings and make their function clear to the general public. At the same time it was hoped to express their cultural value as a part of contemporary industrial society, express their social and economic functions and efface the memory of the damage done in the past. "Only a few of the projects for the various divisions of the company have been completed to date," says De Lucchi. "But in all of them I tried to convey the significance of industrial technology. This is especially clear in the redesigns of the power stations."

To achieve this end De Lucchi created structures on a scale to suit the landscape, using industrial materials such as polycarbonate, aluminum and various kinds of infill paneling in unconventional ways. This policy was backed by the Environment Ministry. Its guidelines recommended greater sensitivity to the environment. It suggested "using native trees and shrubs to screen eyesores and taking greater care in the design of buildings and plant, with a systematic concern for the esthetic qualities of structures, facing materials, and color schemes."

De Lucchi defined the new profiles of the facilities by standardizing the design of the volumes, the visual qualities of the facing materials and a range of color schemes. The sites were also relandscaped, each to a different design, in most cases by the landscape architect Antonio Perazzi. De Lucchi also revised the interiors, replaced furnishings and equipment, and designed new buildings containing offices, staff facilities and information centers.

The color scheme was diversified. The colors of landforms (ochre, red, brown, green) were used for low buildings and structures facing onto landscapes, while aerial colors (grey, blue, aquamarine) were used for highrise and overhead structures. The strictly functional parts (machinery) were given easily recognizable primary colors to make their form and function clear. The same approach underpinned the design of graphics and information panels (with Sezgin Aksu, Geert Koster, Angelo Micheli), which completed this comprehensive redesign of Enel's corporate image. The project formed part of the "Open Power Station" initiative, launched to enable the public to see for themselves how electric energy is produced. Routes for visitors were laid out through power stations. Graphics, blow-ups, pictograms and projections of data and images were used to present the layout of the complexes and the ways that materials and energy flowed through them. The technology was made easy to understand by using the volumes and materials of the structures to display and amplify eloquent graphics.

The first such route was laid out in the Galileo Ferraris power station at Trino Vercellese in 1999 and different versions of it were then installed in over fifty power stations. At Entracque (Cuneo), the project was completed by converting an existing block into an information center for visitors. To make it look the part and fit into its Alpine setting, the building was given a new color scheme and the exterior lined with wood.

The numerous projects commissioned by Enel over the last five years were intended to make their facilities more eco-friendly and improve relations with the public. They included the design of a new pylon—by De Lucchi and Achille Castiglioni (1998–present)—a new meter for homes (2001) and the redevelopment of the company's power stations (2002–present). Both the pylon and the electricity meter were designed as mass produced items bound to become very common. The meter will be installed in thirty million homes by 2005; the pylon (chosen in a competition by invitation and today in the prototype phase) will appreciably alter the Italian landscape.

The redesign of the power stations was commissioned by Enel Terna, a subsidiary set up in 1999, which owns over ninety percent of the national electricity grid. The projects sought to merge these visually very invasive facilities with the landscape and at the same time express their public utility through graphics and information services.

Bibliography: "Progetto di riqualificazione centrali Enel," in *Domus*, 819, October, 1999, pp. 61–63; M. De Lucchi, "La sfida dell'arditezza," in *Crossing*, 2, June, 2001, pp. 56–57; G. Agnolini, "C'è dell'energia nell'architettura," in *Nuova energia*, 1, March–April, 2003, pp. 78–81, in esp. p. 81.

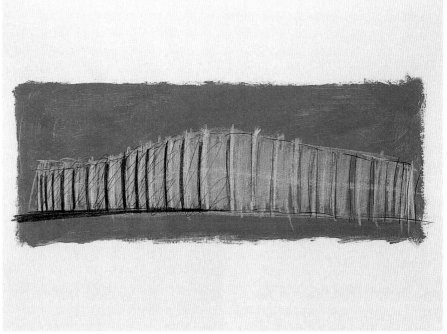

Porto Corsini, drawing
of the Enel power station,
Porto Corsini (Ravenna), 2001.
Drawing for the office block
of the Enel power station,
Porto Corsini (Ravenna),
March 2002.

redevelopment of the
Enel Information Center
Entracque (Cuneo)
collaborators: Sezgin Aksu, Brigid Byrne,
Geert Koster, Aya Matsukaze, Filippo Pagliani
client: Enel Produzione

This project involved the design of a public exhibition pavilion and reception center. It forms part of the visitors' route through the Luigi Einaudi hydroelectric power station at Entracque, which is meant to enable sightseers to understand its workings.

Dating from 1999, the Information Center was installed in a former mixed-use building containing offices and accommodation for technicians. Erected in the sixties when the power station was being built, it was soon abandoned because it no longer had any purpose. Ugo Colombari and Giuseppe De Boni had already reconfigured it for its new function. They strengthened the structure, added shafts for the vertical connections (staircase and elevators), opened up the central section to install a model showing how the turbines are driven by water power. De Lucchi's project retained the structure and the roof of the building, but gave it a new "skin." This consisted of a wooden grid of horizontal slats covering the masonry (painted red), so masking the four rather featureless façades. This cladding is detached from the walls, which rest on a stone plinth

containing the basement. It repeats the original angle of the pitched roof, covered with corrugated iron, and its upper edge is aligned with the outer edge of the eaves.

This arrangement is particularly useful as a way of filtering the natural light that falls on the building during the day, shading the red surface below. At night the building becomes a glowing beacon in the valley, lit up by lamps arranged on the walls to illuminate it from below and above.

Laid out on three floors, the entrance to the pavilion is set 7.45 meters above grade. Visitors pass through a large up-and-over door, which looks as if it was cut out of the wooden grid. It is raised by a system of hydraulic pistons. Through the double-glazing of the entrance a working model of the power station (the centerpiece of the layout of the interiors) can be seen. On this level, besides the café and the sales area, there is the first section of the exhibition with a video zone that leads to the lower floor, which has sections dedicated to the Enel museum and the nature park of the Maritime Alps. The basement houses a lecture room.

Bibliography: "Progetto di riqualificazione centrali Enel," in *Domus*, 819, October, 1999, pp. 61–63; "Michele De Lucchi. Centro di informazioni Enel," in *Casabella*, 680, July–August, 2000, pp. 22–27.

The block, built in the sixties, reclaimed by the project.

The new building faced in wooden slats superimposed on the red rendering. The wooden covering is anchored to the high stone plinth housing the basement.

Views of the building at night.
The light sources that illuminate
it from above and below make
it highly visible from all parts
of the valley.

Disused machinery from
the power station on display
and model of the functioning
of the water generators.

upgrading of the
Enel La Casella power station
Castel San Giovanni (Piacenza)
collaborators: Brigid Byrne,
Gladys Escobar (project leader),
Geert Koster, Federico Seymandi
client: Enel Produzione

This was the first of the environmental enhancement projects for Enel power stations devised in 2000. The company announced it as a trailblazer for the program, but the La Casella project has only been partly completed. The design principles it embodied underpinned the redesign of Enel's other power stations.
La Casella was built in the seventies on a site straddling the municipal territories of Castel San Giovanni and Sarmato (near Piacenza). It was eventually converted to combined-cycle technology, fueled by natural gas with generators driven by gas and steam turbines grouped in "modules" or clusters. Built to a fairly common plan, it consisted of four boilers supplying

as many turbines housed in the machine room. To bring out the fact that this is a major industrial plant, De Lucchi here, as in other power stations, concentrated on the design of the profiles, materials and colors of the structures. He also redefined the interiors and landscaped the grounds, in compliance with the Environment Ministry's desire to cushion the environmental impact. These principles appear in the cardinal points of the project: the screening of the steam generator and the machine shop, the new gas turbine building, the color scheme and the landscape project. This gave the power station, with its original configuration (60 meters tall) left largely unaltered, a highly original appearance. Seeking to model the outlines of the various technical volumes and make them visually uniform, De Lucchi faced the steam generator and the machine room (a rectangle measuring 215 x 47 meters) with a translucent wall of extruded polycarbonate (Makrolon), supported by a galvanized steel and aluminum frame (not yet built). The horizon-

**Model of the power station
with machine room, boiler room
and gas turbine building.**

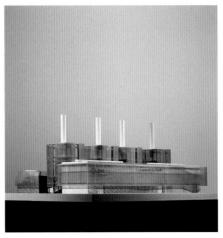

tal arrangement of the panels and the rounded forms created by the new facing increase the transparency of the complex. The gas turbine building was faced with traditional self-supporting metal honeycomb panels, arranged horizontally to stress the monumental quality of the installation without emphasizing its height. The burnt red coloring used for the gas turbine building complies with the general color scheme devised for power stations: primary colors for machinery, earth colors for low buildings and aerial colors for overhead ones.

In addition to redesigning the workspaces, the project added new offices and a porter's lodge. The plan to "renaturalize" the whole area (by the landscape designer Antonio Perazzi) is based on a distinction between formal patterns in areas around the entrances, car parks and offices, and informal vegetation growing naturally in the other areas.

Bibliography: M. De Lucchi, "La sfida dell'arditezza," in *Crossing*, 2, June, 2001, pp. 56–57.

redevelopment of offices
and porter's lodge of the
Enel power station
Porto Corsini (Ravenna)
collaborators: Carlo De Mattia,
Michele Marozzini, Daniele Rossi
(project leader)
client: Enel Produzione

The Porto Corsini power station is located in the industrial zone of the port of Ravenna and overlooks the Candiano canal. Planned in the late fifties by Ignazio Gardella for SADE, its salient feature is its machine room, a clear, plain volume set parallel to the canal and faced with clinker tiles a burnt red color laid with open grouting, lined with pilasters and roofed with a slightly curved concrete vault. Over the years the complex was altered in various ways: a block containing a staff locker room was built in front of it, fire escapes and windows were added, and the clinker was replaced with incongruous materials that ruined the appearance of the façade.

The layout of the complex repeats the classic structure of thermo-electric power stations built in the period, with four boilers, each connected with a turbine, alternator and transformer. The axis of the machine room lies parallel to the channel, with the four boiler towers facing it, while the transformers and distribution cabins are on the landward side.
The conversion project, begun in 2000 and currently nearing completion, involves conversion from the use of heavy fuel oil to a combined-cycle gas turbine station fueled by natural gas. The project was similar to the redesign of the La Casella power station in the same period, the first of the series, but here the project was restricted by lack of space. This made it impossible to convert all the boilers into steam generators and reuse all four turbines in the machine room, retaining the morphology with the boiler-alternator axis unchanged. The attempt to restore the initial configuration had to be abandoned, both because of the high costs involved and because a complex of this type needs to be flexible, so it can be altered

Drawing of the new power island, 2001.

Volumes of the power station. The existing building converted to the machine room will be flanked by the two new blocks, for the boiler and gas turbine.

and updated to include technical and functional innovations. Only two of the original turbines were kept and a new power-generating island was added. This had two steam generators set at right angles to the original axis and two buildings for the alternator and turbines. This meant the size of the machine-room building could be halved, so recouping the section next to the new structures laid out along its smaller side. In this remaining area it is planned to preserve the building designed by Gardella. The two constructions, identical and symmetrical, repeat the design concept, materials and colors used for the La Casella power station, but their layout differs from the other projects. The smokestacks are faced for a third of their height with Makrolon multi UV rings. In the zone below, they are surrounded by an elliptical structure of the same material, like two large outspread wings, which serve to cover the steam generator as far as the gas turbine building. In keeping with the color guidelines, the chimney is painted an aerial color, delicate, filmy bluish-grey, the steam generator deep yellow, and the gas turbine building burnt red.

De Lucchi also revised the layout of the site. He redefined the boundaries so as to clear part of the grounds to the north and south, rearranged the water treatment plant, reorganized the power station, freed a broad strip of ground along the road for the new custodian's lodge and installed a new office block to replace the one originally designed by Gardella, which was unrecognizable and inadequate for current needs. This building, completed with storage depots and laboratories, contains the work areas used by some thirty people, locker rooms for eighty, the canteen and a reception area for guided visits. Set near the new entrance, it consists of two blocks: a parallelepiped, with natural light entering through its shed roof, half embraced by a sinuous glazed front that models its façades.

The office building also provided an opportunity to create the power station's new visual horizon, showcasing human labor and enhancing the powerful production plant. At the opening of the power station on June 1, 2003, De Lucchi explained, "The thread that runs through the project is the quality of the living space: man controls the machine and not the other way round. It is a power station made for the well-being of people, where machinery is not overwhelmed by high technology."

Lucina Caravaggi was commissioned to landscape the project. Her scheme is based on the native flora of the area south of the Po River, with cane brakes, low shrubs and umbrella pines. It has not yet been realized.

Bibliography: Michele De Lucchi, "La sfida dell'arditezza," in *Crossing*, 2, June, 2001, pp. 58–59; G. Agnolini, "C'è dell'energia nell'architettura," in *Nuova Energia*, 1, March–April, 2003, pp. 78–81, esp. p. 81; "La centrale Enel riapre ai cittadini," in *Corriere Romagna*, May 30, 2003, p. 9; "In ottocento alla centrale," in *Il Resto del Carlino*, June 1, 2003, p. 7.

Model of the two
new constructions.
The smokestacks are covered
for a third of their height with
multi UV Makrolon rings, the
steam generator is plastered
yellow, the gas turbine building
is red.
Wooden model (Centre Georges
Pompidou, Paris).

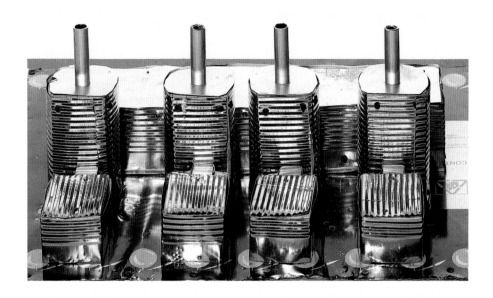

Wooden models of the Enel
power station at Porto Corsini,
Ravenna (Centre Georges
Pompidou, Paris).

Aluminum models of
the new buildings at Enel's
La Casella power station,
Piacenza (Centre Georges
Pompidou, Paris).

upgrading and offices of the
Enel power station
Priolo Gargallo (Syracuse)
collaborators: Carlo De Mattia,
Michele Marozzini, Daniele Rossi
(project leader)
client: Enel Produzione

On May 19, 2004, a new combined cycle gas-fired power station was opened at Pantano Pozzillo in the town of Priolo in the Sicilian province of Syracuse. It replaced the earlier oil-fired facility commissioned in 1979. The conversion formed part of the plan to upgrade Enel's power stations by gradually phasing in the use of new fuels, especially natural gas, in its generators. The changeover to combined-cycle facilities ensures high efficiency and cuts emissions sharply. The upgraded plant consists of two identical combined-cycle groups, each consisting of a gas turbine with its alternator, a heat-recovery steam generator, and a steam turbine with its alternator and condenser.

The project dealt with this plant as well as redesigning the whole area and inserting a new office block. Work began in 2001 and was completed in 2004. Like other Enel projects, it focused on redefining profiles, volumes and colors to reduce the facility's impact on the territory. The paired steam generators and the block housing the double chimney were faced, above a certain height, with multiwall panels of UV-resistant Makrolon, a light, tough, transparent polymer that is also flame-retarding (it withstands temperatures up to 120° C). The panels are treated against UV light on both sides for lasting transparency and protection against the harsh Sicilian sun. The elasticity of the panels is a marked advantage during transport and assembly. For the over 7200 square meters of the façade, panels measuring 6 x 1 meters were used, curved to match the profile and lodged in metal frames. The same material was used for the power stations in Porto Corsini and Piacenza.
The horizontal pattern of the facing and its surface texture make the façade look lighter,

View of the gas turbine building and the heat-recovery steam generator.

View of the heat-recovery steam generator and the smokestacks.

modeling its chiaroscuro effects and proportions. They also provide a very effective contrast with the brighter color scheme used for the rest of the complex, in keeping with the general guidelines for power stations and the graphics. The office building has not yet been built, but the whole site has been fully landscaped, with different types of vegetation which distinguish the zones around the work areas and green belts renaturalized with cultivated fields and woodland.

Bibliography: "Michele De Lucchi. Centrale termoelettrica Enel Priolo Gargallo," in *Casabella*, 723, June, 2004, pp. 74–81.

The gas turbine building and heat-recovery steam generator seen by night.

View from the north-east by night.

Detail of the base of the new
smokestacks with the old
smokestack in the background.

Detail of the covering
of the steam recovery facility
and the smokestacks.

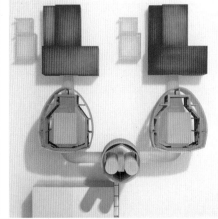
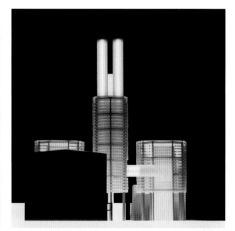
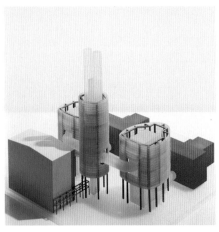
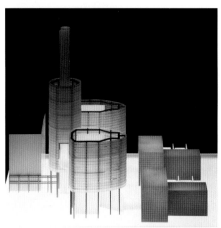

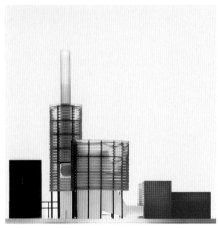
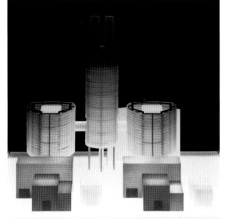
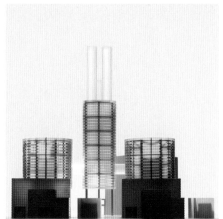

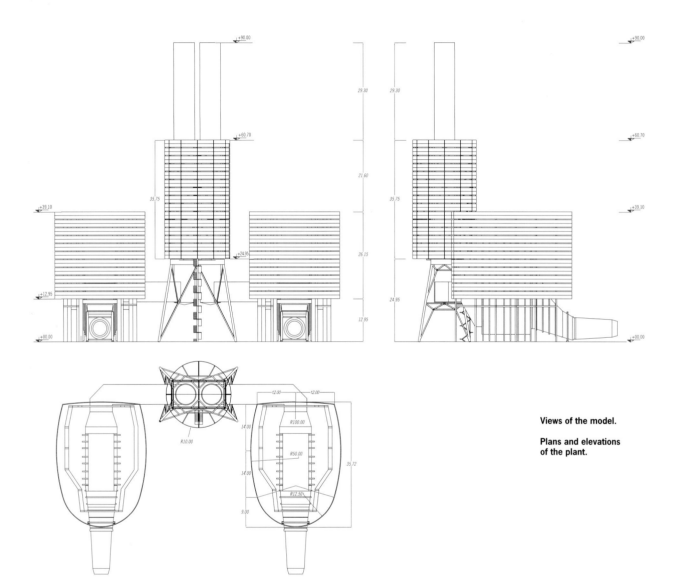

Views of the model.

Plans and elevations of the plant.

upgrading of the
Enel power station
La Spezia
collaborators: Brigid Byrne,
Gladys Escobar (project leader),
Federico Seymandi
client: Enel Produzione

The La Spezia power station was operated from August 1962 by the Edisonvolta company. Set in Vallegrande, a valley lying open to the Gulf of Spezia, it is immersed in one of the most splendid natural settings in Italy, today greatly disfigured. "The city has encroached on the gulf and the industrial area on the valley," De Lucchi wrote in 2001. "Here redeveloping and upgrading the power station means working on a large scale to benefit the whole area."
The power station enjoys an extraordinary logistical position. In the docks at La Spezia, coal used to be (and to some extent still is) unloaded from ships directly onto a long conveyor belt and fed straight into the boilers of the power stations. In fact the conveyor belt and

its supporting framework stamp their distinctive form on the whole plant. It rises from grade at an angle traversing the whole length of the four "castles" of the boilers. The technological upgrading of the complex, begun in 1997, involved replacing two of the units with high output combined-cycle steam generators fueled by natural gas and installing a plant for desulferization, denitrification and capturing of microparticles in the case of the single coal-fired thermoelectric unit that has been retained.
The conversion meant adding various structures, such as machinery, buildings for the turbines, plant for treating smoke and waste water, secondary buildings and auxiliary plant. They made the side facing the valley more ragged and untidy, a major eyesore. The redesign project, begun in 2001 and partly completed, seeks to confer unity and clarity on the profile, starting at 20 meters above grade, by using an anodized aluminum grid that, for structural reasons, follows the forms of the largest volumes. This laminated grid

View of the power station with the covering in anodized aluminum.

Vista of the power station with the new building housing the custodian's lodge and the locker rooms.

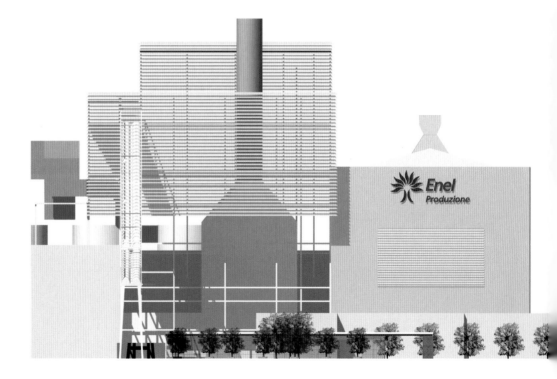

does not weigh excessively on the structures, while its transparency and brilliant finish confer an unexpected lightness on the whole mass. As in the other power stations, the project was completed by a sensitive color scheme.

Antonio Perazzi's landscape project integrates the site (covering some 72 hectares) with its natural setting, exploiting the hillsides and embankment towards the Autostrada. The sense of renewed architectural quality, based on the concept of transparency, includes the redesign of the block housing the custodian's lodge and locker rooms. This is a linear single-story building with fully glazed façades and with a thin roof panel.

upgrading of the
Enel Torre Valdaliga Nord power station
Civitavecchia (Rome)
not built
collaborator: Daniele Rossi
client: Enel Produzione

In late 2003 Enel Produzione had the opportunity to replace its Torre Nord Valdaliga power station at Civitavecchia, at present oil-fired, with a new coal-burning plant. The project involved adapting a very large site subject to stimulating planning restrictions. De Lucchi started work on the project in early 2001. The complex stands on a narrow strip of ground bounded on one side by the sea and the other by the Rome-Livorno railroad line, two barriers that prevent expansion. For this reason it was proposed to set the front of the new facility on an artificial peninsula, specially designed for the purpose, to arrange the tanks and some auxiliary buildings across the tracks on a brownfield site with installations no longer necessary to the new power station. The site

is appropriate for a coal-fueled power station as it backs onto the new port and has wharfs where coal ships can berth alongside the boiler towers. This arrangement, besides creating an interesting design feature, makes it much easier to bring the coal to the power station: it will be conveyed on gigantic flatbed trucks to the tank at the rear of the plant along the railroad tracks. This means the port will not be damaged by the addition of such a large complex.

The plan is divided into two distinct parts: the power station proper, built symmetrically on an axis perpendicular to the sea, and the volume of the coal bunker, which stretches 500 meters to the north along the railroad. The chimney stands 250 meters high at the center of the complex in front of the four vertical boilers 90 meters high and the large machine room. This faces onto the railroad and contains the turbines, alternators and control room. The tracks leading to the transformers and the power station start from the machine room. It is planned to install a system for

Model of the power station.

View of the power station. Behind the smokestack are the four boilers and the machine room.

treating the smoke: after being denitrified in the boiler building, to reduce the nitrogen oxides, emissions will be filtered as they emerge, removing solid particles, and then pass to the desulferizers located at the end of the pipe rack on both the south and north sides, so also reducing the output of sulfurous oxides. The desulferized smoke will be returned to the chimney and expelled into the atmosphere. Further equipment for the treatment and storage of ashes, lime and plaster are set on the side facing the port. A jungle of cables and pipelines, essential to the automation of the plant, traverse the whole structure. "Our first commitment was to organize the forms and dimensions of the buildings, naturally without damaging the production mechanisms and the plant's functioning," stated De Lucchi in 2001. "We worked mainly on the proportions, seeking to reduce the perception of the size of the towers." This was achieved by using horizontal patterns on the façades and painting the volumes light colors, inspired by the shades of air and sky, in keeping with the general color scheme established for all Enel power stations. De Lucchi adds: "All this would never have made sense if we hadn't tried hard to integrate the facility into its natural setting." To do this an embankment was planned to offset the bulk of the coal bunker, especially when seen from ships in port, and areas were set aside for the addition of barriers of natural greenery along the seafront.

Once the preliminary phase has been completed, the project will be developed by Enel's technical office.

upgrading of the
Enel Terna power station
Rome East
collaborators: Filippo Flego, Laura Negrini,
Francesco Otgianu, Enrico Quell
(project leader)
client: Enel Terna

Among the projects De Lucchi is now working on for Enel (Enel Terna, to be precise, owner of the national electricity grid), his redesign of electric substations are particularly interesting. Substations redistribute electric energy for factory, office and home use. They occupy large areas, rigidly enclosed, containing thickets of pylons, masts, cabins, insulators and transformers, various service buildings and powerlines. They are often found in natural beauty spots. Following the groundbreaking project for Rome East begun in 2002, work is now progressing on substations at Tavarnuzze (Florence) and Carpi (Modena).

The Rome East project, covering a site measuring 45,000 square meters, focused on three factors to integrate it with the landscape while clarifying its technical function. The work of cleaning up and rationalizing the structure, for example, involved painting the internal roads a pale green color. Signage was added to make the function of the facility clear. Block-letter signs indicate the course of the electricity flows, and the lines served stand out in dark blue against a sky-grey ground or are directly applied to the asphalt. Apart from changing the color scheme of the service buildings, De Lucchi masked the geometrical metal volumes of the control cabins, ranged in serried batteries, by covering the exterior with an adhesive film printed to create the effect of faded metal. To transform the image of the grey reinforced concrete wall surrounding these areas, some parts were replaced with stands of tall trees clustered in metal "cages," while others were lined with mirror-finish screens that reflect the surrounding landscape. Camouflaging the facility with green barriers was impossible, as vegetation can affect the functioning of substations; the

**Sign showing the direction
of electricity flows.**

**The volumes of the control
cabins.
One of the high "cages"
containing trees, which replace
the reinforced concrete wall.**

problem was solved by planning these five tall cages, made of galvanized steel strengthened with cross-ties and covered with square mesh wire netting to restrain the trees, whose growth has to be periodically pruned back inside them. The mirror-finish surfaces attached to the outside wall are made of polycarbonate with a beehive structure attached to aluminum panels mounted in metal frames and set at a downward angle of about 5 degrees.

The other projects under way embody similar principles. At Carpi a prefabricated building will be added to house the ground control office; and at Tavarnuzze the block of transformers and insulators will be roofed over to make the substation, set in a valley bottom, less conspicuous when seen from the neighboring hills.

High-voltage pylon
Enel Distribuzione
competition (equal first prize)
with Achille Castiglioni
collaborators: Sezgin Aksu, Geert Koster

In 1999 Enel held a competition ("Supports for the Environment") to redesign its traditional lattice tower pylons. It was part of a program to make its installations more eco-friendly and included eliminating old high-tension lines, upgrading power stations and improving substations. Equal first prize, presented in Rome on October 4, 1999, went to Norman Foster and the partnership of De Lucchi and Achille Castiglioni. They were invited to enter separately the year before but eventually decided to pool their ideas. The six projects submitted were judged by two commissions, one to establish their economic feasibility and another to assess environmental impact. A representative panel of forty members of the general public was also called on to express ideas. The projects then went on show at an exhibition in Rome's Palazzo delle Esposizioni, the Centro di Arte Contemporanea Luigi Pecci in Prato and the Milan Triennale. The design of the pylon is now at the prototype stage.

"For both Achille Castiglioni and myself," De Lucchi told *Domus* in 2000, "designing pylons was a fascinating challenge involving high technology and structural engineering. I can't deny we were rather alarmed at first. As architects and designers we have had to work on projects at the very edge of our professional skills but never one so utterly impregnated with math and structural technology, calculations of statics, industrial and general culture [...] It may seem easy to support electric cables. After all, they look a bit like washing lines. Just raise them well clear of the ground, prop them up here and there and they'll be OK. But doing this with powerlines is a completely different kettle of fish [...] You have to ensure the stability of the structure as it passes over rugged ground, goes round curves, and changes direction, all things a powerline has to do [...] Right from the start Achille Castiglioni and I

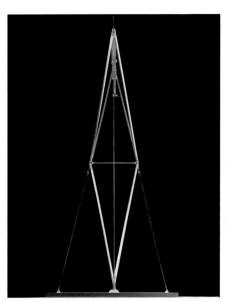 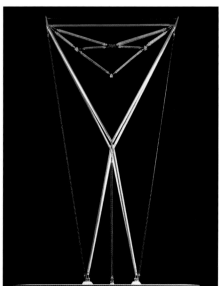

High-voltage pylon, models and photomontage.

wanted to draw a pylon that wasn't the usual lattice mast. It didn't seem right in an international competition to present a truss tower simply of a different shape. So we transformed the standard pylon, made out of numerous parts all the same, into a tensile structure made up of ties and struts. This was our 'support for the environment,' a structure not just very simple but also transparent. Transparency lies at the heart of the project. This is partly to reduce the environmental impact but also because transparent designs look new, modern, contemporary."

A rigorous effort to simplify the framework led to the replacement of the numerous L-shaped profiles of Enel's existing pylons with ten galvanized iron tubes. Eight identical tubes, 32 centimeters in diameter, are joined in pairs at bottom and top and strengthened by two crosspieces and two triangular elements. The pylon's general appearance is rather like one tripod upside down on top of another. The airy structure, standing 41.75 meters high and weighing 26 tons, is stabilized by four braces

anchored to the ground and is considerably less voluminous than the pylons now in use. An alternative version planned for rural settings can be faced with wood (or some other industrial material). Halfway up, the pylon has a perch as a resting place for migrating birds, an initiative launched three years earlier by the electricity company. "The impact of the whole object is a lot less invasive than in the past," states De Lucchi. "Its form is simple but not banal. Its standardization is perceptible but not dominant. The outstanding qualities of this pylon are above all that it's easy to assemble and position, cheap to make and transport, its iconography is novel among pylons for high voltage lines and it uses a static technology still rarely applied."

The design by Castiglioni and De Lucchi (with the engineers Luca Varesi and Giorgio Piliego) is simple in its details and the pylon can be produced industrially. It is almost completely assembled on the ground, so keeping costs low. Upkeep is also simplified because there are few corners and the materials used are freely available. Maintenance workers can climb one

of the uprights using a cabin attached to it at the moment of intervention. At the top, the technician can pass from one end of the support to the other on a catwalk installed for the purpose. Costs can be further reduced by replacing the basic element (a tube 32 centimeters in diameter) with a lattice frame made up of three tubes 8.9 centimeters in diameter and a secondary structure, made up of tubes 4 centimeters in diameter. The parts can be transported on a trailer truck about 19 meters long.

Bibliography: C. Bini, "I tralicci Enel belli come sculture," and "Tralicci griffati, colline salve," in *La Nazione*, October 27, 1999; D. Pecchioni, "Tralicci d'autore sulle colline fiorentine," in *Panorama Casa*, November 28, 1999, p. 8; P. Santoro, "Il traliccio è firmato," in *Donna*, suppl. to *La Repubblica*, 176, November 16, 1999, p. 68; E. Arosio, "Più che un traliccio è un'opera d'arte," in *L'Espresso*, 5, 3, February 2000, pp. 138–39; "Arrivano i pali d'autore," in *La Repubblica*, February 27, 2000, p. 27; M. Bazan Giordano, "Gli alberi dell'Enel," in *L'Arca*, 147, 2000, p. 82; G. Bosoni, "La 'forma' degli elettrodotti tra design, architettura e paesaggio," in *Domus*, 827, June, 2000, pp. 78–85; I. Ciuti, "Tralicci firmati da designer," in *La Repubblica-Firenze*, October 27, 2000, p. 27; F.P., "Design ad alta tensione," in *Ottagono*, 136, February–March, 2000, pp. 64–65; T. Santi, "L'arte corre sul filo," in *Il Corriere di Prato*, January 14, 2000; ST, "Tralicci artistici," in *Il Giornale della Toscana*, January 14, 2000; "Tralicci firmati per la Toscana," in *La Repubblica*, February 13, 2000, p. 23; "I tralicci dell'Enel? Ora sono opere d'arte," in *La Nazione*, January 14, 2000; "Castiglioni-De Lucchi," in *Modulo*, 274, September, 2001, pp. 712–13; S. Polano, *Achille Castiglioni tutte le opere 1938–2000*, Milan 2001, pp. 442–43.

**Photomontage
of the high-voltage pylon.**

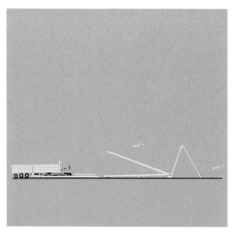

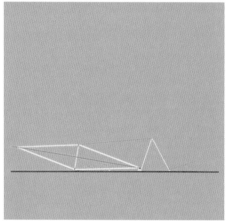

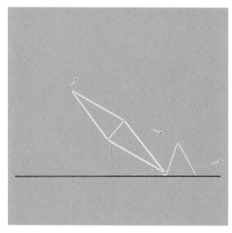

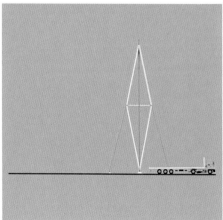

Diagram showing the
phases of assembly
of the high-voltage pylon.

Electricity meter
Enel Distribuzione
production: 2001
collaborator: Sezgin Aksu

By 2005 the new monophase electricity meter designed by De Lucchi in 2001 for Enel Distribuzione should have replaced some thirty million existing household meters, so becoming a sort of symbol of the newly privatized utility. Its new technology enables it to measure consumption and send off a reading electronically, without the need for the electricity company to send around a meter reader. Its form and the way it interacts with the user are also innovative. "This meter speaks the language of technology," stated De Lucchi when he presented it in 2002, "the language of the most advanced electronic products, with soft, rounded forms, smooth, satiny shadows, unexpectedly solid. It is white, unlike all previous meters, at least in Italy, opaque like a whitewashed wall, as if seeking to merge into it, and it stands out on-

ly by the highlights that glance off the corners." Designed to be easy to use, familiar-looking, no longer hidden away under the stairs, it consists essentially of two parts: the electronics housed in the casing at the top and the mechanical switch below. The innovative core of the project is the electronic unit. It consists of an internal panel and an easy-to-read liquid crystal display set behind an elliptical glass front. This is equipped with two LEDs that flash to show energy is being consumed. A circular button can be used to bring up information on the display, including the rate being charged, consumption and the actual amount of power being used in the home. Beneath the button, set in a circular groove, is a spyhole accessible to the meter reader. The potbellied shape of the meter, reflecting the larger volume of the mechanicals, emphasizes the position of the switch. This is the most important working part of the meter, serving to switch the current on and off. Underneath it, a screw-on panel provides access to the contacts inside.

Monophase electricity meter, model and axonometric section.

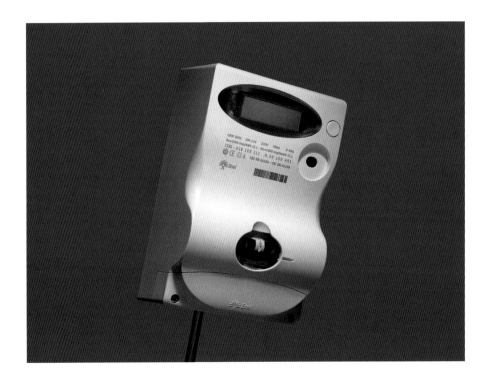

Apart from the interface, the volume of the meter has also been carefully designed. It is compact, measuring 15 x 22 x 10 centimeters, so making it easy to replace the old meters without altering their housing. The new backplate used to fix it to the wall is the same size as on traditional meter; it ensures safe assembly and is proof against tampering.

Bibliography: S. Suardi, "Contatore monofase," in *Interni*, 525, October, 2002, pp. 230–31; A. Bassi, "Michele De Lucchi, il mio progetto," in *Auto & Design*, 138, February, 2003, pp. 71–75, esp. p. 71.

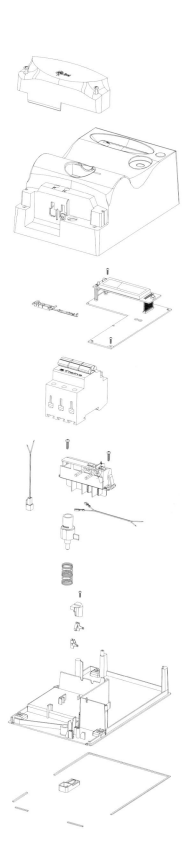

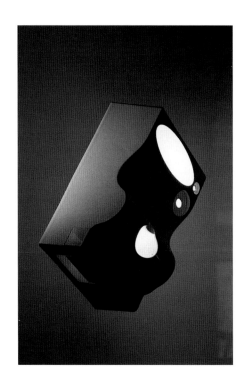

Italian Postal Service 1998–2003

As part of the corporate restructuring of the Italian Postal Service under the management of Corrado Passera, De Lucchi was commissioned to modernize its institutional image. Starting from 1998 he successfully completed this singular project, which had few precedents among public services in Italy, except for the designer's work (in some ways similar) in the same period for Enel. Turned into a joint-stock company in March 1998, the corporation set out to provide the country with an efficient and reliable mail service, capable of balancing its books and supplying services comparable to those in other European countries.

The first contact between the Postal Service and De Lucchi came the previous year, when he designed the PR6 printer produced especially by Olivetti for the corporation. In 1998 the Postal Service commissioned a complete redesign of its corporate identity. This covered the buildings (post office interiors and executive suites, temporary structures and commercial installations), equipment, furnishings, graphics, and corporate communications. The idea was to give visible form to the process of administrative rationalization, technological upgrading and staff training begun by the corporation.

This was another example of service design, like De Lucchi's work for the German Deutsche Bank and Deutsche Bahn in the mid-nineties and his later office concepts for banks. "It is definitely a question of architecture," he wrote in 2002. "Not so much construction as the ability to enhance all the sensorial aspects of a given place. It means being able to design not only walls, materials and furnishings, but above all the so-called 'soft' parameters, meaning color schemes, lighting, heating, scent and so forth, making places look welcoming, efficient, pleasant, convenient, etc. What's more, service design generally involves mass-producing components. This is because service-providers usually own chains of sales points. The more numerous the sales points the more necessary and urgent it is to coordinate them and make facilities of the same class or owned by the same organization distinctive and standardized." For this reason De Lucchi defined a general layout, a basic grid of solutions to be adapted to the individual situation, making it possible to deal appropriately with different contexts while creating the same visual impact.

Among the first projects developed were a series of data transmission kiosks (1999–2000, with Alberto Bianchi, Enrico Quell and Daniele Rossi) and the Telebus (2000, with Alberto Bianchi), transportable postal offices to supply a postal service at crowded events, as during Holy Year in Rome. At the same time De Lucchi began to deal with the most substantial part of the project: some 4,500 post offices were earmarked for improvement out of a total of about 14,000 spread across Italy. He verified the state of these spaces, which had always suffered from constraints imposed by security, the variety of the premises available (some historic buildings, the ground floors of condominium blocks, prefabricated buildings, shops, etc.), the lack of proper maintenance and a corporate mentality which tended to appease the demands of employees rather than provide a public service. Essentially his redesign sought to express a changed attitude to the service's customers, who were no longer treated as an undifferentiated mass of "users."

The offices were redesigned to make the interiors and services user-friendly. New electronic equipment was added in the front and back offices, self-service equipment was installed, a series of information monitors was ranged above the counters and a network linked all the equipment used by staff. In addition, the guidelines for all post offices included better organization of public flows through buildings, greater transparency in office activities and closer contacts between executives and employees, clearer information and better communication. "My objective," De Lucchi told *Domus* in 2001, "was to clear away barriers between staff and customers, setting the customers firmly at the center of the project, giving them more space and better service." The plan identified four zones (entrance, front office, transaction points, internal activities) laid out on the basis of three types of services: two at the transaction points devoted to financial services (Bancoposta) and mail services (Postal Products), identified by dark blue and yellow-green color codes, and a consultancy area. They embody three design themes: security, waiting and information. Closed circuit cameras monitor activities.

The standard redesign starts from the remake of the outer envelope of the office: the windows, freed from shutters and set in new frames with slender profiles of galvanized steel, eliminate the barrier effect. This favors transparency between interior and exterior and provides a useful surface for communicating effectively with the public.

Access is provided by double-entrance rotary doors or automatic sliding doors, depending on the size of the premises and the level of security required by the branch. They open onto the front office, designed to be as spacious, bright and comfortable as possible, with a special emphasis on cutting waiting times. Besides having seats and modern methods of queue management, the post office provides information on video monitors above the transaction points, Internet totems and display stands (1999–2000 and 2000–01, with Daniele Rossi). The display stands are designed as "characters" populating the office. The stand containing the forms, for example, has a central metal pedestal set on a round base and supports a ring of plastic pouches, a circular wooden surface where customers can write standing up, and a metal footrest. It saves clerks at the counter from receiving repeated requests for forms. Great care has been taken to supplement artificial illumination with natural lighting, diffusing appropriate levels of light all through the interiors and concentrating it on work surfaces. Circular lights are embedded at regular distances in the lozenge pattern of the grey panels that cover the false ceiling and a continuous tracklight system is suspended above the counter. This system also houses the cables that power the information monitors.

The visual pivot of the architectural design is the counter with the transaction points separating the public area from the workrooms at the back. The traditional armored glass has been abolished. It protected the clerks but created an irritating visual barrier for the public. Designed to create visual continuity between the clerk seated behind the counter and the customer standing in front, the new counter consists of a frontal element and backrest forming a single standardized unit, easy to manufacture, assemble, store and install, so cutting times and costs to a minimum. A raised platform runs behind it supporting the seating for the clerk, who is separated from the public by three different work surfaces: one for the clerk, one for passing documents across the counter, and one for the customer. They are faced with stainless steel and light-colored birchwood. The back and front are faced with dark blue plastic laminate and separated from the *gres* floor tiles by a steel baseboard.

Another element of the system is the consultancy room. This is transparent and so reflects the bright, airy atmosphere of the interiors. The

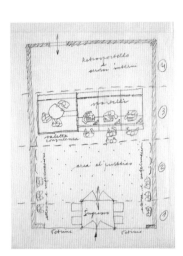

Drawing of the plan of the
standard layout of the post
offices, 1999.

Drawing of the service counter
for the post offices, 1999.
Drawing of the new counter
with the transaction points
in the post offices emphasizing
the visual continuity between
customer and clerk, 1999.

walls are made of glass partitions, with opaque patterns running across the central section to secure the client's privacy.

A preliminary simulation at the Rome-Eur central Post Office involved the creation of two branch offices, one small, the other medium-sized, a financial consultancy room and a self-service area. Various observations were made and alterations suggested by a special team from inside the corporation. They were then embodied in two prototype branch offices in Milan (agencies 15 and 23) and two in Rome (Piazza Vittorio Emanuele and Via della Scrofa).

This was followed by serial production of the components, applied for the first time in 2000 to the Roma 1 post office, an essential step towards the progressive application of the system under the supervision of the corporation's own management. Using calculated variations in the finishes, De Lucchi also designed the interiors of historic post office buildings, like the one in Piazza Cordusio in Milan (2001–02, with Simona Agabio and Alberto Bianchi). "I want to make the most of the Postal Service's older premises," De Lucchi told *Domus*, "preserving the finer architectural structures but feeling absolutely free to redefine their functions and services. Besides freeing the public part I sought to make these spaces flexible, which they were not. I left the monumental architecture as bare as possible, without concealing the technology that had to be installed. The technology is instrumental, the architecture is vital space." The scheme was further adapted to the spaces and the corner elements placed, for example, inside the Uffizi Gallery in Florence, the principal stations in Milan (2000–01, with Simona Agabio and Alberto Bianchi) and Rome (2000–01, with Luca La Torre, Laura Negrini, Francesco Otgianu and Enrico Quell). 2003 also saw the completion of the redevelopment of the Italian Postal Service's head offices in Rome-Eur, where the effectiveness of the whole system was studied in a different architectural and functional setting.

Bibliography: G. Arcuri, "Un laboratorio per il futuro e i nuovi uffici postali," in *il Gabbiano (Mensile delle Poste italiane)*, 52, March, 1999, pp. 17–21; G. Lonardi, "Sportelli tutti azzurri per le Poste 2000," in *La Repubblica*, June 19, 1999, p. 27; T. Cerra, "La nuova immagine delle Poste Italiane," in *Habitat Ufficio*, 100, 2000, pp. 48–51; A. Cirillo, "Legno, metallo e ospitalità le Poste si rifanno il look," in *La Repubblica*, January 25, 2000, p. II; E. Marro, "Le Poste investono 1.500 miliardi per rifarsi il 'look,'" in *Corriere della Sera*, January 20, 2000, p. 25; "La rivoluzione delle Poste con i 'nuovi uffici Md1,'" in *Italia Sera*, May 24, 2000, p. 6; S. Suardi, "Nuove Poste Italiane," in *Panorama Interni*, 7, March 31, 2000, p. 36; M. Urettini, "Le Poste Italiane in vista," in *A Acciaio Arte Architettura*, 5, 2000, pp. 6–15; AA.VV., *ADI Design Index 2000*, Bologna 2001, pp. 263, 274; E. Altea, "A bella posta," in *D Donna*, supp. to *La Repubblica*," July 3, 2001, p. 54; S. Berengo Gardin, "Poste aperte," in *Box*, 20, May, 2001, pp. 62–63; A. Cappellieri, "L'immagine dell'efficienza," in *Domus*, 834, February, 2001, pp. 64–71; C. Fabiani, *"Le poste italiane cambiano look,"* in *mood*, 11, 2001, pp. 122–23; C. Melograni, "Un designer all'ufficio posta," in *La Repubblica*, July 16, 2001, p. 27; *Mostra del XIX Premio Compasso d'Oro*, exhibition catalogue, Bologna 2001, pp. 211–12; "Servicedesign," in *md*, 7, July, 2001, pp. 76–81; "Michele De Lucchi. Futuribile ufficio," in *Modo*, 219, April, 2002, pp. 49–51; "Poste italiane. Insegne a bandiera Uffici postali," in *Ufficio stile*, 19, 2003, p. 58; N.T., "Alle Poste una rivoluzione tinta d'azzurro," in *Il Messaggero, Economia e Finanza* insert, January 6, 2003, p. 13.

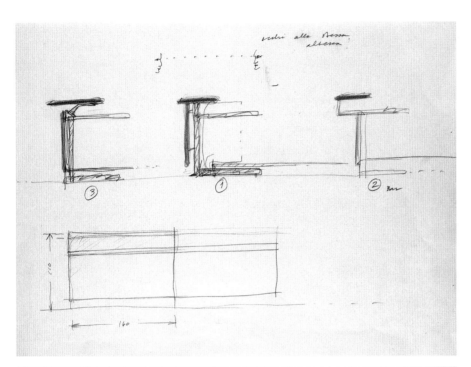

Italian Post Office concept
collaborators: Bastiaan Arler, Alberto Bianchi,
Enrico Quell, Daniele Rossi
corporate identity
Fragile (Michele De Lucchi and Mario Trimarchi)
collaborators: Fulvia Bleu, Massimo Canali,
Annalisa Gatto, Marco Miglio, Elena Riva,
Katrin Schmitt-Tegge
client: Poste Italiane

In 1999 De Lucchi illustrated some of the principles underlying the project. The objective was "to identify the Postal Service with a range of modern services, efficient but also reliable." The priority was to lay out the offices in a way that would ensure security, manage queues and create advertising and information spaces. The counter was the centerpiece of the scheme. "The ergonomics [...] went beyond physical or anthropometric factors," he stated, "to include psychological factors. Once the armored glass screen was removed from the counters, it was essential to create a normal speaking distance between the clerk and the customer. We introduced a transitional surface on the customer's side. The two planes, connected by a trough to prevent items from falling to the ground, create the design support for a relationship of equality. This is also brought out by the fact that though the clerk is seated, a platform raises him to the same eye-level as the customer standing in front of him. In cases where the transaction point has to be protected by armored glass, it can be inserted above the trough, without reducing the two transaction spaces. Apart from the psychological function of the platform, it provides a convenient housing for all the cables needed for operations at the counter. As for signage, we installed luminous panels above the transaction points equipped with a monitor that indicates the services available [...] Lastly, in organizing advertising and general information [...] we had two objectives: to enhance customer service and to find ways to make the promotional spaces a further source of income. Our project creates a hierarchy of wall spaces for placards and posters, information dispensers in the form of totem poles, banners hung from the ceiling or anchored to the floor and monitors with video messages." Enshrining these principles, the redesign project for the Italian Postal Service developed an integrated vocabulary embodied in all its elements, from architecture to interiors and graphics. It applied a uniform visual model and color scheme, used standardized lettering, and replicated the dimensions and position of the graphics and communication systems.

Applications of the corporate identity project, 1998–2003.

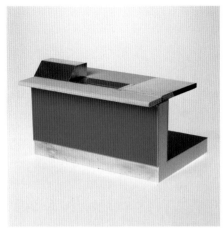
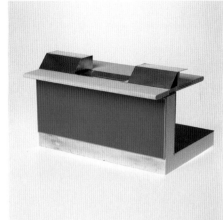
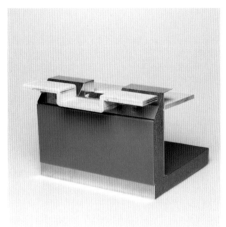
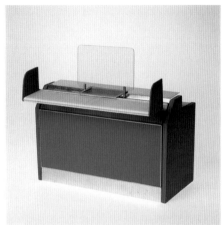

Models of the service counters and standard layout of transaction points in post offices, 1998.

Display stand for forms and Internet totem pole, 1999–2000 and 2001–02.

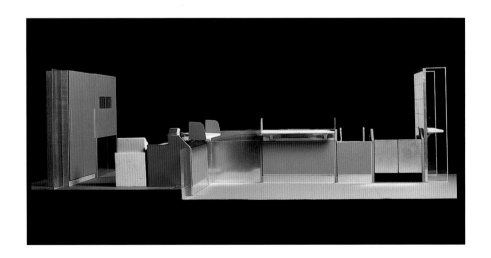

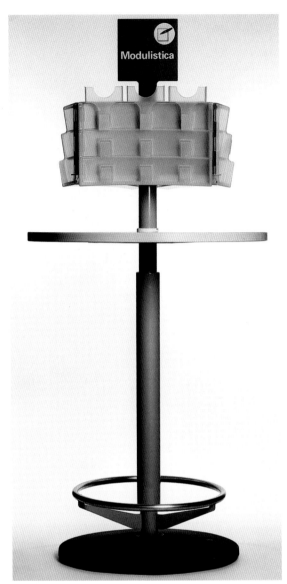

Post office kiosks
collaborators: Alberto Bianchi,
Ada Matsukaze, Enrico Quell, Daniele Rossi
client: Poste Italiane

The redesign of the Italian Postal Service was the most eloquent aspect of a more general shakeup in its customer services. The first step in this direction was the commission given to De Lucchi for the design of the corporation's computer kiosks. These kiosks can be installed in a few hours and used to provide postal services wherever there are large crowds, as for the Holy Year 2000 celebrations (when they were first used), trade fairs or sport events, or during emergencies such as natural disasters.

The kiosk has a simple geometrical form that uses standardized components: It consists essentially of a "shoebox" structure based on a rectangular plan and with a big roof. Supported and bordered by metal profiles symmetrical along one of the median axes, the "shoebox" contains two work stations, an armored unit that also houses the equipment for its functioning (and a washroom), and the zone open to the public.

Access to this space is from both the shorter sides, first along ramps in skidproof sheet metal flanking the kiosk, then through sliding doors (which double as billboards); when they slide open they completely cover the remainder of the two façades. Inside, the customers find themselves between two tripartite walls, glazed in the largest central panel. The exterior of the kiosk alternates opaque and transparent segments, providing a glimpse of the long service shelf inside. The counter that separates the public from the clerks is again designed to put them both at eye level, in keeping with the general guidelines applied to the project for the redesign of the Postal Service.

In the ceiling, the spotlights are recessed in metal panels sloping at the sides. The whole structure is dominated by a light canopy roof made up of eight segments, its fabric stretched taut by a framework of metal struts, which also serves to conceal the air conditioning plant. Again to provide a mobile postal service at special events, in 2000 De Lucchi (with Alberto Bianchi) designed the Telebus, a post office on wheels.

Bibliography: A. Cappellieri, "L'immagine dell'efficienza," in *Domus*, 834, February, 2001, pp. 64–71, esp. pp. 66, 71; N.T., "Alle Poste una rivoluzione tinta d'azzurro," in *Il Messaggero*, *Economia e Finanza* insert, January 6, 2003, p. 13.

Models of the mobile kiosks
and transportable kiosks.
View of a kiosk with the
characteristic canopy roof
made of eight segments.

Entry to the kiosk with
the skidproof ramp outside
and the service counter.

Post offices

1999
Milano 15, Via Vigna
Milano 23, Via San Simpliciano
collaborators: Alberto Bianchi, Paola Silva
Coronel, Enrico Quell, Daniele Rossi
client: Poste Italiane

2000
Roma 1, Via Sicilia
collaborators: Alberto Bianchi, Enrico Quell,
Daniele Rossi
client: Poste Italiane

The branch post offices in Via Vigna and Via San Simpliciano in Milan were the first where De Lucchi applied the definitive design principle developed for the Italian Postal Service. Their completion provided a further opportunity to study the prototypes before the components were mass-produced. The two different, rather compact layouts made it possible to explore possible applications of the scheme for upgrading interiors and exteriors. The interiors were reorganized around four predefined elements: the entrance space with Postamat automated tellers; the front office equipped with technologies for communicating with customers and managing queues; standardized transaction points without the traditional armored glass; separate consultancy rooms.

The project divides the new organization of the services into three areas. There are two counter areas, the first devoted to financial services (Bancoposta) and the second to mail (Postal Products); and one consultancy area, hived off in a separate office divided from the front office by glass walls, with sliding doors and opaque silkscreened central panels to preserve the privacy of the customer.

The plan of Via Vigna provided for six transaction points ranged in a line, a waiting area with seating, and a consultancy room. In the Via San Simpliciano branch the components of the system were arranged in an L shape inside a square space, with seating in the front office where customers can wait. The seedy old post offices everyone in Italy is familiar with are transformed, starting from the relation between interior and exterior: the old metal shutters have been eliminated and the front is line with large transparent windows bearing graphics with the corporation's name. All the details are designed to make the interiors open, welcoming and functional: the grey flooring in *gres* tiles; the appropriate level of illumination provided by lights recessed in the false ceiling (also grey) and on the track system suspended above the counters; the combination of simplified and rounded forms; the textured surfaces and the colors of the furnishings, equipment and graphics, from brushed stainless steel to dark blue plastic laminates and light-colored birchwood.

After appraising and perfecting all parts of the system, in 2000 the first branch offices were laid out using industrially manufactured standard components. The first was the post office on Via Sicilia in Rome, which featured the new graphics. The arrangement, like the prototype in Via Vigna, included rotating doors leading to the front office bounded by a sequence of nine transaction points, of which four were paired to adapt them to the pillared interior, closed off at the far end by the consultancy office.

Bibliography: T. Cerra, "La nuova immagine delle Poste Italiane," in *Habitat Ufficio*, 100, 2000, pp. 48–51; M. Urettini, "Le Poste Italiane in vista," in *A Acciaio Arte Architettura*, 5, 2000, pp. 6–15.

Milano 15 post office, Via Vigna, 1999. One of the post offices used to test the design before mass producing the components.

Interior of the post office featuring standard transaction points without armored glass.

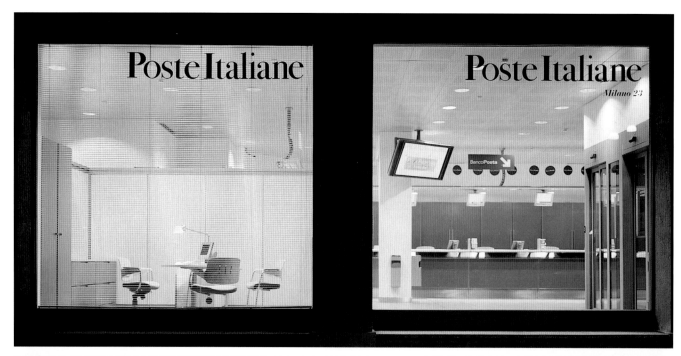

Milano 23 post office,
Via San Simpliciano, 1999.
One of the post offices used
to test the design before mass
producing the components.
Window and consultancy area
with a private office separated
by silkscreened windows.

Views of customer transaction
counters. The materials—dark
blue plastic laminate, birchwood
and stainless steel—make
the space welcoming and
functional.

Roma 1 post office,
Via Sicilia, 2000.
The first post office
to have been furnished
with mass-produced items.
The interior is lit up by lamps
recessed in the false ceiling
and the strip lighting above
the counters.

Detail of a display rack.

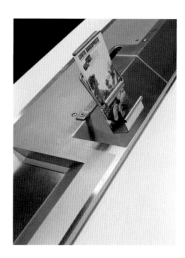

Central Post Office

Piazza Cordusio 1, Milan
collaborators: Simona Agabio, Alberto Bianchi
client: Poste Italiane

The restructuring of the post office in Piazza Cordusio, Milan, is a typical of the project of corporate renewal and image redesign undertaken by the Italian Postal Service, both by the size of the premises and their architectural qualities. It occupies the ground floor of the former Milan Stock Exchange, a massive eclectic building designed by Luca Beltrami and Luigi Broggi in 1899 (of which only the front portal remains) and stands on a square that became the city's financial center in the nineteenth century. It was completely reorganized in the 1980s to provide the Post Office's banking services (Bancoposta). In the general spirit of the modernization program, the project emphasizes the connections between the interiors by making them as bright, transparent and flexible as possible. This is already evident in the entrances, where the doors are transparent sheets of glass set in inconspicuous metal surrounds and surmounted by the corporation's new logo. On crossing the threshold, you enter a large public space rising to double height with the roof borne on sturdy steel columns and illuminated by skylights. This is the heart of the whole system, around which all the other functions are organized. The lighting and color scheme soften the impact of the new installations on the existing structures. For example, the rings of spotlights in the interstices of the star-shaped pattern of the roof girders supplement the natural light shed by the skylights, while the walls have been faced with a clear grey rendering.

The perimeter of this area is surrounded by various workspaces, which were used to try out the standardized furniture designed for post offices located in buildings of historical interest. The counter is lined with sheets of glass painted milk white on the work surfaces and the side facing the public. Behind the L-shaped counter a row of grey laminate closets provides a neutral ground for the system of

View of the public office rising to double height with the steel columns and large skylights.

The entrance and view of the office with standard modular furnishings.

signage and information panels and also screens the spaces behind. The self-service area, consultancy rooms, mail and telegraph store and an exhibition space are placed at the end of the counter, separated from the front office by glass walls with opaque horizontal patterns running across their central sections to ensure clients' privacy. The exhibition space was used to present the "Post Office Project" traveling exhibition, which illustrated the whole plan for the Italian Postal Service with an installation designed by De Lucchi (2001–02, with Simona Agabio, Alberto Bianchi and Gerhard Reichert).

Bibliography: A. Cappellieri, "L'immagine dell'efficienza," in *Domus*, 834, February, 2001, pp. 64–71, esp. p. 68; A. Foppiano, "Poste italiane al Cordusio," in *Abitare*, 421, October, 2002, pp. 188–93.

The transaction counters faced
with painted glass panels.
The grey laminate closets can
be seen in the background.

Details of the upper part
of the counters and the glass
walls of the consultancy rooms.

Head office

Viale Europa, Rome EUR
collaborators: Simona Martino,
Giovanni Battista Mercurio, Laura Parolin,
Enrico Quell
client: Poste Italiane

With the redesign of the interiors of the corpo-ration's headquarters, an immense seventies building in the EUR district of Rome, De Lucchi addressed the question of architecture as a "vehicle of communication," as he declared in a recent conversation, "in which the spatial lay-out expresses the new mentality the company is trying to imprint, in this case essentially on its own employees."
The redesign operation establishes new rules in the arrangement of spaces. Like De Lucchi's other projects for office environments and his general plan for the Postal Service, the design-er sought to create a harmonious and agree-able setting where people can go serenely about their normal tasks. The poky, featureless offices, organized as separate rooms, were transformed into open-plan spaces and the cen-tral service corridor unexpectedly became a lu-minous "tube," its whole length flanked by translucent glass partitions that glow with the changes of daylight at different times of day and the different colors of the artificial lighting. Separated by closets, each houses work sta-tions or conference rooms.
Transparency and visual clarity are also fea-tures of the ground floor: the lobby is wrapped round by extensive strip windows, opaque only where they are covered by the system of com-munication and signage. The main counter has parapets of satin-finish glass, as in the Piazza Cordusio office and others, but its profile is prolonged and surmounted by a handrail made of steel and wood, isolating the public zone.
Access to the floors above is provided by a spiral staircase and two intersecting escala-tors. Another enormous transparent strip win-dow encloses the periodicals library, which is lit by bright globes that stud the ceiling. Light-colored bentwood screens are used to divide up the dining area.

View of the atrium on the ground floor with the counter faced with satin-finish glass.

On the office level the rooms are separated by translucent glass walls.
The glass wall opening onto the periodicals library.

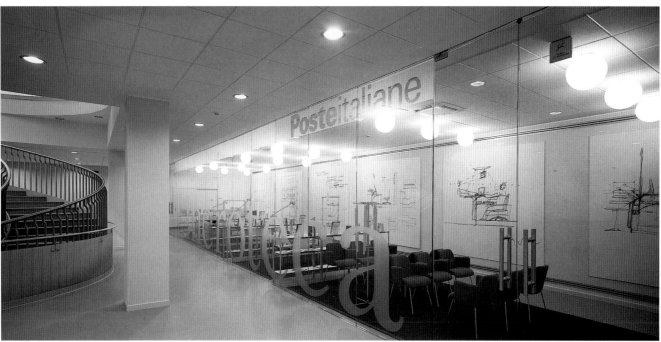

branch offices
Banca 121
collaborators: Giovanni Battista Mercurio,
Angelo Micheli (project leader), Laura Parolin
client: Banca 121

Unlike other redesigns of branch offices, Banca 121 is a financial bank and this project entailed designing a system completely independent of the physical places to which it will eventually be applied. The young company had identified only its first few branch offices but intended to define their image from the very start. Its commercial strategy was perfectly clear: it posited three different kinds of branch bank—"boutique," "store" and "agency"—to which the system would be applied.

A "boutique" is a branch largely offering self-service facilities: it has cash machines permanently on line, a "promo corner" for information and financial offers, Internet points which can be used for amusement and entertainment. An employee may be present to keep an eye on things and deal with occasional requests for assistance. In the "store," automatic facilities are supplemented by an advisory service, providing customers with detailed information about financial products. This calls for private consulting rooms and larger premises. Finally the "agency" offers a full range of services, with the premises highly diversified into reception, promotion, consultancy, investment, rapid service and management zones.

De Lucchi responded with a "technological box," which comes complete with all utilities, equipment, furniture, door and window frames, and can be placed in any kind of setting. The technology remains in full view, stressing the idea of transparent banking. The outstanding feature of the project is the Fugafil netting that lines all the walls and ceilings. This is a synthetic fabric designed for use in filters, still without applications in architecture (it is used, for example, on beach umbrellas or the lining of sports shoes). The netting masks the surrounding architecture without entirely obstructing the view, a simple way of creating distinctive and uniform interiors.

Interiors of the branch bank with the transaction points for customers and the supervisor's office.

Entrance. The walls and the ceilings are lined with Fugafil mesh.

branch offices
Banca Intesa
collaborators: Simona Agabio, Alberto Bianchi, Geert Koster, Giovanna Latis, Simona Martino, Philippe Nigro, Claudia Pescatori, Enrico Quell, Daniele Rossi, Laiza Tonali
corporate identity
Fragile (Michele De Lucchi and Mario Trimarchi)
collaborators: Susanne Gerhardt, Julia Kleiner, Marco Miglio
client: Banca Intesa

The definition of the corporate identity of the Banca Intesa is a continuing project, with some thirty branches completed so far. It is one of a series of commissions De Lucchi received in the early nineties to completely redesign the corporate images of major businesses. The first was Deutsche Bank, followed by projects for the new offices for the Banca Popolare di Lodi and Banca 121 and his work for the Italian Postal Service with its over 14,000 branches. Banca Intesa wanted to rationalize and promote its new corporate identity, still confused behind a series of different bank names and branch offices, which survived long after the merger between three banks (Ambroveneto, Cariplo and Comit). The corporation's brief was to design a new logo and redesign its branches, which meant restructuring over two thousand offices across Italy.

To bring the bank closer to its customers, De Lucchi identified two key principles. Firstly, he stressed graphics and communications with large signs, fields of color and videos, while treating the architecture as a "largely neutral backdrop," using large transparent glass surfaces, both windows and partitions, and reducing constructional materials to a minimum. Color is important. The new brand name, for example, retains the earlier logo with three arches of an aqueduct and adds eleven shades of color in a sequence that ranges from red to green to dark blue. Each color corresponds to a banking service and is used to signal them clearly inside the branches. Secondly, he focused on the customer's convenience, providing

Banca Intesa branch office, Via dei Missaglia, Milan, 2002. A transaction point flanked by colored partitions.

Windows of a branch with the logo featuring different shades of red, green and dark blue.

clear information about the location and functions of the different zones of the bank to speed up transactions, telling operations and consultancy services. The interiors are brightly lit but the consulting rooms are very discreet. To make the project more practical, all parts of the system (architecture, furnishings and graphics) are conceived as industrial products: modular, flexible, interchangeable, easy to produce in series, transport, assemble and reconfigure.

The theoretical model sees the branch office as a set of spaces which, for the sake of uniformity and continuity, have the same kind of flooring, walls and ceilings: self-service area, reception and waiting spaces, transaction counters, consultancy rooms, investment services, back office with private waiting spaces and facilities. The windows of the branches are treated as large transparent screens on which the bank communicates directly with its clients and the public. Appropriate levels of general illumination are provided by lights set in the ceiling. The doors and consultancy rooms are lit by spotlights to improve concentration. Compared with other bank projects, this one places particular stress on the self-service area. The automated devices are embedded in a long curvilinear wall painted with flat colors and with information applied in large lettering. Roller shutters or glass walls divide this space from the front office but fold away to create a single continuous space during normal opening hours.

Bibliography: M. Gabbiano, "L'architetto che vuole portare la luce in banca," in *Affari e Finanza*, *La Repubblica* insert, March 31, 2003, p. 27; "Passera: nuovo marchio per la svolta," in *Corriere della Sera*, March 7, 2003, p. 27; F. Sottocornola, "Così Banca Intesa dà l'addio a BCI," in *Il Mondo*, March 14, 2003, p. 60.

Banca Intesa branch office,
Via dei Missaglia, Milan, 2002.
Front office with the curving
wall with automated telling
machines.
A shutter separates the two
zones when the front office
is closed.

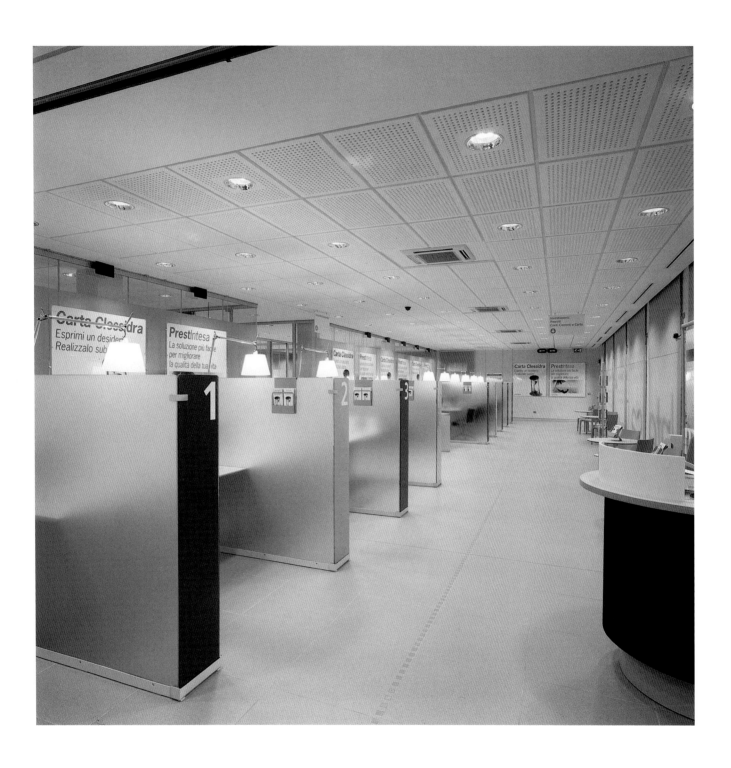

offices
Giorgio Armani
Via Bergognone, Milan
collaborator: Paola Silva Coronel
client: Giorgio Armani

The Milanese designer's new headquarters cover a large site occupied by what was once a Nestlé production facility. The buildings are rather featureless, as can be seen by their elevations—including that of the block set on the streetfront—and plans, which are rectangular and studded with points of support set at regular distances. In all they cover a surface area of over 10,000 square metres. Some of the buildings have one story and some two.

Armani commissioned De Lucchi to redesign all the workspaces—offices, showrooms, tailoring workshops, reception rooms, warehouses—and Tadao Ando to design a theater for fashion shows with an annex for holding receptions. De Lucchi's work "enfolds" Ando's: the theater, preceded by a foyer dominated by a striking curved concrete wall, is set at the back of the lot and reached by a long corridor that runs right through the office building. The two functional blocks face each other discreetly and respectfully, without encroaching. They are separated by a rectangular room with strip windows set in its walls, transparent where they look onto the banqueting room and satin-finished where they face the workplaces. The room is wholly occupied by a pool of water inserted by Ando: it creates a point of light and vibrant detachment, a stage of true purification.

Though the workrooms have specialized functions (each block is assigned to an individual brand in the Armani group), they are linked and integrated by an arrangement that favors continuity, openness, and transparency in spaces. The windows overlooking the internal courtyard have been enlarged to their full height; the entrances and the passages from one zone to another one are fitted with sliding doors and large glass walls. The ceiling slabs between floors have been cut out to define intermediate levels. In particular, the block set in the heart of the whole complex contains an interesting overhead route, with stairs and catwalks independent of the structure enclosing them. The simple, elegant image of the common zones (reception areas, lounges) does not diminish the industrial atmosphere, which evokes restraint and efficiency: for example, the project retains the shed roofs supported on curved concrete girders and the simple façades.

Bibliography: *Milano 2001*, suppl. to *Casabella*, 690, June, 2001, pp. 55–56; A. Foppiano, "Armani/Architettura. Tadao Ando + Michele De Lucchi + Giancarlo Ortelli a Milano," in *Abitare*, 414, February 2002, pp. 96–107.

The office's workrooms look onto an internal courtyard.

Model of the project and passages with the large glass walls that define the office spaces.

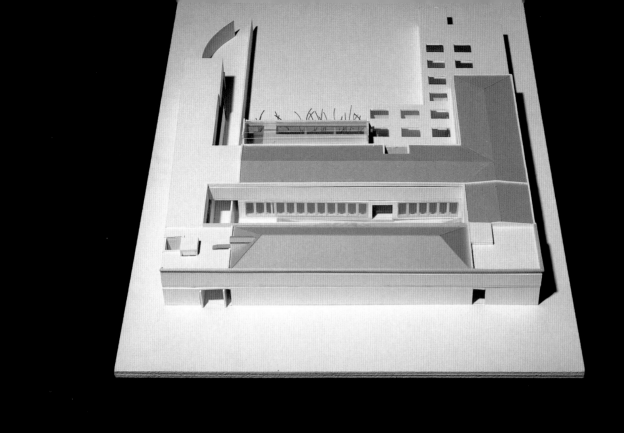

redevelopment of the
Telecom Head Office
Piazza Affari, Milan
collaborators: Giovanni Battista Mercurio,
Angelo Micheli (project leader), Laura Parolin,
Claudio Venerucci
client: Telecom Italia

Telecom's Milan headquarters stand in the distinctive setting of Piazza Affari, the city's business hub. They occupy a building dating from the thirties restructured in the postwar period (next to the more famous and monumental stock exchange building). De Lucchi's project sought first of all to retrieve what remained of the original building. This rather featureless architectural container was laid out as offices set on ten floors (with two levels below ground and its three top floors set back from the cornice). Its plain and rational design actually conceals a sophisticated technological core, which enables advanced operations to be carried out, but the presence of the equipment is never intrusive or exhibited in the forms of the building.

Once again the logic underlying De Lucchi's projects for the office environment is to show "the efficacy of a friendly, harmonious setting" which exploits the full potential of high technology yet remains "a serene workplace." Hence the profusion of glass in the walls to provide the maximum illumination in all the interiors, alleviating the claustrophobia of the corridors between offices and the open-plan space in the center of each floor. Hence the spacious lobby, faced with natural materials, marble and wood and, again, large strip windows and images transmitted by the plasma screens mounted on the walls. And hence the unusual top story, which is set back from the cornice and surrounded by a continuous balcony, with a hanging garden and an extraordinary view over the city.
The rooms on this eighth floor, used for conferencing and receptions, open onto a bright and very informal veranda, covered with *brise-soleils* and walls that open out fully onto the long balcony, with flower stands and wooden flooring. The building ends with yet another

**The thirties building
on Piazza Affari, Milan,
that houses the offices.**

**The press room on the
mezzanine floor.**

level above, a structure in iron and glass that conceals the technical plant of the utilities.

On the semi-ground floor the spaces are distributed around the press room, set in the middle. One or more conference rooms are also planned for each of the upper floors, all laid out as individual offices and open-plan areas. The semi-basement level has been converted into a garage.

This layout was, however, immediately tampered with and today De Lucchi's project is no longer fully visible. Besides this building, the various projects De Lucchi has devised for Telecom since 1999 have included a number of trade fair stands, graphic designs and the organization of the Future Center in Venice (2002, with Angelo Micheli, project leader, Massimo Canali, Giovanni Battista Mercurio, Laura Parolin, Mercedes Jaén Ruiz).

The walls bounding the offices
are in etched glass.
On the right, the top floor faces
onto a continuous balcony
with a hanging garden.

The open-plan layout of offices.

Apartment in Milan
collaborators: Angelo Micheli, Silvia Suardi

The spacious apartment, originally laid out on a traditional plan with a passage running down the middle, was completely remade by eliminating all the partitions along the main front and replacing the suite of rooms with a single reception room divided from the other interiors by a continuous curved wall. This is a true wall, ending in a rectilinear segment, which screens the end room, laid out as a study. The front door looks as if it has slipped to one side because of the wall: when you enter the apartment, its convex form looms up as if prompting you to go around it and so take stock of its presence.

The solemnity of the wall, "a boundary wall, wall open to the sky, garden wall that you can take in at a glance and appreciate for its proportions and texture," as De Lucchi states, is enhanced by the expert use of natural and artificial light. The wall does not touch the ceiling and lets in the light from the big french windows opening onto the passage behind. In the same way the attic has a false ceiling but its edge does not touch the outer walls. It houses recessed spotlights pointing down for direct light but it also acts as a reflector screen for diffused light from lamps, nestling in its upper side, so that it looks very light, almost seeming to float.

The large opening set in the wall about a third of the way down its length, described by the designer as "an emperor's portal," links the reception room and passage, which has an irregular plan. The corridor is very dignified and architecturally independent, as confirmed by various details of the project. In first place the floor, laid with solid oak boards, continues the flooring of the drawing room. All the rooms have sliding doors (including the private quarters of the apartment on the opposite side and the "gallery" of long wardrobes lining the wall). They are opaque or semitransparent so as not to break up the spatial continuity. Much of the furniture is made to measure, in stone and painted glass, from the shower cabin to the bookcase running through the study. The big drawing room is furnished with fine designer furniture.

The colors and materials are warm and natural: the extensive plastered surfaces are painted, the shelves in the bathrooms are made of amber-colored stone, the doors are lacquered in warm tones of grey. This natural atmosphere is supplemented by the comfort furnished by the quiet presence of technology: the interior is climate controlled, secure, with doors and windows controlled by highly sophisticated technology.

Bibliography: S. Suardi, "La casa e il suo muro," in *Interni*, 520, April, 2002, pp. 208–11.

View of the passage. The floor is laid with solid oak boards, the rooms have opaque or semitransparent sliding doors. The large aperture set in the curved wall of the living room.

View of the living room bounded by the curved wall, with light filtering through from the french windows. At the far end is the wall screening the study.

Literature café and Fastweb foyer
Largo Franco Parenti, Milan
collaborator: Giovanna Latis
client: Fondazione Pier Lombardo

The Fastweb Foyer is the first part completed to date of a plan for the architectural and functional enhancement of the Teatro Franco Parenti. In 1996 the theater was transformed into a foundation and a project evolved for a "Citadel of the Performing Arts." This set the theater within a larger complex of cultural facilities on a site covering over 5,000 square meters.

The foyer is on the mezzanine floor of an adjacent building and linked to the theater lobby, but is also an independent space with separate access. Laid out on a rectangular plan, it has a number of different functions which blend quite naturally with each other: internet stations set on columns, lounge-corners for using Web TVs, a bookstore and café-restaurant. At each end there are two more flexible spaces: a private lounge, separated by a sliding wall, and a zone that can be used for live shows, connected with the restaurant and lined with large strip windows facing onto the entrance passage. The foyer as a whole forms a sort of open-plan space used for a range of activities, its fluid arrangement emphasized by the furnishings (all specially designed except for the seating), and by the materials lining the walls and floors.

The woodwork is left in its natural colors: the floors are oak, the chairs and bar counter are beech, the internet columns and tables spruce (with small bas-reliefs by Emilio Tadini, poet and painter, let into the square café tabletops), the bookcases and doors are in medium-density fiberboard. These natural materials contrast pleasantly with the plain cement rendering of the walls and the more hi-tech inserts (the plain iron and brass fittings of the bar counter, the aluminum of the armchairs in the library, the metal tracks fixed to the ceiling to support the lighting). The conical Andrée pendant lamps, in transparent glass, were designed for the foyer and can be raised and lowered by a pulley system.

Bibliography: G. Latis, "Fastweb Foyer," in *Interni*, special issue enclosed with *Panorama*, 18, November 29, 2002, pp. 21–22; s.ch., "Una multisala di 5 mila metri quadrati con bar, libreria e cinque palcoscenici," in *La Repubblica*, January 17, 2003, p. IX.

The dining room has Internet points on the right. The room is separated by a sliding wall.

The main room features a bookcase and square tables with bas-reliefs imbedded into the tops by the artist Emilio Tadini.

lamps
Logico
Artemide
production: 2001
collaborator: Gerhard Reichert

The design of Logico reflects De Lucchi's studies of light diffusion. It is a series of lamps made of organic glass shapes that slot together, as in a three-dimensional jigsaw puzzle. The glass has a refined finish and coloring that makes it look like ice. The lamps reveal the possibility of finding a modular joint between the complex geometries of non-orthogonal forms, so that the composition creates new and sinuous configurations and sheds different kinds of light. The diffuser—made out of glass paste mixed with opal salts distributed uniformly—has a hole in the top for the flex and the attachment for the bulb fitting, while the bottom edge is flat. Conceived in a number of dimensions, the lamps can be used individually or combined in line (in groups of three) or radially (on 90- and 120-degree axes). Complex to assemble, the mold was carefully designed to calculate precisely the tolerance of the slots. Logico is a whole family of lamps that includes pendant, ceiling, table, floor and wall versions, in three dimensions.

Logico lamp, Artemide, 2000–03, pendant version.

Ways of combining the diffusers.

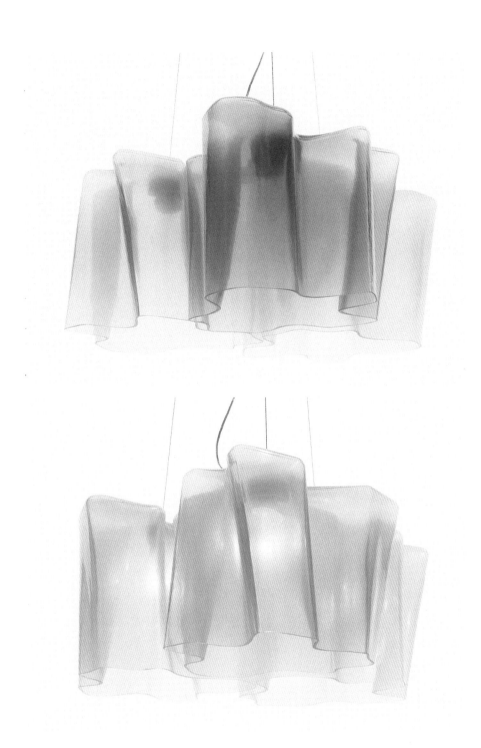

lamps
Castore
Artemide
production: 2003–04
collaborator: Huub Ubbens

The Castore series, presented in 2003, was the completion of a family of lamps that grew out of an adaptation of the diffuser used for the Dioscuri lamp (1999–2000). This was an etched opalescent globe of blown glass fitted with an almost invisible wall bracket made of thermoplastic resin, and produced in ceiling/wall and free-standing versions.

Continuing his personal reworking of archetypal shapes, De Lucchi again entrusted the expressive effect to a perfectly white sphere but enhanced the overall design with refined supports and details. The tapered stem, which the designer added to the new versions (pendant, table and floor models) again uses the fitting from Dioscuri, made of white thermoplastic resin. By filtering the light it mitigates the transition from the brightness of the diffuser to the shadowy zone of the lamp's structure, and at the same time sheds a soft light on a part of the lamp that is usually opaque. The dimmer switch, particularly on the floor model, is a simple tapered joint between the two stems (in the table version it is set in the base). It regulates the lamp's brightness, memorizes the last brightness level chosen and offers a choice between local and remote control. The series, which includes the Calice version, is versatile, its use not being restricted to the home. For greater stability the lamps are fitted with circular bases in zama metal alloy.

Bibliography: M. Romanelli, "Anticipazioni. Euroluce 2003," in *Abitare*, 427, April, 2003, pp. 210–11; DS, "Milano 2003. Michele De Lucchi," in *Domus*, 858, April, 2003, pp. 130–31; "Castore. Michele De Lucchi" and "Un creador con enorme personalidad," in *Arquitectura y diseño*, 42, May, 2004, p. 11.

Dioscuri lamp, Artemide, 1999–2000, the wall-mounted version.

Castore lamp, Artemide,
2003–04, the floor, pendant
and table versions.

exhibit designs
Scuderie del Quirinale
Rome

2000
**"Sandro Botticelli. Painter
of the Divina Commedia"**
collaborators: Enrico Quell, Silvia Suardi
client: Agenzia Romana per il Giubileo

2001
**"Renaissance. Masterpieces
in the Italian Museums"**
collaborators: Enrico Quell, Silvia Suardi
client: Agenzia Romana per il Giubileo

2002
**"Rembrandt. Paintings, Engravings
and Reflections in the Seventeenth
and Eighteenth Century in Italy"**
collaborators: Enrico Quell, Silvia Suardi
client: Azienda Speciale Palaexpo
del Comune di Roma

For each of these three exhibitions at the Scuderie del Quirinale in Rome, De Lucchi devised a distinctive exhibit design, in harmony with their themes. He sought to transfigure the familiar setting, while respecting Gae Aulenti's architectural conversion (in 1997–99) of Ferdinando Fuga's building into a venue for temporary exhibitions.

The first of the exhibitions presented some one hundred illustrations of the *Divina Commedia* drawn on parchment by Sandro Botticelli. The technique of the sequence might today be described as cinematic, innovative in its format and probably used as a visual aid during public readings of Dante's poem. Commissioned by Pierfrancesco de' Medici (1463–1503), the illustrations were first brought together at an exhibition in Berlin; after being presented in Rome the exhibit was reassembled in London.

The show was arranged on two levels. The ground-floor rooms recreated the historical and artistic context of this unique codex. Paintings were placed on neutral-colored false walls or on prismatic display cases with rounded edges set on simple rectangular supports that contained textual materials. The paintings illustrated the Florence of Lorenzo il Magnifico, the humanistic fervor of relations between Pierfrancesco de' Medici and Botticelli. The exhibition included the sole known source for the parchments in a work called the *Anonymous Magliabechiano* (c. 1540) and a room devoted to Florence under Savonarola. The last two sections, providing an introduction to the theme of the exhibition, were devoted to the art of drawing in the age of Botticelli—from Filippo Lippi to Leonardo da Vinci—and to the figure of Dante in fifteenth-century Florence. Each of the exhibits was carefully related to its backdrop, whether painted or wooden, and enhanced by artificial lighting.

The heart of the exhibition was on the upper floor. Its rooms were traversed by a sinuous plasterboard wall, evoking Dante's interpretation of the afterlife. Along it were ranged the exhibits, each at the same height on a plane set at a slight angle to the wall, and each containing a single sheet bearing a drawing by Botticelli, with beside it the printed text of the corresponding *canto*. The whiteness of the space, increased by the choice of diffuse lighting, facilitated the viewing of the materials: sheepskin parchments with drawings made in a lead pencil. In some cases, Botticelli had added green or red ink to convey a sense of depth or perspective.

A year later De Lucchi prepared one hundred and sixty pieces, lent by sixty Italian museums, to recount the Renaissance to the Japanese, coming from the same exhibition in the Japanese capital. To enable visitors to perceive, within the narrative scheme, which work was most important in each group and which the secondary items, De Lucchi applied a material "which had a grey pictorial effect in imitation of *pietra serena*," using it to line the false walls and stands used for displaying the objects. This made it possible to bring together works of different kinds and sizes—from paintings to carvings, religious items and suits of armor—enhancing the most valuable items even if they were small, again with the help of the lighting, which was angled or diffused to suit each exhibit. The panels were divided up horizontally by narrow grooves set at regular distances: these marks served to position the works, their containers and above all their labels at standard heights from the floor, even when they were set against white walls.

**Installation of the exhibition
"Sandro Botticelli. Painter
of the Divina Commedia,"
Scuderie del Quirinale, Rome,
2000, second floor rooms.**

The exhibition "Rembrandt. Paintings, Engravings and Reflections in the Seventeenth and Eighteenth Century in Italy" presented a detailed analysis of the Dutch master's complete output of engravings. A selection of oil paintings was included to allow immediate comparison between the expressiveness of different techniques, and also some works by Italian painters directly inspired by the artist.

It was important for visitors to be able to examine the engravings closely, since each line was significant. The works arrived already framed (with an ivory-colored mount, a frame of smooth, light-colored wood and protective glass). De Lucchi mounted them on lecterns set at 45-degree angles and supported on plain wooden stands about one meter high set on slender legs. The lecterns were set back some twenty centimeters from the front edge of the stands, which formed a supporting shelf, so allowing visitors to lean over the engravings and even rest their elbows on the stands. Magnifying glasses were handed out at the entrance, so increasing the minuteness with which details could be analyzed. De Lucchi completely eliminated natural light and focused the lighting directly on the works. The stands were painted light grey, while the surfaces of the lecterns were coated with a gold film which diffused the light and so created a continuous bright band running through the half-light of the interiors. In addition to respecting the recommended levels of illumination and rendering the atmosphere in the rooms soft and warm, this arrangement created a pleasant contrast with the hard lines of the engravings. The outer edges of the stands were lined with dark blue drapes in fireproof velvet, both to proportion their height to the visual band which was the center of focus and to screen the light sources. These were spotlights with 50 watt halogen twin-plug bulbs mounted on a low-voltage electrified track fixed about 3.5 meters above the level of the works, so focusing them directly on the surface of the exhibits without creating glare or areas of shadow. The paintings were generally hung on false walls painted in colors that

created a contrast with the white walls of the rooms and illuminated through shaping devices. The halogen lamps were fitted with different opticals and bulbs of different brightness to suit the dimensions of the works, the height they were set at and the geometrical relations between the light sources and the surfaces illuminated. A very low-voltage electrified system was again used to power the captions set beside the paintings. They were enclosed in an aluminum structure screwed to the panels at an angle of about 30 degrees, faced with a special diffusing adhesive film and by a panel of silk-screened polycarbonate with the texts in negative.

Bibliography: F. Giuliani, "Botticelli, 92 disegni d'Inferno e Paradiso," in *La Repubblica* (Rome), September 14, 2000, p. VII; R. Sleiter, "Il Rinascimento? Per qualcuno è tutto uno sballo," in *Il Venerdì*, 2001, pp. 120–24; A. Reggiani, "Rembrandt a Roma. L'eleganza della semplicità," in *Luce e Design*, 2, April, 2003, pp. 70–74.

Installation of the exhibition "Sandro Botticelli. Painter of the Divina Commedia," Scuderie del Quirinale, Rome, 2000, ground floor and second floor rooms.

Installation of the exhibition "Renaissance. Masterpieces in the Italian Museums," Scuderie del Quirinale, Rome, 2001, views of the rooms.

Detail of the false wall textured with paint to imitate *pietra serena* and view of the room.

Installation of the exhibition "Rembrandt. Paintings, Engravings and Reflections in the Seventeenth and Eighteenth Century in Italy," Scuderie del Quirinale, Rome, 2001, exhibit design for the engravings and paintings.

Detail of the display stand for the engravings with a gold leaf finish.

redevelopment of the public spaces of the
Milan Triennale
Palazzo dell'Arte, Milan
collaborators: Brigid Byrne, Paolo Fromage,
Aya Matsukaze
client: Milan Triennale

De Lucchi returned as a designer to the Milan Triennale, a symbolic place in his career. In 1973 he had made his provocative debut there as "Designer in General" and in 1983, when Memphis was at its height, he presented a plastic prefabricated holiday home (at the exhibition "The Houses of the Triennale. Eight Projects for Contemporary Domestic Interiors," curated by Franco Raggi and Francesco Trabucco). September 23, 2002 saw the opening of his redesign of the ground floor of the Palazzo dell'Arte, which took in the atrium, ticket office, wardrobe, bookstore, coffee-shop and temporary exhibition areas.
Replacing the previous arrangement by Umberto Riva, De Lucchi responded to the need to reorganize the spaces functionally by opening up the interiors and seeking to recreate as faithfully as possible the original layout by Giovanni Muzio (1933). "And so it has happened that this extraordinary architecture has been brought to light again," stated the designer in 2002. "The space designed by Muzio is large and modern, its geometry is symmetrical but not pedantic, its proportions are monumental but carefully controlled." The decision to "clean and remove," restoring whiteness and transparency, renders the atmosphere of the interior limpid. The walls are refined, plastered, smoothed and painted white; the marble has been washed and damage made good. Cables, plumbing and various utilities have been stowed away out of sight and wherever possible eliminated. The floor has been smoothed and parts worn by use changed.
When you approach from Viale Alemagna, you pass through the porch and the glass front of the entrance, guided by the central axis, where eight large glass panels present information about the exhibition program at the entrance to the atrium. In contrast with earlier arrangements,

**Sketch of a vista
of the coffee shop.**

**The entrance with, at
the sides, panels that display
information on the program
of events and the coffee shop
at the far end.**

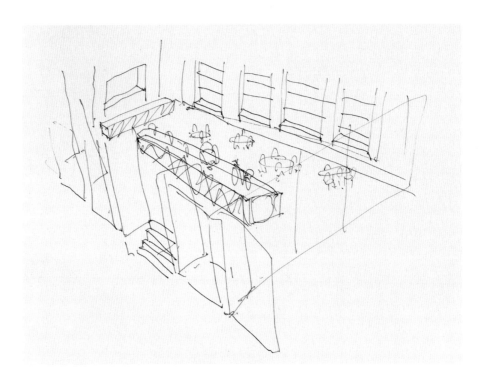

this space has now recovered its value as a large central distribution area. First it widens out, making the Gallery of Architecture and the Gallery of the "curve" directly accessible and housing the ticket counter and wardrobe. Then it reveals the impluvium, where the bookstore is laid out, and gives access to an imposing staircase; finally it guides the visitor towards the coffee shop that stretches across its far end. In the bookstore the books are placed on nine tables arranged in a regular checkerboard pattern in the covered area of the impluvium. A dais housing exhibits from the Triennale's design collection and periodically updated masks the large area of the coffee shop. This is furnished with different models of seating and has large strip windows overlooking the park. Extensive windows, bordered by slender metal profiles, separate the coffee shop from the atrium and a side room. The lighting, in a harmonious rapport with the architecture, uses both cylindrical ceiling lamps, arranged in a regular pattern to create diffused light (combining transformer and fluorescent light in a single element for low energy consumption and high light output), and suspended spotlights—as in the bookshop—where the light sources are left in view.

"The new arrangement of the ground floor of the Palazzo dell'Arte," wrote Alberto Bassi in *Casabella* in 2003, "prompts reflections of a more general kind about the contemporary language and form of architectural projects and installations in museums, but also of exhibitions and artistic-cultural initiatives. If [...] we have entered the age of hyper-merchandising museums, then we will accept the relationship between these places devoted to celebrating art, architecture, design, culture and whatever else and the spaces where goods are displayed and sold. [...] In short, the places devoted to the exhibition of the arts and culture increasingly resemble showrooms, and vice versa; and the same is true of the places where we live, work and travel more or less rapidly [...] These are ways of showing, designing, or displaying more easily assimilated and attuned to the contemporary cultural sensibility. The equivalence between museum and showroom, inspired by a minimalism that may be cold or halfway between the playful and the

info-entertainment, clearly does not exhaust the issue. The difference in innovation and quality seems to be—perhaps is again, as always—due to the care taken over in presentation."

De Lucchi here indicates a practical path, expressing himself in the architecture and the exhibit design with a vocabulary of the greatest relevance. "The program for the retrieval of the Palazzo dell'Arte envisions further intervention [...]," he stated, "in a logic of formal clarity and the remove of permanent obstructions, because it is part of our contemporary sensibility to enjoy clean, open, simple, spaces where the function is better combined with feeling."

The same approach permeated an earlier project, never built, for the Triennnale's new documentation center (1998, with Brigid Byrne, Aya Matsukaze, Filippo Pagliani). This was to be a courtyard rising double height faced with bare brick, remodeled and converted into a utilities room and storage space, where De Lucchi sought to restore Muzio's original layout by reusing the original materials. At present he is working on the remainder of the building.

Bibliography: A. Besio, "Luci, bar, bookshop. La nuova Triennale," in *La Repubblica*, August 28, 2002, p. XVI, and "In mille festeggiano la nuova Triennale," in *La Repubblica*, September 24, 2002, p. XI; G. Borella, "Il nuovo look della Triennale," in *Corriere della Sera*, September 29, 2002, p. 57; T. Giacobone (ed.), "Triennale per Eames design," in *Interni*, October, 2002; F. Irace, "Doppia modernità felice," in *Il Sole 24 Ore*, September 29, 2002, p. 39; A. Morello, "Dall'acustica ai book shop. Sarà una grande Triennale," in *La Stampa* (Milan), August 1, 2002, p. 2; A. Bassi, "Michele De Lucchi: il nuovo ingresso alla Triennale di Milano," in *Casabella*, 708, February, 2003, pp. 100–05; "Coffee Design-Triennale Milano," in *Brutus*, 38, May, 2003, pp. 36, 50; M. De Lucchi, "Fondazione Triennale-Milano," in *The Plan*, suppl. to *Gli spazi del sapere*, 2, April, 2003, pp. 22–29; A.F., "Atrio della Triennale," in *Abitare*, 426, March, 2003, pp. 132–35; M. Mussapi, "Se il bar diventa vetrina del design," in *Fuoricasa*, January–February, 2003, pp. 54–56; P. Panza, "Il ministro Urbani: 'Alla Triennale il Museo del design,'" in *Corriere della Sera*, January 21, 2003, p. 50.

The Gallery of Architecture and the Gallery of the "Curve" containing the ticket office and wardrobe.

The coffee shop furnished with chairs of various models and large windows facing the park.

Diocesan Museum

Ivrea (Turin)
collaborators: Angelo Micheli (project leader),
Federico Seymandi, Silvia Suardi
client: Diocesi d'Ivrea

Set within the sixteenth-century bastions of the city of Ivrea, the new diocesan museum—a project now in the preliminary phase—is planned to replace the existing museum in the church of San Nicola da Tolentino. The 1732 square meters of surface area of the new building are set on two levels, mainly on the semi-basement and ground floors. The decision to put part of the premises below ground takes advantage of the masonry of the bastion and helps soften the impact of the building on its surroundings, as well as linking it rationally with existing points of access. The distributive center of the whole complex is a large atrium on an oval plan and flat roof, permeable on both levels by the vertical

connections and openings in the attic story. Borne on a colonnaded structure, large windows relate the interior to the existing structure and also illuminate it with natural light. The atrium also links three different interiors: the former gymnasium converted to use as a museum, a car park in the square in front of the seminary and a small exhibition building erected above ground level. The last of these, a narrow block recognizable by its mixtilinear profile, catches the eye because it emerges from the flat profile of the complex. It is in effect conceived as a container for a single precious object that is illuminated only by the natural illumination shed by an elongated skylight projected to capture the endless daily and seasonal variations of light. The design of the outside paving and garden is characterized by a checkerboard pattern that links old and new points of access, regularizing and making perceptible the dimensions of the open spaces.

Rendering of the atrium and of the "casket."

Museo della Città

Palazzo Pepoli Vecchio, Bologna
collaborators: Brigid Byrne, Silvia Suardi
client: Fondazione Cassa di Risparmio
di Bologna

Invited by the Fondazione Cassa di Risparmio di Bologna to submit a design to the competition for a Civic Museum, De Lucchi made use of a spatial concept from the art world in the works of Anish Kapoor, an Indian sculptor who trained in London, which mimicked the effect of craters on the floors and walls of rooms.

The premises of the museum were in a medieval building, Palazzo Vecchio Pepoli, which covers an area of some 6,000 square meters and is laid out around a spacious central court on an almost square plan. This space, to be converted into an exhibition area, was substantially divided into two superimposed areas separated by a ring-shaped service gallery set about 15 meters above grade. Taking the courtyard as the organizing feature, the plan envisions a gigantic mushroom-shaped structure anchored to the ground and expanding onto the gallery above, so freeing the center of the courtyard, which will be occupied by a garden, while a floor is to be added on the intermediate level, where access is also provided by a spiral staircase. This arrangement makes the windows set in the façades on the courtyard a bright filter between the rooms of the historical building and the new exhibition loggia. The flexible grid made of metal and glass respects the stereometry of the internal façades, enhances the architectural matrix of the building and solves the problem of expanding the rooms, becoming the fulcrum of movement through the museum. The competition, to which a dozen Italian architectural firms were invited (Mario Bellini and Associates, Studio Cerri and Associates, Studio Michele De Lucchi, Studio Iosa Ghini, Studio Mendini, MCA Integrated Design, Miguel Sal & C., Zacchiroli Architetti Associati and Piero Sartogo Architetti Associati), assigned the commission to Mario Bellini in February 2004. The projects were put on display at an exhibition, "Ideas for the City Museum," presented at Palazzo Saraceni in Bologna in May 2004.

Model showing the internal mushroom-shaped structure.

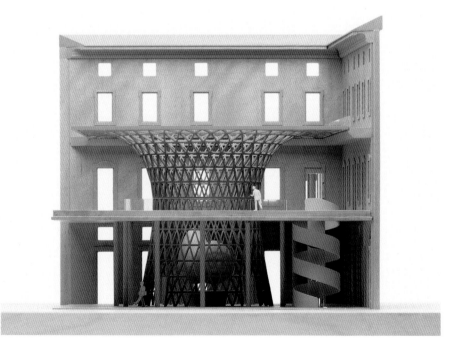

appendices

Anthology of writings

Speech of a Designer in General

Listen to me – Listen to me!
I am a Designer in General and in General a Designer.
I give the world the beauty of useful things.
I am paid so you can live amid beauty – amid comfort – amid softness – amid the functional – amid the colorful – amid the cheerful.
I am with you in the quest for balance and harmony between artistic beauty and natural beauty.
I furnish cities – the countryside – the landscape – roads – buildings – homes – rooms – bathrooms – kitchens – tables – chairs – forks – dishes – food – ideas – flavors – thoughts – culture.
I design you.
I – designer – love nature and will fight to the end with all my strength to defend the blue of the skies – the deep blue of the oceans – the green of the meadows – the white of the snows – the red of sunset. And in so doing I defend you, mankind, because you, too, are nature and your life is fostered by the delicious fruits of the garden, the milk from the cows that browse in the cool forest glades.
Make way for the designer.
Leave technology to me, because I know how to make good use of it so it will be useful and not harmful. Entrust me with your problems – I will solve them – I – I alone – and never trust anyone else.
(From the text of a performance presented in front of the Milan Triennale, September 1973)

Notebook architecture
I don't remember it clearly but in one of his stories Chekhov tells the tale of a Russian soldier, in I'm not sure which war. Amid the cannonades and the shooting, he managed to fill a notebook with beautiful thoughts. His comrades in the trenches, who had seen it, were impressed by the beauty, the simplicity and significance of the contents of this notebook. The soldier then died and his body was found many days later. The damp of the trench had irreparably ruined his notebook and it was now illegible, useless. A man had been destroyed and his notebook with him, all his ideas, his feelings, everything he had to communicate, improvidently entrusted to flimsy sheets of paper.
This is the problem of memory, the fascinating problem of memory, of things preserved, kept, transcribed, stored away, so that he or someone else will be able to reread, revise, and

love them again one day. Psychoanalysis also examined the question and came to recognize the importance of memory for all those who do not feel they are fully alive. Whoever needs to reassure himself of his reality, in his body and mind, who needs to feel he exists, materially as well as spiritually, surrounds himself with objects and things that reflect or relate to real events, things experienced or thought and identified with an object, that live in the object. And so people, some people, surround themselves with things, their homes are filled with things associated with new memories, organized with things that are important for their memories, emptied of things whose memories no longer serve any purpose, no longer relevant, that can or must be rejected.

The memories of architects, in general of those who design, may be more highly developed than other people's: perhaps they most feel the urge to preserve memories. But I could be wrong.

Sketches and drawings of projects, jottings, drawings made for their own sake or drawings of things that seem important—these constitute the rich and orderly memories of designers. It could be, of course, that all this passion for preserving memories derives from the idea that some day in the future all these things will be exhibited or published.

(From a review of the volume *La memoria invece* by A. Natalini, in *Modo*, 19, 1979, pp. 49–52)

Introduction

There are some strange figurative tensions, lying outside the rules of the moment, often even outside the normal run of events, that push up beneath the crust of normality and sometimes explode and spread across the planet.

Solid is a phenomenon of this type; it is an earth movement that spontaneously began to tremble and is now starting to spread. The people who produced this new phenomenon were ten or so young designers, some Italian, others foreign, who arrived in Milan attracted by the energy that the city is emanating at the present time. Many young people pass through the Milanese design firms: they come from schools in distant cities and are bursting with enthusiasm, gentleness and goodwill, eager to be put to the test and start working in design.

These young designers are insatiable consumers of images, irreducible consumers of figurative communication. These young designers are armed with an extraordinary determination to realize the ideas they have in their heads. These things are very concrete, precise, geometrical, substantial—in fact Solid. Conceptualism is now only a distant memory and this new form of communication is no longer literary but figurative, no longer metaphysical but real, no longer oblique but direct and as immediate as possible. The new designers believe that figuration is a leading instrument of communication and cultural progress; the avant-garde now passes through concrete, practical, solid objects. The Solid designers ally themselves with those who maintain the importance of design in the cultural avant-garde. Design has now acquired the nobility of an institution and competes with the traditional disciplines in driving images beyond the limits of the established figurative languages.

Young design today possesses great vitality in producing avant-garde models. If you think about it, you'll see that it's the design movements that in recent years have produced the major breakthroughs.

Movements like the now historical Alchymia and Memphis and the new groups in Milan, Paris, London, New York and Berlin have renewed the idea of the world far more than other more conceptual artistic exhibitions. One of the things that has most impressed the Solid designers is geometry, which has penetrated in depth into their vocabulary, with its theorems and its axioms. Geometry is perhaps the true discovery of this new generation: a fresh, new geometry, which does everything, which changes and mutates and adapts to feelings and different attitudes. It may be romantic geometry or sarcastic geometry; at times cold and detached, at others sweet and passionate. It is pure and cutting geometry or soft and refined: it is provocative or captivating, pure or polluted, rich or frugal, abstract or decorative.

Geometry is everything: geometry is language above all else. The unrestrained decorativism of the early eighties has passed away, the phantasmagoric world of colors is everywhere at an end; the world of the ephemeral and of figurative excess has faded. Geometry also means order, physical and mental order that can be moved and articulated, that can push against the limits of the comprehensible, but always with fixed and inviolable rules. Geometry is pure matter; the materials (nearly always natural) are solid shapes, full or hollow volumes but always defined with great clarity. Each particle has been broken down to be better studied and "solidified": a knife blade, the handle of a screwdriver, the lip of a jug, the stem of a glass, a tablecloth (which becomes a sheet of steel).

The rule of Solid seems to be: geometry produces material, material produces volume, volume produces function, and everything else is just details. The order of addition has changed, as if this time it were a sum whose result magically changes. While in canonical design the designer explores forms to satisfy functions, in Solid design the new designers reuse simple old functions to recreate forms and play with them in a figurative exercise that seems to be unending [...] It's very strange and fascinating to be able to speak today of new design and new avant-gardes based on simple and humble domestic objects that never, or rarely, have been the center of much discussion. It is strange and wonderful to envision new images of the world in a fork or a coffee cup.

Design is an extraordinary new instrument of figurative communication. It is only recently—all too recently—that it has made an effort to appeal to ordinary people. It is too soon today to pass judgment on the significance of Solid or even to give a full definition of it: for the time being (fortunately) it is still many things all together.

It is definitely a group of young designers of a generation that is so new it still lacks a name. It is clearly a group of many designers (eight) from very different places united by the same desires and the same decisive intention.

It definitely a collection of products for the home, for day and night, morning and afternoon, eating and working, reflecting and creating.

It is definitely a collection of objects that are bought not because people need them but because they can't do without them.

It is definitely a firm, a small firm that produces precious things, useful in use and out of use.

It is definitely an idea: that even by making small, common, everyday objects you can communicate new and different ideas.

It is definitely a demonstration: that in design, research into solid and volumetric figuration can be extremely modern and striking.

It is definitely a gesture of optimism about the future and the ability of design not just to produce beautiful things but also to produce practical and tangible progress.

(Published in the catalogue of the exhibition "Solid," edited by Michele De Lucchi, Milan 1987, pp. 11–15)

Ettore Sottsass, who is not my teacher

When I went to study architecture I would leave from Padua and travel by the train that used to pull into Platform 1 in Florence. On one of the first trips I bought my first architectural magazine, a copy of *Casabella*, because it seemed to be full of beautiful things. Since I got a lot of pleasure out of it I wrote my name on the front so no one would snitch it at the university. That issue of *Casabella* was devoted to Sottsass and that day I first encountered the idea that architecture amounts to far more than simply putting up buildings. Between the "pavilions" hung on the dolomitic cliffsides and "rafts" floating on the peaceful rivers of the "Planet as Festival," quite unconsciously I understood the ideological path I was to take.

I met him on the iron bridge of a derelict railroad in the countryside near Vicenza, where we had gone to talk about the work we had to do and which we eventually did. I worked for him for a number of years: then he wanted us to be divided for ever and for ever united by Olivetti. He has devoted his life to the quest for riches, but not money. In his eyes, riches are plastic and figurative values, and they are a condition of materials and forms when they are extraordinarily new. Money certainly has never interested him. His only use for it is as something that enables him to socialize with other people. It is not unusual, when dinner's over, to hear him heave a sigh and say to himself, "Well, today we managed to scrape together the money to pay for a meal."

He scolded me when I got married because he hated all constraints and perhaps he sees time as the biggest constraint. And even for the most beautiful things there is never enough time and it flows away. There's never enough time, or when there is it's always too much. Only one thing overcomes time: freedom, freedom from everything. He doesn't want to be considered a master and so he doesn't want me to see myself as his pupil. He has never taught in schools of architecture, but with his glamour he has influenced and won over more than one generation and he still has an intense, continuing relationship with young architects and designers. He is willing to accept arrogance and pride if they are shown by people who possess a vision capable of overwhelming the world. He loves snobbishness as a quality of those who are able to stand apart from the daily struggle to survive. Survival is not his problem because surviving is not a heroic condition of life. He believes life needs to be lived with intensity in the soul, yet he sees the soul as a combination of chemical substances mixed in some gland in the neck.

I've spent the summer designing: in September, back in Milan, I'll show him what I did and, as happens every year, I'll wait to hear what he says and above all I'll wait to see the drawings he will have done at Filicudi. Today we no longer say much to each other but our great silent conversation continues on the surfaces of our drawings. With him I learned the importance of drawing and how the design grows out of drawing. The project is drawing and drawing is the most complete formula of communication. It is always deeply moving, delicate and profoundly engrossing, this moment when we compare drawings. The moment is coming closer, my watercolors are ready. Who knows whether we will still be on the same wavelength?

(In "Maestri: Musatti, Carlson, Berio, Sottsass," Milan 1990, now in *Ettore Sottsass*, exhibition catalogue, Milan 1999, p. 34)

On the ecology of design

I believe that ecology and the proper use of materials have made a deep impression on the designers of my generation and we are all ready to declare our concern over the health of the world and the dwindling resources that remain. This subject, though it actually tends to come and go depending on the fashion of the moment, is deeply felt and many designers wonder what they can do, apart from being more careful and seeking to spread a greater awareness of the limited nature of natural resources among the business community. I believe that design is not just a question of giving beautiful forms to objects and choosing fine materials that go well with each other: it is definitely a lot more. For example, it is a system of communication, a means of expression, a tool of business and above all a form of education. I love the idea that a designer object can encourage a concern for the quality of objects and so foster values bound up not only with the beauty and intelligence embodied in products but above all with their potential for reuse.

Among peasants there's an image that expresses this concept clearly. A fine straight tree branch becomes first a strong stake to support the vine. Then, when the point wears out and it is no longer any use in the vineyard it is used to prop up a fence. Then it breaks and is used to support a broken table leg, then it becomes a rung of a ladder, and in the end it is burnt in the kitchen stove and here too it helps warm the room. In this respect design can do a lot because it is not necessary to wait for wonderful and beautiful new recycled materials to become available to design wonderful and beautiful products. With simple details, with little things made well, not wastefully, you can create a new concern for the meaning of objects and a new awareness of them and so prolong the lifetime of materials.

But not all materials are important and necessary.

I'd like to say that the most beautiful and extraordinary material that exists, the most precious and rare, the most malleable, flexible and recyclable is not plastic or aluminum or metal alloys or resins or ultra-technological compounds that no one has yet invented. It is space, air, the air we breathe and where we walk, buy and sell and which we sculpt as if it was wax. And as long as we have plenty of it we never worry about it but when it begins to run short we'll never know where to go and get some more and we can't produce it in a factory.

And then there is another material, a very expensive one that we already don't have enough of and what we have we waste and unfortunately it isn't recyclable (but that's actually a stroke of luck). This is time, the hours and days that we waste doing wrong-headed and dangerous things and it's not just hours and days and hours thrown away but hours and days spent doing ourselves harm. Air and time are paradoxically the least solid and tangible materials but the ones we waste most and that exist most on earth in the form of quality to be retrieved. And they exist not just in the form of material qualities but above all sensory and spiritual qualities, if we can still speak of spiritual qualities. (Text published in Danish and English, with the titles "Synligt genbrug i design" and "The Visibility of Recycling in Design," in *Re-f-use*, exhibition catalogue, Dansk Design Center, 2000, pp. 14–15)

Make fun of reality

Bruno Munari taught me that a project is something born in the head. It is light, impalpable, airy, but very concrete, very tangible, easy to communicate, terribly contagious. With his *Traveling Sculptures*, *Useless Machines*, *Books*, *Talking Forks*, *Paper Eyeglasses* and all the rest of his work, he taught me that reality is no use, it's not in the least functional, and nothing will ever succeed in making it functional. You have to make fun of reality, at most it's good for a laugh. He taught me that projects are not necessarily related to things or even if they have to be, they are things whose intrinsic content, whose material, the preciousness of metals, the smoothness of surfaces, whose forms, count for nothing. Because it's other things that count: ideas, enthusiasm, hopes and desires. And Bruno Munari was capable of putting all these things in them. And the strength of someone capable of thinking differently.
(In *Su Munari*, edited by B. Finessi, Milan 1999, p. 147)

On freehand drawing

I've always liked drawing and the most important decisions in my life have been strongly influenced by this urge. The choice of the work I do definitely stemmed from the hope of being able to hold a pencil in my hand every day. I've drawn a lot all my life but not as much as I would have liked or as much as I'd like to now. Having to cope ever more frequently with managerial problems has gradually distanced me from drawing, and it is only because of a wholly personal insistence of my own that I still manage to practice this skill.

When I began to study architecture everything was still done by hand, using a pencil on cartridge paper, or India ink on glossy paper and so forth, sheet after sheet, tracing after tracing, polishing it up to correct the errors, change details, prepare presentations for clients or planning offices with "red" copies with the "radex," and so on.

The first office I opened in Florence was crammed with rolls of paper, Koh-i-Noor nibs, pencils and pencil-sharpeners, three-pronged thumbtacks and razor blades that served to scratch off the India ink and make corrections. I loved the atmosphere in the office, so personal, like a craft shop, a place organized to turn out projects made up of drawings, scores of drawings, rolls of drawings. All this has gone. I bought my first computer in January 1986.

I couldn't live without a computer today. How many have I had? Can't say! At least a hundred and they keep on arriving, new ones, even more advanced, replacing the "old" ones, meaning ones bought no more than three years ago. You don't even have time to grow attached to one and used to its presence before they take it away!

My sheet anchor lay in my 47 notebooks of drawings, a line that runs through all my work and makes its development comprehensible through the succession of changes. I'm still using number 48! I keep them in my bookcase together with the small notebooks, the diaries, the folders where I organize the drawings using various systems, sometimes by project, sometimes by type of product, and sometimes by the name of the business or the client.

I'd like above all to address the generation of architects and designers now growing up, who understand far better than I do the sense of fulfillment that a skillful use of technology can give you today, who know far better than me about parametric programs, who know how to represent with extreme fidelity everything that is still only virtual. To all of them I'd like to say how much virtual reality can also be represented in a drawing, how important it was for me to carry around my bag containing a tin of watercolors and a bundle of brushes, how much I enjoyed those unrepeatable moments with a pencil in one hand and a brush in the other.

And an eraser in my pocket, because of all the mistakes I made. (text from 1999)

Being irreverent to delve more deeply

Hans Höger: What made you study architecture?

Michele De Lucchi: There were some serious reasons and some that are anecdotal. Which would you like me to tell you about? One of the reasons for doing architecture was that I wanted to do something different from my twin brother. Because being twins and having spent eighteen years of our lives together, the choice of a faculty was also, you might say, a decision to separate. It was a perfectly deliberate and serene decision for both of us. One day, talking with my father, I was the first to say: "I'll do architecture." And my brother: "OK, then I'll do chemistry." Of course the opposite could have happened. If he'd said: "I'll do architecture," I'd have said, "OK, then I'll do chemistry." And in that case I would have been the chemist and he would have been the architect.

HH And what were the serious reasons?

MDL The serious reasons were that I've always liked drawing. At any rate I always thought I would do something in life that was bound up with drawing. Unfortunately, the way things are now, drawing plays less and less of a part in what I do. Yet, despite all the computers and technology, despite the fact that the work I do is more managerial coordination than design proper, I always think that the heart of my work lies in drawing, in picking up a pencil and doing a drawing. So it's true that before deciding to take up architecture, despite my twin brother, I was set on being a painter. And if my father had not insisted that I had to study architecture, I would have enrolled in the academy to study painting. Because the thing I like most of all is painting.

HH Instead of which you work as an architect. Is this work like you imagined it when you enrolled to study architecture?

MDL No, the profession as I imagined it is quite very different from what I actually do. But it doesn't trouble me. It isn't a problem—quite the contrary. I feel quite proud to think I managed to practice a profession at a time when the profession was changing completely. Being an architect is no longer a question of designing houses. It means making a profound contribution to the decisions that affect the physical, visual and constructional aspects of the world today—whether they are products or installations, temporary or permanent.

HH In the very years when you were studying there developed a special cultural climate that brought to the surface new ideas about the role of the architect and the profession.

MDL True. I feel I was lucky to arrive in Florence in the very years when Florence was livelier than ever, in all sorts of ways.

I was lucky to get to know some of the leading figures in this cultural ferment, Adolfo Natalini and Andrea Branzi, who then introduced me to Sottsass, Mendini, Pesce and many others. But I must say I've always managed to end up where things were changing most. I've always jumped onto the bandwagon of change. I feel it's essential if you're going to be a designer.

HH You were still a student when you founded the Cavart group. Was that an attempt to speed up the changes somehow, to make them happen?

MDL First and foremost it was a way of looking for a different approach to things. Cavart was closely bound up with the idea of the quarry. The group was set up to organize a competition, to reclaim a trachyte quarry near Padua. We chose the name Cavart because we wanted to design, but not so much by adding one thing to another, houses to houses, condominiums to condominiums, but by paring them away, so it was like quarrying. The quarry was a sort of metaphor for removal. The quarry was like an extraordinary, wonderful stage, created simply by taking away the rock. A similar concept today lies behind a lot of projects. Large urban areas on the outskirts of Italian cities could be reclaimed today simply by not building yet more architecture but simply removing some of it. The problem the architect has to work with today is no longer natural materials to be made artificial. It is a wholly artificial world he has to manipulate. It is no longer necessary to defend ourselves against reality. Rather we have to create new significances.

HH The dissertation you presented for your degree was titled *Vertical Housing* and it theorized some houses that were developed not horizontally but vertically. What led you to work on this project?

MDL I have to say that this project was deeply embedded in the context of radical architecture. Radical architecture did not raise the question of architectural design in itself but it questioned the reasons lying behind architectural design. So what led me to devise the "vertical housing" was not the idea of wanting to solve specific problems but to invent a fictitious project which might stimulate ideas and creativity among other people. I believe this concept is still extremely relevant. And also at Memphis, for example, it wasn't the individual objects that were significant so much as the phenomenon that we created and the enthusiasm with which students across the world studied and endorsed this way of doing things.

HH What part does provocation play in this type of work?

MDL Clearly it's not an end in itself but serves to attract attention and stimulate reactions. In a way I feel the approach adopted by radical architecture still continues in the present and constitutes a peculiarly Italian path in design and also to research.

HH How would you describe this Italian path to design and architecture?

MDL It's clearly an approach that rejects purely formal solutions. It seeks to give a meaning, one that can be expressed in words, to the things it produces. Sottsass, for example, with some of his apparently most formalistic projects, can only explain them by involving you in the almost sacral and ceremonial aspects of the situations from which he takes his cues and to which he relates them. I find it significant that Sottsass doesn't just design objects or architecture but also writes books: books of metaphors in which the words determine the images, not the other way around. You find the same thing in the work of Andrea Branzi or Alessandro Mendini, who is essentially a born editorialist. And I see it also in my own work and in my relations with clients, where the thing I do best, even compared with colleagues from other countries, is proposing something that is not just a solution to a specific problem or a response to a brief but which has a larger significance.

HH In the nineties, you began to do a lot of work for big multinationals, like the Deutsche Bank, Enel, the German Railroads, the Italian Postal Service and Olivetti. The size of these corporations enabled you to realize important projects. At the same time they must have been extremely complex organizations and communicating with them can hardly have been easy.

MDL True. You have to avoid getting tangled up in red tape or organizational and logistical problems, because they are the real restrictions on the development of a project. I try to talk directly with these corporations, always at the highest level. In fact, whenever I fail to make contact with the top management my contribution tends to be inexorably limited. I always feel that businesses are very similar to people. And if you can't succeed in reaching a person's head, you can't do much. You can tickle a person's appetite, stimulate a reaction, but if you can't get through to his head you won't be able to do much with him. An architect or designer can have a lot of power within a business, because the things he does affect everyone: not just the identity of the business but all its ambitions in the world at large. The great work an architect has to do is not build logically and rationally, because that's not enough. The great work lies in being able to create projects charged with passion, energy, desire. A project could be the most beautiful in the world, but if it is not imbued with this type of enthusiasm, it won't have the strength to come alive.

HH Where do you draw the inspiration for your work, what are the sources of your enthusiasm?

MDL My problem nowadays is to free some vital spaces of time and place to dedicate to inspiration, to recharge my batteries. Because these continual contacts with big organizations and the endless proliferation of commitments and networking leave me little time for anything else. And you can recharge your energies by doing the simplest things: by keeping informed, by observing what is happening around you, by reading. The last time I called on Sottsass he persuaded me to reread Nietzsche's *Birth of Tragedy*. It gave me a tremendous kick to explore certain passages again with a different outlook. So reading is immensely important. And another thing is figurative development, meaning the evolution of all those images that we feel are part of the products turned out today, the advertising that accompanies these products, people's esthetic choices, corporate identities, the visual languages of newspapers, everything that helps define the contemporary world. But apart from all this there's another side of my personality and life that fosters professional inspiration. This side is simplicity, rural life, the natural world at Angera, where I live. My family and the countryside are part of those values that give me a certain security in looking at things. In this respect designing flower vases is just as important to me as designing telephones for Siemens.

HH For this year's Milan Furniture Show you conceived and designed an exhibit on Ettore Sottsass. Would you like to tell us about your friendship?

MDL Well I'm sorry we're kept so busy that we see little of each other. When I did that exhibition for the Furniture Show, my real worry was not doing the exhibition but the fear that perhaps Ettore wouldn't like what I did. I knew that even if he didn't like it he would simply say, "Michele, you're an idiot, you don't understand a thing," and that would be that. But I would have been very sorry to discover we're no longer on the same wavelength. Luckily that didn't happen, because he really liked it. Ever since I've known him, I've received a very profound education from Ettore and I feel that he still has a lot to teach me. For example, these books he's doing now, these metaphorical books, are really such a highly distilled essence of architectural quality that you realize that to create architecture it's not necessary to design a skyscraper in Singapore. Or rather, there are some people who manage to do much more in architecture with five words and a drawing than by using a complex technological system. And I realize that in his latest works Ettore has succeeded in condensing his message about the practice of architecture and design far more completely than in the past.

HH Memphis was an important chapter of your work together. Do you feel it's possible to speak of the legacy of Memphis, say in relation to the current situation?

MDL In stylistic terms I really can't say, and perhaps I'm not even particularly concerned to try and assess that side of it. But as a movement Memphis is still a landmark, because to date there's never been anything with the same kind of provocative and purposeful force. What strikes me as its outstanding message was its power to free thinking about design from the ideas associated with Ulm and the good old Functionalist school. There had never been an alternative before. Memphis cleared the field of a monopoly that was very restrictive and inhibiting. And it did this with a charge of irreverence lacking today. It's lacking because no one knows how to go about being irreverent now. Or for the right reasons. Being irreverent just for the sake of protest is no big deal. Being irreverent as a way of digging deeper into things and not being satisfied is a far more rare attitude.

HH Another great designer you've worked with on various occasions is Achille Castiglioni.

MDL Yes, and Castiglioni is also irreverent when he does his most extraordinary things. And he's irreverent with a kind of irony and playfulness that you won't find in the things Sottsass does. What has always fascinated me about Sottsass is the way he transforms things into drawing and simplifies everything through drawing. His drawings are of an extraordinary purity. But Castiglioni doesn't draw. He replaces drawing with a kind of dramatic verve. In thinking, in conceiving, in the way he approaches a project, he transforms everything into an extremely captivating behavior that becomes a project in a way that's pure magic. Castiglioni tackles all the thorny points in a project and the problems to be solved as if they were an opponent's judo moves and he has to respond to them. He redoubles his opponent's strength and turns it against him. If there was a judo competition for ideas, Castiglioni would surely be black belt and world champion. All his projects are a bit like that. Take the Arco lamp. The problem was to bring a lamp down over a table, and he simply stood the problem on its head by attaching the lamp to a stem set on the floor. Or his wonderful ready-mades. In fact he invented designer ready-mades.

HH In the eighties you were busy working in Japan, where you were commissioned to design products but above all architecture. What was the experience like in those years?

MDL The thing that gave me most trouble in Japan is a certain type of naivety which means they expect the architect or designer to come up with a decisive solution to every problem, but without ever questioning themselves, their firm, their project, even before talking things over with the architect. And then in

Japan they feel great respect for the *griffe*, the big name, so they take it for granted that anything done by someone with a reputation is necessarily better than anything else, without analyzing it and reasoning about its specific qualities. In terms of organization and of their commitment to work, you can compare Japan in some ways with Germany. I've never seen people so dedicated and fascinated by what they're doing as in Japan and Germany. But the great difference is that in Germany they work step by step, seeking to frame their work in an overall plan. In Japan, instead, they jump from one idea to another at high speed and great nonchalance and even quite carelessly, without following a thread of development. It happens even in big companies. Just think about the battle over the CD-ROM and the Minidisk.

HH Do you have a special way of approaching a new project?

MDL No, in the sense that there's no recipe, though sometimes I'd like to have a system so I'd know how to set about all the projects that arrive, I'd know what to do. But it's not like that, and perhaps it's just as well. If I you have a single system you might end up with a set of standard stylistic features and rules for applying them. It would lead you to repeat yourself and limit your curiosity to explore the differences between one project and another, between one problem and another. I think there are various different paths leading towards a new project. Apart from a logical, rational, analytical approach there's another way, which consists in raising the stakes. What I call the counter-brief. With the counter-brief you reformulate the client's brief, more or less provocatively, depending on the situation, and this is useful as a way of verifying the coherence, the ambitions and the real objectives behind a specific project. Then the counter-brief is very useful also because the exercise of reformulating a problem is already one possible way of exploring possible solutions and ways of moving beyond it.

HH Your work covers a great range of different subjects. For many years you designed electronic products for Olivetti and a few months ago you presented a new collection of Murano blown-glass vases. You design architecture but also graphics. Does this wide range of projects reflect a systematic choice or is it something that has just emerged over the years?

MDL It's just emerged over the years, but it's also because I've always seen the architect's work not just as dealing with housing, but as a way of solving the problem of survival in the industrial world. Most of my clients are businesses, corporations, organizations, and they normally have a single big problem, which is to survive. And I've always tried to ensure my profession made its contribution to help this happen. Businesses ask me to develop products, design graphics, design architecture, but the challenge is their ambition to grow. I've always tried not to specialize, and at the same time not to take on just major projects. I find it very important to achieve a balanced mix because to my mind it's just as useful to design a flower vase as a multifunctional office machine. As I see it, one thing contributes to the design of another, and so forth. The greatest difficulty lies in passing from product design to designing spaces. All the same, today I'd say the problem of spaces or products is not bound up with a specific problem of void or solids. It's much more a specific problem of the function and the potential for transformation these things possess. Underlying everything is the concept of the continuous transformability of the conditions in which the world lives and in which businesses have to work. Scope for success today no longer stems from production capacity but the ability to produce ideas, develop them and realize them. I feel the sense of being an architect today lies in being more capable of playing a part in the business world.

HH And what do you expect from the future?

MDL The future as I see it is very positive, despite the dark clouds looming. I'd really like to sweep away those clouds immediately. The clouds are caused by problems like pollution and more generally the sustainability of growth on our planet. I think we should make an effort to be optimistic, but with a profound awareness that certain problems need to be faced immediately. Much that will be extraordinary in the future lies in the awareness of human beings. I like to close my lectures with a quote from Brodsky: "Esthetics is the mother of ethics." The search for beauty cannot be separated from the quest for a profound awareness of the values and non-values in things.

(Interview by Hans Höger, published in *Domus*, 819, October, 1999, pp. 54–63)

Design in Olivetti. A tradition that never fades

I never knew Adriano, I hardly could have known him, since when he died I still hadn't decided what to study when I grew up. All the same I've encountered him many times because his presence is still alive in all of Olivetti and even today, so many years after his death, he is still deeply missed. And even though I never knew him and never worked with him, I miss him too. In my office in Milan, I put up a photo of him behind my desk, next to my drawings and the photos of my children. Every so often someone asks me if that's my father and sometimes I unabashedly say yes. After all, his utopia is very close to me and apart from developing my character in my professional life, it has also lent me strength in moments of indecision or difficulty.

I went to see Ettore Sottsass, because it was Ettore who took me on at Olivetti [...] That was another big gift from Adriano: he gave me the opportunity to meet Sottsass, who has always been my master, though he doesn't like the idea. We talked about Adriano's utopia and its value today, of how deeply industry feels the absence of someone like him, capable of injecting some enthusiasm into the future of industrial civilization. The debate over the social significance of technology and technological progress is at a standstill. The only place where it's still discussed is the stock exchange because "technology" means "finance" and so human destiny is also a victim of the ups and downs of the stock index.

There are clearly no longer those ideals and that social philosophy, that questioning of technological research and its human significance, which Adriano would surely have endorsed. Today everything is done for instant profit, because it's more difficult to tell right from wrong, the beautiful from the ugly, what makes sense from what doesn't. If there is something unusual about Olivetti and there still is, surely, even though the manufacturing side has been supplanted by the financial, it's [...] a sense of doing things that go beyond the value of the company's shares on the Milan *bourse*. I don't know the reason for this, I don't even know if it's true or just an illusion, but the fact is that I've never experienced this emotion and I've never drawn this richness of conviction from any other firm. [...] I'm convinced Adriano believed deeply in progress, and so do I. The most recent freedom, which enables us to work anywhere (at home, in the car, on the train), ceases to be freedom if we feel compelled to work at the times we used to devote to ourselves or our thoughts. Ahead of us lies a period of unexpected freedom but with equally unexpected enemies, treacherous and ambiguous, such as stress, speed as an end in itself, sterile and useless competition. It is with these thoughts and ideas that Adriano would have confronted the subject of design today. He would have felt that all the electronics packed into the innumerable machines that surround us and that we use every day are a great benefit we possess, and that it's up to us to make them accessible to everyone, because they can bring us benefits and enhance the quality of our private and social life.

The problem is above all how to embody these ideas in products, with all the difficulties involved in production, sales, marketing, advertising. At Olivetti they really believe in the soul of the business and they are all aware that it's essential to give a meaning to things, to products, to ideas. I work a lot with other people, with people in marketing, in design, in production, and I try to discuss the significance of each product with them. This helps a lot because ideas and solutions often emerge by themselves and when the ideas are right the form springs from it automatically, effortlessly, and it's immediately convincing, without any need for explanations or complicated formal theories. The language of these concepts is not in the least abstract. It is made up of a subtle but precise symbolism with specific references to recognized signals, visible not only in electronics but also in other advanced sectors of industry. [...] The ability to discover these concepts and embody them in forms was what I learned in those years and I believe they most fully express the significance of the designer's work for industry today. Doing design doesn't mean sculpting objects but above all giving them a significance that is communicative, functional and ergonomic. We should never forget that we live in a period when industry, though it gives us a great deal, is under attack. Industrial products have matured and their value is continually subject to scrutiny by contemporary society. This is precisely the role Olivetti attributed to design: to conceive quality and be capable of expressing it.

The concept of design is therefore complex and very variable and it's not easy to describe it in a few words. From the Olivetti tradition I assimilated directly the idea that design concerns life and people, and not just industry.

[...] The designers at Olivetti were always architects and in Olivetti the designers were always called architects: even to the simplest employee at Scarmagno the designer is an architect. And this is no accident but symptomatic of the fact that in Olivetti it doesn't make sense for a designer to know how to design products without understanding the physical and social setting of a product, whether in the showroom or in use. In his profession an architect acquires a wider range of interests and a more complex esthetic sense, which is not confined to repeating "something is beautiful if we like it and ugly if we don't." Adriano was a pioneer in this and if industrial designers had not existed he would have invented them. He saw that good design calls for a basic technical skill, but it's not enough to be a skilled technician. Underlying everything is the ability to draw and ensure that things are produced, but the work also calls for a strong personality, someone who is capable of playing an authoritative part in developing a product, because a firm's major interests and powerful passions gravitate around issues bound up with design. Adriano also had the insight to see that design is not a corporate function that can be developed within industry alone. Design is born, develops and flourishes in the midst of ordinary everyday life and its task is to relate business to life, to combine production, marketing and research with what is happening in the world and with what the world normally expects industry to produce. In the end design is a firm's philosophy. It lies at the center of the debate over the reasons for industrial production, for continuing to design, produce and sell. It's important to ask yourself why we are making products, and what significance we should attach to products in this world, which is already so full of things that it doesn't know where to put them any more. And Adriano's great strength was not only that he asked these questions fifty years ahead of his time but he made them part of the company's life, ensuring that the idea would continue to develop even when he was no longer there...
(Tribute to Adriano Olivetti, published in *La Sentinella del Canevese*, April 19, 2001, p. 25)

List of works

The works are arranged chronologically on the basis of the year of the design and listed in this sequence: product design, retail design, exhibit design, graphics and architecture.

1973

Performance: *Designer in General*, Milan Triennale

1975–76

Vertical housing
Prototype and models of the Cavart seminars, Monselice (Padua) and Vicenza

1975–77

Mobile architecture
Prototypes

1976–80

Design and organization of the *Reconstruction of Interiors* section at the exhibition "Italian Design in the Fifties"; editorial coordination of the conference catalogue
Client: Centrokappa, Noviglio (Milan)

1978

La Spaziale lamp
Production: 1980
Client: Alchymia

Sinerpica lamp
Production: 1979
Client: Alchymia (until 1992), Belux (until 2000), Vitra Design Museum

1978–79

Tarkin chair
Prototype
Collaborator: Masayuki Matsukaze
Client: Thema

1979

I Peli wall tiles
Prototype
Client: Alchymia

Sinvola lamp
Production: 1979
Client: Alchymia

Sputnik rug
Prototype
Client: Alchymia

Models of electrical appliances
Client: Girmi

1979–81

Monitor workstations
and supports for Modulo computers
Production: 1979–81
with Ettore Sottsass
Client: Olivetti Synthesis

1980

Atlantic desk pedestal
Production: 1981
Client: Memphis

Kristall table
Production: 1981
Client: Memphis

Oceanic lamp
Production: 1981
Client: Memphis

Pacific closet
Production: 1981
Client: Memphis

Riviera chair
Production: 1981
Client: Memphis

Carafe
Production: 1980
Client: Cleto Munari
Graphic design of the volume *Elogio del banale*, Edizioni Studio Forma

1980–87

Patterns for plastic laminates
and fabrics
Production: 1980–87
Client: Abet Print

1981

Bathroom accessories
Production: 1981
Client: Fontana Arte

Fortune table
Production: 1982
Client: Memphis

Lido sofa
Production: 1982
Client: Memphis

Sebastopole table
Production: 1982
Client: Memphis (produced by UP&UP, later UpGroup)

45CR office system
Production: (1981)
with Ettore Sottsass
Client: Olivetti Synthesis

Long Beach sofa
Prototype
Client: Poltrona Frau

Artù and Peter Pan armchairs
Production: 1981
Client: Thalia

Designs for hi-fi sets

Study for Pensione Adriatico,
Adriatic riviera

1981–83

Fiorucci stores
with Ettore Sottsass
Client: Fiorucci

1981–85

Rossana kitchen 214
Production: 1985
Client: RB Rossana

1981–86

Icarus office system
Production: 1982
with Ettore Sottsass
Collaborator: Theo Gonser
Client: Olivetti Synthesis

1982

Antares vase
Production: 1983
Client: Memphis (produced by
Toso Vetri d'Arte)

First chair
Production: 1983
Client: Memphis

Grand lamp
Production: 1983
Client: Memphis

Phoenix bookcase
Production: 1983
Client: Memphis

President table
Production: 1983
Client: Memphis

Transit trolley
Production: 1983
Client: Memphis

Vega lamp
Production: 1982
(from 1986 Fontana Arte)
Client: Vistosi, then Fontana Arte

Designs for computers

Designs for a gondola

1982–83

Calcutta table
Production: 1983
Client: UP&UP (later UpGroup)

Delhi bench and Kampur hi-fi
Production: 1984
Client: UP&UP (later UpGroup)

Kandla jewel holder,
Misore and Sholapur vases
Production: 1985
Client: UP&UP (later UpGroup)

1982–85

Cyclos lamps
Production: 1984–85
Client: Artemide

1983

Diomede lamp
Prototype
Client: Artemide

Bambù lamp
Production: 1983
with Simone Drost and Evelien van Veen
Client: Bieffeplast

Rotor, Round and Roll lamps
Production: 1984
Client: Bieffeplast

Continental table
Production: 1984
Client: Memphis

Flamingo bedside table
Production: 1984
Client: Memphis

Horizon bed
Production: 1984
Client: Memphis

Polar table
Production: 1984
Client: Memphis

Erfon and Horton chairs, Pool sofa
and Sfayra armchair
Production: 1984
Client: Matau

Exhibit design "Holiday Home,"
Milan Triennale
Client: Enichem

Exhibit design "Research into an Office
Interior," Milan Triennale
with Ettore Sottsass
Client: Olivetti Synthesis

1984

Tender lamp
Production: 1985
Client: Bieffeplast

Milan tables and chairs
Production: 1985
Collaborators: Ferruccio Laviani,
Angelo Micheli
Client: Elam

Set of rigid suitcases
Prototype
Collaborators: Ferruccio Laviani,
Angelo Micheli
Client: Mandarina Duck

Burgundy table
Production: 1985
Client: Memphis

Celery and Tomato dishes
Production: 1985
Client: Memphis

Dorian and Ionian table mirrors
Production: 1985
Client: Memphis

Scarlet partition
Production: 1985
Client: Memphis

Jewelry
Production: 1985
Client: Cleto Munari

Misty table and Cadetti side tables
Production: 1985
Client: Morphos
(Acerbis International division)

Polis chair
Production: (1985)
Client: Poltronova

Ardito table
Production: (1984)
Collaborators: Ferruccio Laviani,
Angelo Micheli
Client: RB Rossana

La Festa table
Production: 1984
Client: RB Rossana

La Rotonda chair
Production: (1984)
Collaborators: Ferruccio Laviani,
Angelo Micheli
Client: RB Rossana

Designs for floors and tables in marble
(Impallinato, Zebrato and Be)
Client: Up&Up (now UpGroup)

Study for tile
Client: Ceramiche Marazzi

1985

Enameled jewels
Production: 1985
Client: Acme

Discoli dinner service, Discolaccio tray
and Superdiscolo fruit stand
Production: 1985–86
Client: Alessi/Tendentse

Pianeta bed
Production: 1985
Client: Elam

Witness sofas
Production: 1985
Client: Mazzoli

Cairo table
Production: 1986
Client: Memphis

Madrid corner cabinet
Production: 1986
Client: Memphis

Delphos office system
Production: 1985
with Ettore Sottsass
Collaborator: James Irvine
Client: Olivetti Synthesis

1985–86

Meccanica lamp
Production: 1986
Collaborators: Ferruccio Laviani,
Angelo Micheli
Client: Belux

1985–87

Computer monitor
Production: 1987
Collaborator: Eric Gottein
Client: Olivetti

1985–88

Nuovo Banco Ambrosiano branch office,
Corso Magenta, Milan
Collaborator: Nicholas Bewick
Client: Nuovo Banco Ambrosiano

1985–89

House, Via dell'Osservanza, Bologna
collaborators: Elisa Gargan,
Angelo Micheli (project leader)

1986

Furniture collection
Production: 1986
Client: ADL (Artieri del Legno)

Euclide table
Production: 1986
Client: Glass Design

La Residenza sulla Terra
furniture collection
Production: (1987)
Collaborators: Nicholas Bewick,
Ferruccio Laviani, Geert Koster,
Angelo Micheli
Client: Malobbia International

Kim chair
Production: 1987
Client: Memphis

Rug
Prototype
Client: Memphis

Via Solferino chair
Prototype
Collaborator: Mario Rossi Scola
Client: Promochair

Avalon chair and Missouri table
Production: 1987
Client: Tisettanta

Poster for "International Exhibit
of Historical Cities"
Client: Whic Kyoto

1986–87

Signifeé store, Omotesando
Tokyo (Japan)
Collaborators: Ferruccio Laviani,
Angelo Micheli
Client: Signifeé

1986–88

Platone bookstore
Production: 1988
Client: Glass Design

1986–90

PL Componenti stand, Sasmil,
Milan Trade Fair
Collaborator: Geert Koste
Client: PL Componenti

1986–present

Tolomeo series of lamps
Production: 1987
with Giancarlo Fassina
Client: Artemide

1987

Motel and Terrace chairs
Production: 1987
Client: Bieffeplast

Tecnico table
Production: 1988
Client: Cappellini International

Eyeglasses
Production: 1988
Collaborator: Angelo Micheli
Client: Charmant

Kleberoller dispenser
Production: 1987
Collaborators: Ferruccio Laviani,
Angelo Micheli
Client: Pelikan

Madrigali 3 bed
Production: 1987
Client: Poltrona Frau

Design coordination and art direction
of the Solid collection
Production: 1987
Collaborators: Nicholas Bewick,
Ferruccio Laviani, Angelo Micheli
Client: RB Rossana

Grand Place store, Osaka (Japan)
Collaborators: Ferruccio Laviani,
Angelo Micheli
Client: Batsu

Lazy Susan store, Osaka (Japan)
Collaborators: Sanae Kimura,
Angelo Micheli
Client: Lazy Susan

Memphis showroom, New York
Collaborator: Ferruccio Laviani
Client: Memphis

Olivetti Synthesis stand, Eimu,
Milan Trade Fair
Collaborator: Geert Koster
Client: Olivetti Synthesis

1987–88

Talete table
Production: 1988
Client: Glass Design

Credito Commerciale branch office,
Mantua
Collaborators: Ferruccio Laviani,
Angelo Micheli
Client: Credito Commerciale

1987–90

Zerbino hairdryers
Production: (1990)
Collaborators: Angelo Micheli,
Tadao Takaichi
Client: Matsushita Electric Works

Vases with black and white patterns
Production: 1987
Collaborator: Elisa Gargan
Client: Produzione Privata (produced
by Ceramiche San Marco)

1987–93

Mandarina Duck stores (first generation)
Collaborator: Nicholas Bewick
Client: Mandarina Duck

1988

Clack tables, Clock stool, Click
lamp and coat stand
Production: 1988
Client: Bieffeplast

Lazy Susan clocks
Production: 1988
Collaborators: Elisa Gargan,
Tadao Takaichi
Client: Lazy Susan

CD 6300 automatic telling machine
Production: (1990)
Collaborator: Mario Trimarchi
Client: Olivetti–Siab

Through the Wall cash dispenser
Production: 1988
Collaborator: Mario Trimarchi
Client: Olivetti-Siab

Highlighter
Model
Collaborator: Ferruccio Laviani
Client: Pelikan

Design coordination and art director
of the Solid collection
Production: 1988
Collaborators: Nicholas Bewick, James
Irvine, Ferruccio Laviani, Angelo Micheli
Client: RB Rossana

Moda drinks distributor
Production: 1988
Collaborator: Angelo Micheli
Client: Rhea Vendors

IN Express stores, Tokyo (Japan)
Collaborator: Tadao Takaichi
Client: Renown

Pulloveria stores
Collaborator: Nicholas Bewick
Client: Americanino

RB Rossana stores
Collaborator: Ferruccio Laviani
Client: RB Rossana

Exhibit design
"Cos'è l'immunologia?,"
Galleria Vittorio Emanuele II, Milan
Collaborator: Angelo Micheli
Client: City of Milan

Kyoto Keisei Housing office block,
Kyoto (Japan)
not built
Collaborator: Tadao Takaichi
Client: Keisei Housing

Kyoto Recruit Project residential
building, Kyoto (Japan)
not built
Collaborator: Tadao Takaichi
Client: Recrute Corporation

1988–89

Alfex stores
Collaborator: Ferruccio Laviani
Client: Alfex

Packaging for Alla Festa
Collaborator: Sanae Kimura
Client: Pola

1988–90

Pens
Prototypes
Collaborators: James Irvine,
Ferruccio Laviani
Client: Pelikan

The World's Most Beautiful House
Competition
Collaborators: Akiko and Tadao Takaichi

1988–91

De Lucchi furniture line (chest of
drawers, secrétaire, bed, cabinet,
writing desk, chair)
Production: 1988
Collaborators: Elisa Gargan,
Mario Rossi Scola
Client: Consonni International Masters

Segmenti office accessories
Production: 1989–91
Collaborator: Tadao Takaichi
Client: Kartell

1989

Abate chair
Production: 1989
Client: Bieffeplast
Empire office system
Production: 1989
Client: Bieffeplast

Collection of eyeglasses
Production: 1989
Collaborators: Sanae Kimura,
Angelo Micheli
Client: Charmant

Scenario ceramics
Production: 1990
Collaborators: Sanae Kimura,
Angelo Micheli
Client: Floor Gres Ceramiche

Sintesi bathroom accessories
Production: (1992)
Collaborator: Tadao Takaichi
Client: Interform mfg

Lazy Susan tea service
Production: 1989
Collaborator: Sanae Kimura
Client: Lazy Susan

PBA handles
Prototypes
Client: PBA

Wooden objects
Production: 1990
Collaborator: Elisa Gargan
Client: Shizuoka City

Moments store, Oporto (Portugal)
Collaborator: Nicholas Bewick
Client: Moments

Solid showroom, Stezzano (Bergamo)
Collaborator: Emanuela Botter
Client: RB Rossana

Product presentation corner
Collaborators: Nicholas Bewick,
Kenneth Fraser, Gianluigi Mutti
Client: Mandarina Duck

Mandarina Duck stand, Mipel,
Milan Trade Fair
Collaborator: Nicholas Bewick,
Kenneth Fraser
Client: Mandarina Duck

Olivetti Synthesis Stand, Eimu,
Milan Trade Fair
Collaborator: Geert Koster
Client: Olivetti Synthesis

Carigi automatic branch office
Production: 1989
Collaborator: James Irvine
Client: Cassa di Risparmio di Genova
e Imperia (produced by Olivetti)

500 Forest Country Residence
residential building, Shizuoka (Japan)
not built
Collaborators: Angelo Micheli,
Tadao Takaichi
Client: Tokyu Corporation

Deutsche Bank branch offices
Competition (first prize)
Collaborators: Taku Arai,
Jonathan Barnes, Nicholas Bewick
(project leader), Hanno Giesler,
Denise Houx, Angelo Micheli,
Michele Rossi, Christian Schneider
Client: Deutsche Bank

1989–90

La Fenice kitchen
Production: 1991
Collaborator: Mario Rossi Scola
Client: RB Rossana

Section of the civic museum,
Groningen (The Netherlands)
Collaborators: Geert Koster,
Ferruccio Laviani, Angelo Micheli
Client: City of Groningen

1989–91

Olivetti System & Networks research
center, Bari
with DEGW
Collaborator: Nicholas Bewick
Client: Olivetti

La Fenice building, Osaka (Japan)
Collaborator: Tadao Takaichi
Client: Intergroup

1989–92

Eura lamp
Production: 1992
Collaborator: Tadao Takaichi
Client: Yamagiwa

1990

Elia sofa and poltrona, Giona sofa
Production: 1990
Collaborator: Elisa Gargan
Client: Arflex

Ascanio bedside table, Atena shelf,
Celeo writing desk and Demetria
console table
Production: 1991
Collaborator: Elisa Gargan
Client: Glass Design

Sangirolamo office system
Production: 1991
with Achille Castiglioni
Collaborators: Ferruccio Laviani,
Angelo Micheli
Client: Olivetti Synthesis

Mascagni sofa and Melodia table
Production: 1991
Collaborators: Elisa Gargan,
Tadao Takaichi
Client: Origin Fukujama

Rossini and Vivaldi sofas
Production: 1991
Collaborator: Ferruccio Laviani
Client: Origin Fukujama

White vases
Production: 1990
Collaborator: Elisa Gargan
Client: Produzione Privata

Candlesticks
Production: 1990
Collaborators: Elisa Gargan,
Mario Rossi Scola
Client: Produzione Privata

Table bookcase
Production: 1990
Collaborator: Elisa Gargan
Client: Produzione Privata

Vases with black and white patterns
Production: 1990
Collaborator: Elisa Gargan
Client: Produzione Privata
(produced by Ceramiche San Marco)

Vases in marble and stone
Production: 1990
Collaborator: Elisa Gargan
Client: Produzione Privata

Haseko Urbest stores, Osaka
and Kobe (Japan)
Collaborator: Tadao Takaichi
Client: Haseko Urbest

Exhibit design "Children's Bedroom,"
Salon des Artistes Decorateur, Paris
Collaborator: Elisa Gargan
Client: Salon des Artistes Decorateur

Exhibit design "Rubens," Palazzo
della Ragione, Padua
Collaborator: Angelo Micheli
Client: City of Padua

Olivetti Synthesis stand, Orgatec,
Cologne trade fair
Collaborators: Emanuela Botter,
Geert Koster, Ferruccio Laviani
Client: Olivetti Synthesis

RB Rossana stand, Eurocucine,
Milan Trade Fair
Collaborators: Emanuela Botter,
Ferruccio Laviani, Mario Rossi Scola
Client: RB Rossana

Graphics for the cover of
Art Deco
Client: Gakken

Graphics for the Martini Prefabbricati
corporate book
Collaborators: Emanuela Botter,
Ferruccio Laviani
Client: Martini Prefabbricati

Logo for the Design Zentrum Bremen
Collaborator: Mario Rossi Scola
Client: Innoventa

Bancacontinuaovunque
prefabricated branch office
Collaborators: Nicholas Banks,
Angelo Micheli, Mario Rossi Scola,
Mario Trimarchi
Client: Olivetti

AV Mazzega factory, offices and
showroom, Mogliano Veneto (Treviso)
not built
Collaborators: Angelo Micheli,
Tadao Takaichi
Client: AV Mazzega

Study for Casa Lunga
Collaborator: Akiko Takaichi

Study for Casa Rotonda
Collaborator: Akiko Takaichi

1990–91

Finenovecento furnishings
Production: 1991
Collaborator: Mario Rossi Scola
Client: Design Gallery

Glass vases
Production: 1991
Collaborator: Mario Rossi Scola
Client: Cleto Munari

Exhibit design for "Techniques
Discrètes. Le design mobilier en Italie
1980–90," Paris, Musée des Arts
Décoratifs
with Achille Castiglioni
Collaborators: Ferruccio Laviani,
Angelo Micheli
Client: Ice, Assoarredo, Union des Arts
Décoratifs

Sanpo House, Gumma (Japan)
Collaborator: Tadao Takaichi

1990–92

Exhibit design "Elégantes Techniques,"
Cultural Center;
Chicago
with Achille Castiglioni
Collaborators: Jonathan Barnes,
Ferruccio Laviani, Angelo Micheli
Client: Assoarredo,
Union des Arts Décoratifs

Commercial and residential building
TK Project, Tokyo (Japan)
not built
Collaborator: Tadao Takaichi

1990–93

BPA automatic branch office,
Portugal
Collaborators: Nicholas Bewick
(project leader), Angelo Micheli
Client: Banco Portugues do Atlantico

1990–

graphics for Produzione Privata
catalogues
Client: Produzione Privata

1991

Gaia lamp
Production: 1991
Collaborator: Mario Rossi Scola
Client: AV Mazzega

Luna lamp
Production: 1993
Collaborator: Mario Rossi Scola
Client: AV Mazzega

Sigira lamp
Production: 1991
Collaborator: Mario Rossi Scola
Client: ClassiCon

Tap
Prototype
Collaborator: Angelo Micheli
Client: Ideal Standard

Frame photo–holders
Production: 1992
Collaborator: Tadao Takaichi
Client: Interform

Alba armchair
Prototype
Collaborator: Mario Rossi Scola
Client: Moroso

Sofas and armchairs
Joyce collection
Production: 1991
Collaborator: Elisa Gargan
Client: Moroso

NTT chairs
Production: 1991
Collaborator: Tadao Takaichi
Client: NTT Japan
(produced by Cassina Japan)

Paper On office stationery
Production: 1991
Collaborator: James Irvine
Client: Olivetti-Baltea

LSX 5000 computer
Prototype
Collaborator: James Irvine
Client: Olivetti

Pearwood coat stand, table and bed
Production: 1991
Collaborator: Mario Rossi Scola
Client: Produzione Privata

Macchina Minima no. 7 lamp
Production: 1991
Collaborator: Mario Rossi Scola
Client: Produzione Privata

Pendant lamp
Prototype
Collaborator: Mario Rossi Scola
Client: Produzione Privata

Porta-evidenze
Stamp
Production: 1991
Client: Rex (produced
by Cleto Munari)

Manager Restaurant NTT, Tokyo (Japan)
Collaborator: Angelo Micheli,
Tadao Takaichi
Client: NTT Japan

1992

Pensiero Libero bookstore
Prototype
Client: Alias

Libro lamp
Prototype
Client: Belux

Bel Dì sofa
Production: 1992
Collaborator: Mario Rossi Scola
Client: Brunati Italia

Handle
Prototype
Client: Fusital

Saltimbanco bench
Production: 1992
Collaborator: Mario Rossi Scola
Client: Play Line

Expo kitchen
Prototype
Collaborator: Mario Rossi Scola
Client: RB Rossana

Gourmet saucepans
Production: 1993
Collaborator: Mario Rossi Scola
Client: Sambonet

Handle
Prototype
Client: Valli and Colombo

Carpet patterns
Production: 1992
Client: Vorwerk

Exhibit design for
"Il Soggiorno nella Casa Neoeclettica,"
Abitare il Tempo, Verona
Collaborator: Mario Rossi Scola
Client: Abitare il Tempo

Y Project design museum,
Tokyo (Japan)
not built
Collaborator: Tadao Takaichi

The Spreebogen Urban Design Ideas,
Berlin (Germany)
Competition
Collaborators: Pio Barone Lumaga,
Nicholas Bewick (project leader), Alberto
Bianchi, Angelo Micheli, Michele Rossi
Client: Federal Republic
of Germany and Land Berlin

1992–93

Philos laptop PC
Production: 1993
Collaborator: Hagai Shvadron
Client: Olivetti

Ginger and Fred salt and pepper
shakers,
Duo Piccante oil and vinegar flasks
Production: 1994
Collaborator: Masahiko Kubo
Client: Rosenthal

1993

Libera lamp
Production: 1994
Client: Artemide

Wooden table
Prototype
Collaborator: Mario Rossi Scola
Client: Consonni International Masters

Hobbit computer
Prototype
Collaborator: Mario Trimarchi
Client: Olivetti

M6 Suprema series computer
Production: 1993
Collaborator: Mario Trimarchi
Client: Olivetti

Echos 40 laptop
Production: 1994
Client: Olivetti

ETP typewriter
Production: 1993
Collaborator: Alessandro Chiarato
Client: Olivetti

PWP typewriter
Prototype
Collaborator: Simon Morgan
Client: Olivetti

Cash register
Production: 1993
Collaborator: Bruce Fifeld
Client: Olivetti

Thermal cash register
X2T and X3T
Prototypes
Collaborator: Alessandro Chiarato
Client: Olivetti

Minicad automatic telling machine
Production: 1993
Collaborator: Mario Trimarchi
Client: Olivetti–Siab

DM 109 printer
Production: 1993
Collaborator: Alessandro Chiarato
Client: Olivetti

PR 60 bank printer
Production: 1994
Collaborator: Alessandro Chiarato
Client: Olivetti

JP 103 inkjet printer
Prototype
Collaborator: Simon Morgan
Client: Olivetti

JP 270 inkjet printer
Production: (1993)
Collaborator: Alessandro Chiarato
Client: Olivetti

PG 304 laser printer
Production: 1993
Collaborator: Alessandro Chiarato
Client: Olivetti

1993 chair
Production: 1993
Collaborators: Elisa Gargan,
Mario Rossi Scola
Client: Produzione Privata

Trefili lamp
Production: 1993
Collaborator: Mario Rossi Scola
Client: Produzione Privata

Workshop*
Ivrea (Turin); Eindhoven (The
Netherlands)
Collaborators: Alessandro Chiarato,
Torsten Fritze, Masahiko Kubo,
Mario Trimarchi
Client: Olivetti-Philips

"Citizen Office" exhibit design,
Vitra Design Museum, Weil am Rhein
(Germany); Design Forum of Nänikon
(Switzerland, 1995); Italian Cultural
Institute, Moscow (Russia, 1996)
Collaborator: Geert Koster
Client: Vitra Design Museum

KTK Project commercial complex
and hotel, Shiga (Japan)
not built
Collaborator: Tadao Takaichi
Client: Kalasuma Town Kaihatsu

1993–94

Multimedia kiosks
Production: 1995
Collaborators: Antonio Macchi Cassia,
Enrico Quell
Client: Olivetti-Mael Tecnost

Echos 20 laptop
Production: 1995
Client: Olivetti

1994

Handles
Prototypes
Collaborator: Mario Rossi Scola
Client: Forges

Serie 4000 office system
Production: 1995
Collaborators: Nicholas Bewick
(project leader), Hanno Giesler,
Christian Schneider
Client: Mauser Office

Silver computer
Collaborator: Mario Trimarchi
Client: Olivetti

OFX 1000 fax
Production: 1995
Client: Olivetti

OFX 1001 fax
Production: 1995
Client: Olivetti (produced
by Olivetti for Bosch and others)

NP 9 palmtop
Prototype
Collaborator: Alessandro Chiarato
Client: Olivetti

MS 6050 automatic telling machine
Production: 1995
Collaborator: Enrico Quell
Client: Olivetti-Mael Tecnost

Pronto cell phone
Production: 1994
Collaborator: Enrico Quell
Client: Olivetti-Mael Tecnost

M 711 terminal for municipal police
Production: 1994
Collaborator: Enrico Quell
Client: Olivetti-Mael Tecnost

Exhibit design for
"Information Room," Furniture Show,
Milan
Collaborator: Paolo De Lucchi
Client: Interiors

Exhibit design "Tipo & Contro Tipo.
Furniture Design in Italy 1987–97,"
Hong Kong and Beijing (China)
with Achille Castiglioni
Collaborator: Angelo Micheli
Client: Ice and Assoarredo

Yokohama port terminal,
Yokohama (Japan)
Competition
Collaborator: Brigid Byrne,
Filippo Pagliani
Client: City of Yokohama

1994–95

PR2 bank printer
Production: 1995
Collaborator: Johannes Kiessler
Client: Olivetti Lexicon

Packaging for Ciba Dailies
Collaborators: Torsten Fritze (project
leader), Masahiko Kubo
Client: Ciba Vision

Study for the Festival Office
with Nicholas Bewick, Torsten Fritze
Collaborators: Eric Castets,
Michael Corsar, Paolo De Lucchi
Client: Domus Academy

Interiors of the De Lucchi office,
Via Pallavicino 31, Milan
Collaborators: Paolo De Lucchi,
Angelo Micheli
Client: Studio De Lucchi

1994–96

Interlife series of furnishings
Production: 1996
Collaborator: Mario Rossi Scola
Client: Interlübke

Envision computer project
Production: 1994
Collaborators: Felipe Alarcao,
Alessandro Chiarato
Client: Olivetti

Video for multimedia computer
Production: 1996
Collaborator: Masahiko Kubo
Client: Olivetti

1994–97

Mandarina Duck stores
(second generation)
Collaborators: Geert Koster,
Mario Trimarchi
Client: Mandarina Duck

1994–2001

Lighting Field lamps (prototypes),
subsequently Le Marionette
Collaborators: Alberto Nason,
Mario Rossi Scola
Production: 2001
Client: Artemide (Prototypes);
Produzione Privata

1995

Tessalo lamp
Production: 1995
Client: Artemide Litech

Fireplace
Prototype
Collaborators: Michael Corsar,
Torsten Fritze
Client: Edilkamin

Tape dispenser, scissors
and paper cutter
Production: 1995
Collaborator: Tadao Takaichi
Client: Interform

Automatic ticket dispensers 1 and 2
Collaborator: Enrico Quell
Client: Olivetti–Tecnotour Eltec

PR4 retail printer
Production: 1996
Collaborator: Johannes Kiessler
Client: Olivetti

Eidos and Pegaso office systems
Production: 1995
Collaborator: Geert Koster
Client: Olivetti Synthesis

Bottiglia vases
Production: 1995
Collaborator: Mario Rossi Scola
Client: Produzione Privata

Samsung trophies
Collaborator: Johannes Kiessler
Client: Samsung

Fiera di Brescia, Brescia
Competition
Collaborators: Nicholas Bewick,
Filippo Pagliani
Client: Ente Fiera Brescia

Deutsche Bahn ticket halls
Competition (first prize)
Collaborators: Nicholas Bewick
(project leader), Brigid Byrne,
Michael Corsar, Alessandra Dalloli,
Gladys Escobar, Torsten Fritze,
Christian Hartmann, Annelaure Lesquoy,
Enrico Quell, Daniele Rossi,
Michele Rossi, Katia Scheika,
Steffen Schulz, Trond Sonnergren
Client: Deutsche Bahn

1995–96

JP 170 inkjet printer
Production: 1996
Collaborator: Alessandro Chiarato
Client: Olivetti

JP 790 inkjet printer
Production: 1996
Collaborator: Johannes Kiessler
Client: Olivetti

MdL95 kitchen
Production: 1996
Collaborator: Mario Rossi Scola
Client: RB Rossana

ORS cash register
Prototype
Collaborator: Johannes Kiessler
Client: Siemens/Nixdorf

Interiors of the Deutsche Bahn station,
Aschaffenburg (Germany)
Collaborators: Nicholas Bewick
(project leader), Brigid Byrne,
Michael Corsar, Alessandra Dalloli,
Torsten Fritze, Christian Hartmann,
Steffen Schulz, Trond Sonnergren
Client: Deutsche Bahn

1995–99

Sistemare filing system
Production: 1997
Collaborators: Nicholas Bewick,
Gerhard Reichert
Client: Mauser Office

1996

Telemaco lamp
Production: 1996
Client: Artemide

Campus School furnishings
Prototypes
Collaborators: Michael Corsar,
Torsten Fritze (project leader),
Hanno Geisler
Client: Casala

Echos P 120 laptop
Production: 1996
Collaborator: Felipe Alarcao
Client: Olivetti

Modulo series computer
Production: 1996
Collaborator: Felipe Alarcao
Client: Olivetti

Xana computer
Production: (1996)
Collaborators: Felipe Alarcao,
Masahiko Kubo
Client: Olivetti

Vase
Prototype
Client: Pampaloni Argentieri

Acquatinta lamp
Production: 1996
Collaborator: Mario Rossi Scola
Client: Produzione Privata

Caolina lamp
Production: 1996
Collaborator: Mario Rossi Scola
Client: Produzione Privata

Workshop Domestic Chips,
Ivrea (Turin)
Collaborators: Torsten Fritze,
Johannes Kiessler, Masahiko Kubo,
Enrico Quell, Mario Trimarchi
Client: Olivetti

Museum Shop, Galleria Nazionale d'Arte
Moderna (GNAM), Rome
Collaborator: Michele Rossi
Client: Reunion Des Musées Nationaux

Mauser showroom, Waldeck (Germany)
not built
Collaborator: Nicholas Bewick
Client: Mauser Office

1996–97

Echos PRO laptop
Production: 1997
Collaborator: Felipe Alarcao
Client: Olivetti

OFX 500 and OFX 500-2 fax machines
Production: 1997
Collaborators: Masahiko Kubo,
Johannes Kiessler
Client: Olivetti

Xtrema laptop
Production: (1998)
Collaborator: Felipe Alarcao
Client: Olivetti

Mandarina Duck showroom,
Piazza Arcole, Milan
Collaborators: Sezgin Aksu,
Geert Koster
Client: Mandarina Duck

Interiors of the Deutsche Bahn station,
Frankfurt (Germany)
Collaborators: Nicholas Bewick
(project leader), Brigid Byrne,
Michael Corsar, Alessandra Dalloli,
Torsten Fritze, Christian Hartmann,
Steffen Schulz, Trond Sonnergren
Client: Deutsche Bahn

1996–98

Conrad Creative Seminar House,
Wernberg Koblitz (Germany)
Collaborators: Nicholas Bewick (project
leader), Marco della Torre, Daniele Rossi
Client: Conrad Family

1997

Goto vase
Production: 1997
Client: Barovier & Toso

Aria lamp
Production: 1998
Collaborator: Alberto Nason
Client: Enel (produced by Produzione
Privata)

Chair no. 1 chair
Production: 1997
Collaborator: Mario Rossi Scola
Client: Kembo

Piero computer
Production: 1997
Collaborator: Masahiko Kubo
Client: Olivetti

Basequadra vases
Production: 1997
Collaborators: Alberto Nason,
Mario Rossi Scola
Client: Produzione Privata

Petali centerpiece
Production: 1997
Collaborator: Mario Rossi Scola
Client: Produzione Privata

Pluvia vase
Production: 1997
Collaborator: Mario Rossi Scola
Client: Produzione Privata

Treforchette lamp
Production: 1997
Collaborator: Mario Rossi Scola
Client: Produzione Privata

Exhibit design for the "Design Team of
the Year 1997 Award," Essen (Germany)
Collaborator: Johannes Kiessler
Client: Design Zentrum Nordrhein
Westfalen

Limburg station
(Germany)
Competition
Collaborators: Nicholas Bewick,
Filippo Pagliani
Client: Deutsche Bahn

1997-98

Aleppo lamp
Production: 1998
Client: Artemide

JP 883 inkjet printer
Production: 1998
Collaborator: Masahiko Kubo
Client: Olivetti

Luna bed
Production: 1998
Collaborator: Silvia Suardi
Client: Poltrona Frau

PR6 printer
Production: (1998)
Collaborator: Johannes Kiessler
Client: Poste Italiane
(produced by Olivetti)

Montedoro stand, Florence
Collaborators: Alberto Nason,
Mario Rossi Scola
Client: Montedoro

Rome subway
Competition
Collaborators: Alberto Bianchi,
Angelo Micheli, Enrico Quell
Client: ATAC

1997–2000

Enel stand, Fiera del Levante, Bari
Collaborators: Enrico Quell, Silvia Suardi
Client: Enel

1998

Hoof chair
Prototype
Collaborator: Gerhard Reichert
Client: Arflex

Scatole Magiche home computers
Prototypes
Collaborator: Paolo De Lucchi
Client: Clac (Centro Legno Arredo Cantù)

Table leg
Prototype
Client: Feria Internacional del Muebel
a Valencia, Asociaciòn Nacional de
industriales y Exportadores de meubles
de Espana (Anieme), Instituto Espanol
de Comercio Exterior (Icex)

Calcolatrice Divisumma 12
Production: 1998
Collaborator: Sezgin Aksu
Client: Olivetti

M700 (Anna) computer
Production: 1998
Collaborator: Masahiko Kubo
Client: Olivetti

Artjet 10 inkjet printer
Production: 1999
Collaborator: Masahiko Kubo
Client: Olivetti

Artjet 20 inkjet printer
Production: 1998
Collaborator: Masahiko Kubo
Client: Olivetti

Multifunction printer
Studio Jet 300
Production: 1998
Collaborator: Masahiko Kubo
Client: Olivetti

Artù furniture system
Production: 1998
Collaborator: Silvia Suardi
Client: Poltrona Frau

Acquaparete lamp
Production: 1998
Client: Produzione Privata

Tokyo lamp
Production: 1998
Collaborator: Alberto Nason
Client: Produzione Privata

Exhibit design of the "Virtual Basilica,"
Assisi (Perugia)
Collaborators: Gladys Escobar,
Enrico Quell
Client: Enel

Exhibit design at the Futur Show,
Bologna
Collaborators: Silvia Suardi,
Mario Trimarchi
Client: Bologna Fiere

Upgrading of the visitors' route through
Enel power stations
Collaborators: Sezgin Aksu,
Geert Koster, Angelo Micheli
Client: Enel Production

Centro per le Arti Contemporanee,
Via Guido Reni, Rome
Competition
with Achille Castiglioni, Italo Lupi
Collaborators: Brigid Byrne,
Filippo Pagliani
Client: Soprintendenza Speciale Arte
Contemporanea

Footbridge for Holy Year, Rome
Competition
Collaborator: Filippo Pagliani
Client: Agenzia Romana
per il Giubileo

IUAV premises in the Magazzini
Frigoriferi building,
San Basilio, Venice
Competition
Collaborators: Brigid Byrne,
Filippo Pagliani
Client: IUAV

Linz station (Austria)
Competition
Collaborator: Filippo Pagliani
Client: Deutsche Bahn

1998–99

OMS corporate identity
Collaborators: Massimo Canali,
Angelo Micheli
Client: Olivetti Multi Service

Packaging for Olivetti electronic
products
Fragile (Michele De Lucchi
and Mario Trimarchi)
with Bruna Gnocchi, Matteo Nannucci,
Elena Riva
Client: Olivetti

Visual path at the Enel power station,
Trino Vercellese (Vercelli)
Collaborators: Sezgin Aksu,
Geert Koster, Angelo Micheli
Client: Enel Production

Signage for urban routes, Brescia
Collaborators: Angelo Micheli (project
leader), Eliana Pasquini
Client: City of Brescia

Banca Popolare di Lodi branch offices
Collaborators: Gladys Escobar,
Angelo Micheli (project leader),
Silvia Suardi, Claudio Venerucci
Client: Banca Popolare di Lodi

1998–2000

OFX 300 multifunction fax
Production: 2000
Collaborator: Masahiko Kubo
Client: Olivetti

Mandarina Duck store,
Via Montenapoleone, Milan
Collaborators: Paolo De Lucchi,
Geert Koster
Client: Mandarina Duck

Exhibit design for "4:3. Fifty Years
of Italian and German Design,"
Bonn (Germany)
Collaborators: Brigid Byrne,
Aya Matsukaze, Filippo Pagliani
Client: Bonner Bundeskunsthalle

Holy Year Information Center 1,
Museo del Risorgimento, Rome
Collaborators: Gladys Escobar,
Enrico Quell
Client: Agenzia Romana
per il Giubileo

Holy Year Information Center 2,
Via della Conciliazione, Rome
Collaborator: Enrico Quell
Client: Agenzia Romana
per il Giubileo

Redevelopment of the
Enel Information Center, Entracque
(Cuneo)
Collaborators: Brigid Byrne, Geert
Koster, Aya Matsukaze, Filippo Pagliani
(project leader)
Client: Enel Production

Redevelopment of the
Interiors of the Enel Information Center
and Auditorium,
Montalto di Castro (Viterbo)
Collaborators: Geert Koster,
Enrico Quell
Client: Enel Production

1998–2001

House, Bologna
Collaborators: Alberto Bianchi, Angelo
Micheli (project leader), Eliana Pasquini

1998–2003

Poste Italiane corporate identity
with Fragile (Michele De Lucchi
and Mario Trimarchi)
Collaborators: Fulvia Bleu, Massimo
Canali, Annalisa Gatto, Marco Miglio,
Elena Riva, Katrin Schmitt-Tegge
Client: Poste Italiane

Post offices for Poste Italiane
Collaborators: Bastiaan Arler, Alberto
Bianchi, Enrico Quell, Daniele Rossi
Client: Poste Italiane

1998–present

High-voltage pylon
Competition (equal first prize)
with Achille Castiglioni
Collaborators: Sezgin Aksu,
Geert Koster
Client: Enel Distribuzione

Documentation center at the Triennale,
Palazzo dell'Arte, Milan
Collaborators: Brigid Byrne,
Aya Matsukaze, Filippo Pagliani
Client: Milan Triennale

1999

Acme pen
Production: 1999
Collaborator: Massimo Canali
Client: Acme

Compaq laptop
Prototypes
Collaborators: Sezgin Aksu,
Philippe Nigro
Client: Compaq

Materic kitchen
Prototype
Collaborator: Gerhard Reichert
Client: Dada Cucine

Trabiccolo coach for surfing the Net
model
Collaborator: Stefano Prina
Client: Hi-wood

Modifon computer and switchboard
Prototype
Collaborator: Masahiko Kubo
Client: ICS for Olivetti

Allavoro and Attivo office chairs
Production: 1999
Collaborator: Gerhard Reichert
Client: Mauser Offices

Beds
Prototypes
Collaborator: Gerhard Reichert
Client: Molteni

Jet-Lab 600 multifunction fax
Production: 2000
Collaborator: Masahiko Kubo
Client: Olivetti

OFX 560 fax
Production: 199
Collaborator: Masahiko Kubo
Client: Olivetti

Collection
A che cosa servono i vasi da fiori?
Production: 1999
Collaborator: Alberto Nason
Client: Produzione Privata

Acquamiki lamp
Production: 1999
Collaborator: Alberto Nason
Client: Produzione Privata

Candela lamp
Production: 2000
Collaborator: Alberto Nason
Client: Produzione Privata

Cubetta lamp
Production: 1999
Collaborator: Alberto Nason
Client: Produzione Privata

Pensando ai Poeti Sufi collection
of lamps
Production: 2000
Collaborator: Alberto Nason
Client: Produzione Privata

Quattropieghe lamp
Production: 1999
Collaborator: Alberto Nason
Client: Produzione Privata

Vassoio and Vassoietto trays
Production: 1999
Collaborator: Alberto Nason
Client: Produzione Privata

Cordless phone
Concept
Collaborators: Mario Trimarchi,
Masahiko Kubo
Client: Siemens

Exhibit design
"A mano libera. Disegni senza
computer," Ivrea (Turin);
Hamburg (Germany)
Collaborator: Silvia Suardi
Client: Olivetti, Telecom Italia

Exhibit design "Ettore Sottsass,"
Salone del Mobile,
Milan Trade Fair
Collaborator: Geert Koster
Client: Cosmit

Merloni stand, Domotechnica,
Cologne (Germany)
Collaborators: Enrico Quell, Silvia Suardi
Client: Merloni Elettrodomestici

Telecom stand, Motor Show, Bologna
Collaborators: Geert Koster,
Angelo Micheli, Enrico Quell
Client: Telecom Italia

Graphics for a Unilever brochure
Collaborators: Massimo Canali,
Angelo Micheli
Client: Unilever

Graphics for the catalogue
of the exhibition
"A mano libera. Disegni senza
computer"
Collaborator: Silvia Suardi
Client: Olivetti, Telecom Italia

Graphics for the exhibition
"Leonardo. The Last Supper"
Collaborators: Massimo Canali,
Angelo Micheli
Client: Olivetti

Railway ticket hall, Mazzoni wing
of the Stazione Termini, Rome
Collaborators: Brigid Byrne, Enrico Quell
Client: Grandi Stazioni

Post offices: Milano 15, Via Vigna,
Milan; Milano 23,
Via San Simpliciano, Milan
Collaborators: Alberto Bianchi,
Paola Silva Coronel, Enrico Quell,
Daniele Rossi
Client: Poste Italiane

Casa di Bianco, Cremona Ludoteca
and offices
Competition
Collaborators: Aya Matsukaze,
Angelo Micheli (project leader)

Museo Civico degli Eremitani, Padua
Competition
Collaborator: Filippo Pagliani
Client: City of Padua

1999–2000

Dioscuri lamp
Production: 2000
Client: Artemide

Milestone and Palme outdoor lamps
Production: 2001
Collaborator: Gerhard Reichert
Client: Artemide DZ Licht

Furnishings for Poste Italiane
Collaborator: Daniele Rossi
Client: Poste Italiane

Illuminated sign for the Stazione
Centrale, Milan
Competition
Collaborators: Brigid Byrne, Gladys
Escobar, Aya Matzukase, Philippe Nigro
Client: City of Milan

Corporate identity per OIS
Collaborators: Massimo Canali,
Angelo Micheli
Client: Olivetti-OIS

Post office kiosks
Collaborators: Alberto Bianchi,
Ada Matsukaze, Enrico Quell,
Daniele Rossi
Client: Poste Italiane

2000

Logico lamps
Production: 2001
Collaborators: Gerhard Reichert
Client: Artemide

Design Report 2000 trophy
Production: 2000
Collaborator: Alberto Nason
Client: Design Report
(produced by Produzione Privata)

Domotic control system
Prototype
Collaborator: Masahiko Kubo
Client: Domustech

Notepen pen
Production: 2000
Collaborator: Alberto Nason
Client: Moccagatta,
Pogliani & Associati (produced
by Produzione Privata)

Leger shelf
Prototype
Collaborator: Gerhard Reichert
Client: Molteni&C

Piazza di Spagna sofa and bed
Production: 2000
Collaborator: Silvia Suardi
Client: Poltrona Frau

Telebus for Poste Italiane
Collaborator: Alberto Bianchi
Client: Poste Italiane

Ciao lamp
Prototype
Collaborator: Alberto Nason
Client: Produzione Privata

H vases (Hermosa, Hansa, Handel)
Production: 2001
Collaborator: Alberto Nason
Client: Produzione Privata

Mandarina Duck stores (third generation)
Collaborators: Angelo Micheli,
Silvia Suardi
Client: Mandarina Duck

Installation of the pope's dais at the
Sports Jubilee, Stadio Olimpico, Rome
Collaborators: Giovanni Battista
Mercurio, Rolando Zorzi
Client: City of Rome

Exhibit design
"Sandro Botticelli. Pittore della Divina
Commedia," Scuderie del Quirinale,
Rome
Collaborators: Enrico Quell, Silvia Suardi
Client: Agenzia Romana per il Giubileo

Telecom stand, São Paolo
and Rio de Janeiro (Brazil)
Collaborators: Geert Koster,
Enrico Quell
Client: Telecom Italia

Telecom stand, SMAU 2000, Milan
Collaborators: Geert Koster,
Enrico Quell
Client: Telecom Italia

Graphic design of the volume
Olivetti 1901–1998
with Mario Trimarchi (concept)
Collaborator: Katrin Schmitt-Tegge

Interiors and graphics for the library
Centre Céramique, Maastricht (Holland)
Collaborators: Alberto Bianchi,
Massimo Canali
Client: Gemeente Maastricht

Redevelopment of Telecom offices,
Corso Italia, Rome
Collaborators: Angelo Micheli,
Enrico Quell
Client: Telecom Italia

Roma 1 post office, Via Sicilia, Rome
Collaborators: Alberto Bianchi,
Enrico Quell, Daniele Rossi
Client: Poste Italiane

Gallery of Stazione Termini,
Rome
Competition (first prize)
not built
Collaborators: Brigid Byrne,
Laura Negrini
Client: Grandi Stazioni

Milan subway, red line
Competition
Collaborators: Alberto Bianchi,
Angelo Micheli

2000–01

Xana 410 computer
Production: 2001
Collaborator: Sezgin Aksu
Client: Olivetti (produced by ICS)

Multimedia monitor
Production: 2001
Collaborator: Sezgin Aksu
Client: Olivetti (produced by ICS)

Multifunction printer
Copy Lab 200
Production: 2001
Collaborator: Masahiko Kubo
Client: Olivetti

Orione sofa
Production: 2001
Collaborator: Philippe Nigro
Client: Poltrona Frau

Desk set and wastepaper
basket/umbrella stand
Production: 2001
Collaborator: Philippe Nigro
Client: Poltrona Frau

Internet totem pole for Poste Italiane
Production: 2001
Collaborator: Daniele Rossi
Client: Poste Italiane

Banca 121 branch offices
Collaborator: Giovanni Battista Mercurio,
Angelo Micheli (project leader),
Laura Parolin
Client: Banca 121

Apartment, Milan
Collaborators: Angelo Micheli,
Silvia Suardi

Interiors of the Oracle demo room,
Sesto San Giovanni (Milan)
Collaborator: Gladys Escobar
Client: Oracle Italia

Interiors of a section of the municipal
museum, Groningen (Holland)
Collaborators: Geert Koster,
Giovanna Latis
Client: Groninger Museum

Restructuring of the Enel Power head
office, Via Carducci 3, Milan
Collaborators: Giovanni Battista
Mercurio, Angelo Micheli (project
leader), Laura Parolin
Client: Enel Power

Olivetti headquarters, Piazza di Spagna,
Rome
Collaborators: Francesco Otgianu,
Enrico Quell, Silvia Suardi
Client: Olivetti

Post office, Stazione Centrale, Milan
Collaborators: Simona Agabio,
Alberto Bianchi
Client: Poste Italiane

Post office, Stazione Termini, Rome
Collaborators: Luca La Torre,
Laura Negrini, Francesco Otgianu,
Enrico Quell (project leader)
Client: Poste Italiane

Post office, Galleria degli Uffizi, Florence
Collaborators: Simona Agabio,
Alberto Bianchi
Client: Poste Italiane

Giorgio Armani offices, Via Bergognone,
Milan
Collaborator: Paola Silva Coronel
Client: Giorgio Armani

Telecom offices, Parco dei Medici,
Rome
not built
Collaborators: Giovanni Battista
Mercurio, Angelo Micheli (project leader)
Client: Telecom Italia

2000-02

Atlantico entryphone
Production: 2001
Collaborators: Marco Gillio, Masahiko
Kubo (project leader), Aya Matsukaze
Client: Urmet Domus

Il Chioso, Angera (Varese)
Collaborators: Giovanna Latis,
Angelo Micheli, Claudio Venerucci
Client: Hortus

Restructuring of Telecom head office,
Piazza Affari, Milan
Collaborators: Giovanni Battista
Mercurio, Angelo Micheli (project
leader), Laura Parolin, Claudio Venerucci
Client: Telecom Italia

2000–03

Upgrading and offices of the Enel power
station, Priolo Gargallo (Syracuse)
Collaborators: Carlo De Mattia, Michele
Marozzini, Daniele Rossi (project leader)
Client: Enel Production

2000–04

Vasi di Natale
Collaborator: Alberto Nason
Client: Produzione Privata

Upgrading of Enel's La Casella power
station, Castel San Giovanni (Piacenza)
Collaborators: Brigid Byrne,
Gladys Escobar (project leader),
Geert Koster, Federico Seymandi
Client: Enel Production

2000–present

Hospice and day-care center
for Alzheimer's patients
Villa Sclopis, Salerano (Turin)
Collaborators: Paolo Fromage,
Angelo Micheli (project leader),
Fabiola Minas, Claudio Venerucci
Client: Associazione Casainsieme

Redevelopment of offices
and custodian's lodge
Enel power station,
Porto Corsini (Ravenna)
Collaborators: Carlo De Mattia, Michele
Marozzini, Daniele Rossi (project leader)
Client: Enel Production

Redevelopment of
Teatro Franco Parenti, Milan
Collaborator: Giovanna Latis
Client: Fondazione Pier Lombardo

2001

Sempronio lamp
Prototype
Collaborators: Gerhard Reichert
Client: Artemide

Electricity meter
Production: 2001
Collaborator: Sezgin Aksu
Client: Enel Distribuzione

Ceramic basket with leaves
Production: 2001
Client: Este Ceramiche e Porcellane

Urban furniture for Milan
Prototypes
Collaborators: Simona Agabio
Philippe Nigro
Client: IGP Decaux

Gioconda calculating machine
Production: 2001
Collaborator: Sezgin Aksu
Client: Olivetti

Logos calculating machines
Production: 2002
Collaborator: Sezgin Aksu
Client: Olivetti

OFX 570 Fax
Production: 2001
Collaborator: Masahiko Kubo
Client: Olivetti

2001 chair
Production: 2001
Collaborator: Gerhard Reichert
Client: Produzione Privata

Fata and Fatina lamps
Production: 2001
Collaborators: Alberto Nason
Client: Produzione Privata

Macchina Minima no. 8 lamp
Production: 2001
Collaborator: Alberto Nason
Client: Produzione Privata

Glass table with blown glass leg
Collaborator: Alberto Nason
Prototype
Client: Unifor

Telecom 187 stores
Competition
Collaboratorss: Geert Koster,
Giovanna Latis
Client: Telecom Italia

Exhibit design "Renaissance.
Masterpieces in the Italian Museums,"
Scuderie del Quirinale, Rome
Collaborators: Enrico Quell, Silvia Suardi
Client: Agenzia Romana
per il Giubileo

Telecom stand, Smau 2001, Milan
Collaborators: Geert Koster,
Enrico Quell
Client: Telecom Italia

Corporate identity for the
Food for Life campaign
Collaborators: Massimo Canali,
Angelo Micheli
Client: Unilever

Corporate identity for Moccagatta
& Pogliani
Collaborator: Massimo Canali
Client: Moccagatta & Pogliani

Interiors of the Enel Information Center,
Brindisi
Collaborators: Gladys Escobar,
Geert Koster
Client: Enel Production

Museo Abet Laminati, Bra (Cuneo)
unbuilt
Collaborator: Alberto Bianchi
Client: Abet Laminati

Museum of Information, Milan
unbuilt
Collaborators: Giovanni Battista
Mercurio, Angelo Micheli (project leader)

Upgrading of the
Enel Torre Valdaliga Nord power station,
Civitavecchia (Rome)
unbuilt
Collaborator: Daniele Rossi
Client: Enel Production

Enel Paesaggio wind farm
Competition
Collaborators: Birgid Byrne,
Masahiko Kubo
Client: Legambiente
and Erga Gruppo Enel

Footbridge over the Tiber, Rome
Competition
Collaborators: Brigid Byrne, Enrico Quell
Client: City of Rome

2001–02

Artù chair
Prototype
Collaborator: Sezgin Aksu
Client: Poltrona Frau

Orione mirror, Tri coat stand,
Volino table
Production: 2002
Collaborator: Philippe Nigro
Client: Poltrona Frau

PT Shop for Poste Italiane
Collaborators: Simona Agabio,
Alberto Bianchi
Client: Poste Italiane

ÒCardboard TreeÓ exhibit design,
Lucca; Ricicla, Fiera di Rimini
Collaborator: Alberto Nason
Client: Comieco

Design of the "Post Office Project"
traveling exhibition
Collaborators: Simona Agabio,
Alberto Bianchi, Gerhard Reichert
Client: Poste Italiane

Graphics for Ras information campaign
Collaborators: Massimo Canali,
Mercedes Jaén Ruiz, Angelo Micheli
Client: Ras

Coop sales points image
Competition
Collaborators: Giovanni Battista
Mercurio, Angelo Micheli (project
leader), Laura Parolin
Client: Coop

Enel auditorium and foyer, Viale Regina
Margherita 137, Rome
Collaborators: Giovanna Latis,
Francesco Otgianu, Enrico Quell
Client: Enel

Literature Café and Fastweb Foyer,
Largo Franco Parenti, Milan
Collaborator: Giovanna Latis
Client: Fondazione Pier Lombardo

Central Post Office, Piazza Cordusio 1,
Milan
Collaborators: Simona Agabio,
Alberto Bianchi
Client: Poste Italiane

2001–03

Apartment building Padua
Collaborators: Giovanna Latis,
Daniele Rossi, Federico Seymandi
Upgrading of the Enel Edi Power
electric power station, Chivasso (Turin)
Collaborators: Paolo Fromage,
Angelo Micheli (project leader),
Fabiola Minas
Client: Enel Production

Poste Italiane head office,
Viale Europa, Rome Eur
Collaborators: Simona Martino,
Giovanni Battista Mercurio,
Laura Parolin, Enrico Quell
Client: Poste Italiane

2001–present

Upgrading of the Enel power station
La Spezia
Collaborators: Brigid Byrne,
Gladys Escobar (project leader),
Federico Seymandi
Client: Enel Production

2002

Foglia outdoor lamp
Production: 2002
Collaborator: Gerhard Reichert
Client: Artemide DZ Licht

Cartoccio necklace
Production: 2002
Collaborator: Philippe Nigro
Client: Atelier Van Cleef & Arpels

Battista furniture accessories
Production: 2002
Collaborator: Sezgin Aksu
Client: Caimi Brevetti

Koala signage and communication
system
Production: 2002
Collaborator: Sezgin Aksu
Client: Caimi Brevetti

2002 chair
Prototype
Collaborator: Gerhard Reichert
Client: Produzione Privata

Ipy Grande lamps (Trepalle and Trellissi)
Production: 2002
Collaborator: Aya Matsukaze
Client: Produzione Privata

Ipy pendant lamps
Production: 2002
Collaborator: Nora De Cicco
Client: Produzione Privata

Lagrande lamp
Production: 2002
Collaborator: Alberto Nason
Client: Produzione Privata

Exhibit design for
"Chaos and Order – Love and Hate,"
Studio aMDL, Via Pallavicino 31, Milan
Client: Produzione Privata

Exhibit design for "Michele De Lucchi:
Dopotolomeo," Church of San Lorenzo,
Aosta
Collaborator: Silvia Suardi
Client: Regione Val d'Aosta

Exhibit design for
"Rembrandt. Paintings, Engravings
and Reflections in the Seventeenth
and Eighteenth Century in Italy,"
Scuderie del Quirinale, Rome
Collaborators: Enrico Quell, Silvia Suardi
Client: Azienda Speciale Palaexpo
del Comune di Roma

Telecom stand, Smau 2002, Milan
Collaborators: Geert Koster,
Giovanna Latis, Enrico Quell
Client: Telecom Italia

Corporate identity Banca Intesa
branch offices
Fragile (Michele De Lucchi
and Mario Trimarchi)
Collaborators: Susanne Gerhardt,
Julia Kleiner, Marco Miglio
Client: Banca Intesa

Image of Credem Bank branch offices
Competition
Collaborators: Carlo De Mattia,
Giovanna Latis, Michele Marrozzini,
Giovanni Battista Mercurio,
Angelo Micheli (project leader),
Philippe Nigro, Daniele Rossi
Client: Credem

Banca Intesa branch offices
Collaborators: Simona Agabio,
Alberto Bianchi, Geert Koster,
Giovanna Latis, Simona Martino,
Claudia Pescatori, Enrico Quell,
Philippe Nigro, Daniele Rossi
Client: Banca Intesa

Interiors of the Telecom Future Centre,
Venice
Collaborators: Massimo Canali,
Mercedes Jaén Ruiz, Giovanni Battista
Mercurio, Angelo Micheli (project
leader), Laura Parolin
Client: Telecom Italia

Redevelopment of the public
spaces of the
Milan Triennale, Palazzo dell'Arte, Milan
Collaborators: Brigid Byrne,
Paolo Fromage, Aya Matsukaze
Client: Milan Triennale

Redevelopment of the Enel Terna
power station, Rome East,
Collaborators: Filippo Flego,
Laura Negrini, Francesco Otgianu,
Enrico Quell (project leader)
Client: Enel Terna

Banca Intesa branch office,
Via dei Missaglia, Milan
Collaborators: Simona Agabio,
Alberto Bianchi, Geert Koster,
Giovanna Latis, Simona Martino,
Philippe Nigro, Claudia Pescatori,
Enrico Quell, Daniele Rossi, Laiza Tonali
Client: Banca Intesa

2002–03

Atis desk set, Felix decanter and pitcher

Production: 2004
Collaborator: Alberto Nason
Client: Arnolfo di Cambio

Altar of the Church of Santa Maria
Assunta in Angera
Production: 2003
Collaborator: Alberto Nason
Client: church of Santa Maria Assunta
in Angera

Ipy Parete lamp
Production: 2003
Client: Produzione Privata

Meteora lamp
Production: 2003
Collaborator: Alberto Nason
Client: Produzione Privata

Study for Open Space House,
Maastricht (Holland)
Collaborators: Simona Agabio,
Alberto Bianchi
Client: Vesteda

Interiors of the Telecom Future Centre,
Milan
unbuilt
Collaborators: Giovanni Battista
Mercurio, Angelo Micheli (project leader)
Client: Telecom Italia

Interiors of Omnia Invest head office,
Via Abruzzi 25, Rome
Collaborators: Filippo Flego, Enrico
Quell (project leader)
Client: Immsi

2002–04

Series of Laetitia goblets
Production: 2004
Collaborator: Alberto Nason
Client: Arnolfo di Cambio

Betelgeuse lamp
Prototype
Collaborator: Gerhard Reichert
Client: Artemide

Artista lamp
Production: 2003
Collaborator: Alberto Nason
Client: Produzione Privata

Orientale lamp
Production: 2003
Client: Produzione Privata

Sculptures Pinnacoli, Pinnacolina,
Pinnacolona
Production: 2003
Client: Produzione Privata

2002–present

Multi-socket box
Sotto-Sotto
Collaborator: Philippe Nigro
Client: Danese Milan

Banca Intesa branch office,
Laboratory, Via Cernaia 10, Milan
Collaborators: Geert Koster,
Giovanna Latis, Simona Martino,
Philippe Nigro, Claudia Pescatori,
Enrico Quell, Daniele Rossi
Client: Banca Intesa

Artistic director of restoration work
on the Palazzo delle Esposizioni,
Via Nazionale, Rome
Collaborators: Filippo Flego,
Enrico Quell (project leader)
Client: Azienda Speciale Palaexpo

Enel Terna power station, control
building, Carpi (Modena)
Collaborators: Laura Negrini, Enrico
Quell (project leader), Emanuele Villani
Client: Enel Terna

Enel Terna power station,
Tavarnuzze (Florence)
Collaborators: Filippo Flego,
Laura Negrini, Francesco Otgianu,
Enrico Quell (project leader)
Client: Enel Terna

2003

Layout container system
Production: 2004
Collaborator: Philippe Nigro
Client: Alias

Straight lamp
Production: 2004
Client: Artemide

Lapiccola lamp
Production: 2004
Collaborator: Alberto Nason
Client: Produzione Privata

Teapot
Prototype
Collaborator: Alberto Nason
Client: Produzione Privata

MDL office system
with Giovanni Battista Mercurio
Production: 2004
Collaborator: Angelo Micheli
Client: Unifor

Grigi vases
Prototypes
Client: Produzione Privata

Viacard column
Competition
Collaborators: Sezgin Aksu,
Angelo Micheli
Client: Autostrade SpA

Installation "Design-Italia" exhibition,
Milan
Collaborator: Silvia Suardi
Client: Design-Italia

Exhibit design
"Dans le sens industriel," La Galerie
d'Architecture, Paris (France)
Collaborators: Giovanna Latis,
Philippe Nigro
Client: La Galerie d'Architecture

Exhibit design "Michele De Lucchi,"
Centre Georges Pompidou,
Paris (France)
Collaborators: Giovanna Latis,
Philippe Nigro
Client: Centre Georges Pompidou

Exhibit design "Traces, of Nature, Time,
Hand and Spirit. Michele De Lucchi
and Ernst Gamperl Explore their
Favourite Materials: Wood and Glass,"
Studio aMDL, Via Pallavicino 31, Milan
Client: Produzione Privata

Rancilio stand, Host, Milan Trade Fair
Collaborators: Angelo Micheli,
Laura Parolin
Client: Rancilio

Auditorium, Montalto di Castro (Viterbo)
Competition with Studio Galdo
Collaborators: Filippo Flego,
Laura Negrini, Enrico Quell
Client: City of Montalto di Castro

Interiors of the Unilever offices, Milan
Competition
Collaborators: Giovanni Battista
Mercurio, Angelo Micheli (project leader)
Client: Unilever

Museo di Forte di Bard, Bard (Aosta)
Competition with Studio Rosset
Collaborators: Giovanni Battista
Mercurio, Angelo Micheli, Silvia Suardi
Client: Finbard

Museo di Gaeta, Gaeta (Latina)
Competition
Collaborators: Laura Negrini,
Enrico Quell
Client: City of Gaeta

2003–04

Castore and Castore Calice lamps
Production: 2003–04
Collaborator: Huub Ubbens
Client: Artemide

Ipy and Acquamiki suspension system
Production: 2004
Collaborator: Alberto Nason
Client: Produzione Privata

La Conica lamp
Prototype
Collaborator: Alberto Nason
Client: Produzione Privata

Mondadori stand system
Collaborators: Gregoire Beetz,
Mercedes Jaén Ruiz, Angelo Micheli
(project leader), Laura Parolin
Client: Mondadori

Interiors of the Fondazione Carive,
Dorsoduro, Venice
Collaborators: Giovanni Battista
Mercurio, Angelo Micheli (project leader)
Client: Fondazione Venezia

Museo della Città, Palazzo Pepoli
Vecchio, Bologna
Competition
Collaborators: Brigid Byrne, Silvia Suardi
Client: Fondazione Cassa
di Risparmio di Bologna

2003–present

Apartment building, Padua
with Alessandro Pedron
Collaborator: Marcello Biffi

Interiors of the Enel offices,
Viale Regina Margherita, Rome
Collaborators: Giovanni Battista
Mercurio, Angelo Micheli (project leader)
Client: Enel

Interiors of the Novartis offices,
Basel (Switzerland)
Collaborators: Giovanni Battista
Mercurio, Angelo Micheli (project leader)
Client: Novartis

Diocesan Museum, Ivrea (Turin)
Collaborators: Angelo Micheli (project
leader), Federico Seymandi,
Silvia Suardi
Client: Diocese of Ivrea

Interiors of the Neues Museum,
Berlin-Museuminsel (Germany)
Competition (first prize)
Collaborators: Sezgin Aksu,
Giovanna Latis, Gerhard Reichert
Client: Neues Museum Berlino

Bibliography

1970

S.W., "Michele De Lucchi all'Antonianum," in *Il Gazzettino*, March 3.

1972

"Michele De Lucchi alla Venezuela," in *Il Gazzettino*, January 12.

1974

Domus, 530, January (cover)
"Michele De Lucchi," in *Schema informazione*, Galleria Schema magazine, 2, Florence.

M.A. Teodori, "L'architetto lanciafiamme," in *L'Espresso*, 2, pp. 104–11.

1975

A. Branzi, "Tecnologia o eutanasia," in *Casabella*, 397, pp. 17–18.
Karma Film (edited by), *Filmstudio-Politecnico*, Dimensione super 8, Filmstudio Notebooks, Artist's Cinema section, 2, Rome, p. 104.

1976

A. Branzi, "Radical Note" and "Relazione su alcuni frammenti," and F. Raggi, "Masturbazione o autocastrazione, I rabdomanti," in *Casabella*, 411, pp. 10–13.

1977

B. Orlandoni, G. Vallino, *Dalla città al cucchiaio*, Turin.

G. Avogadro, "Lo stile boom entra in museo," in *Il Giorno*, September 30, p. 25.

1978

C. Donà, "Biennale, Triennale, Quadriennale etc. etc.," in *Modo*, 12, July–August, pp. 49 ff.

1980

A. Branzi, "Triennale anno zero," in *Domus*, 604, March, pp. 36–38.

"Michele De Lucchi designer," in *Linea Uomo*, 14, September, p. 43.

N. Gasperini, "Intervista a Michele De Lucchi," in *Donna*, 2, April.

A. Piaggi, "Neues Design aus Italien, in *Vogue Deutsch*," 8, August, p. 188.

1981

B. Radice, *Memphis. The New International Style*, Milan, pp. 19–23.

C. Jencks, "The new international style e altre etichette," in *Domus*, 623, December, pp. 41–49.

A. Mendini, "Caro Michele De Lucchi," in *Domus*, 617, May, p. 1.

1982

P. Sparke, *Ettore Sottsass Jr*, London, pp. 69–79.

"Convegno Ufficio stile/Consul: 'L'office automation e la progettazione e l'arredamento dei posti di lavoro nella realtà aziendale,'" in *Ufficio stile*, 4, June, pp. 14–16.

U. La Pietra, P. Scarzella, "Il progetto e la piastrella," in *Domus*, 632, October, pp. 58–65, esp. p. 64.

1983

E. Chiggio, E. Francalanci (edited by), *Memphis*, Padua.

R. Zorzi, *Olivetti Synthesis: per una storia del design*, Milan, pp. 15–35.

G. Cutolo, "Michele De Lucchi e Gigi Lanaro," in *Gap casa*, May–June, pp. 94–97.

S. De Pozzo, M. Dini, "Post post post. E poi?," in *Panorama*, October 31, pp. 146–59, esp. p. 157.

"Maison Figurative (figurée) ou éclectique," in *Habiter c'est vivre*, November, pp. 242–43.

"Milano capitale del design," in *L'Unità* (Milan-Regione), October 23.

A.C. Quintavalle, "Nuova immagine vuol dire idea diversa del vivere," in *Corriere della Sera*, October 23, p. 17.

R. Sias, "Michele De Lucchi," in *Ufficio stile*, 3, March, XVI, pp. VI–VIII.

1984

A. Branzi, *La casa calda*, Milan, pp. 139, 141, 144, 152.

B. Radice, *Memphis. Ricerche, esperienze, risultati, fallimenti e successi del nuovo design*, Milan.

D. Baroni, "Anni '80. Il paesaggio domestico," and B. Pedretti, "Un futuro possibile," in *Interni*, 346, December, pp. 58–59, 60–61.

S. Basso, M. Espanet, "L'architetto giusto per ogni casa," in *Capital*, 10, October, pp. 17–26, esp. pp. 24–25.

R. Di Caro, "Nasce il nuovo stile," in *L'Espresso*, 15, April 15, pp. II–IX.

M. Dini, "Jolly pigliatutto. Una matita tutta punk," in *Panorama*, January 2, pp. 82–84.

"Italian Neo Futurism," in *Axis* 10, winter, pp. 16–23, 42–45.

G. Quartieri, "Sistema è…," in *Office layout*, suppl. to *Office Automation*, 6, June, pp. 10–15.

P. Sayer, "Michele De Lucchi son of Sottsass," in *Designer's Journal*, May.

1985

AA.VV., *Michele De Lucchi. Design. 1978–1985*, exhibition catalogue, Komplement.

S. Bayley (edited by), *The Conran Directory of Design*, London, p. 114.

G. Celant, "Michele De Lucchi," in *The European Iceberg*, exhibition catalogue, Art Gallery of Ontario, Toronto, Milan, pp. 226–27, 345.

G. Gramigna, *Repertorio 1950–1980*, Milan.

"Michele De Lucchi," in *Progettando l'ufficio. Storia, documenti e riflessioni sull'ufficio*, Pordenone, pp. 51–54.

C. Sabino, A. Tondini, *Italian Style*, London, pp. 267–278.

B.B.A. (Beatrice Barbiellini Amidei), "Un anticonformista di successo," in *Il piacere*, 9, September, p. 52.

"Montreal: un congresso per promuovere il design," in *Casa Vogue*, 160, February.

P. Sparke, "Source Milanese," in *Observer*, *Italy Awaits* issue, May 12, pp. 32–33.

1986

Italia diseño 1946/1986, exhibition catalogue, Museo Rufino Tamayo, Mexico, p. 153.

"Michele De Lucchi," in *FP*, 8, September, pp. 48–66.

"Michele De Lucchi," in *FP Fusion Planning*, 8, September, pp. 50–65.

"Michele De Lucchi," in *The Sun*, monographic issue dedicated to Italy, 299, pp. 28–31.

1987

AA.VV., *Designed by architects in the 1980s*, Barcelona.

B. Radice, *Gioielli di architetti*, Milan.

F. Shimizu, Studio M. Thun (edited by), *The Italian Design*, Tokyo, pp. 50–52.

P. Starck (edited by), *The International Design Yearbook 1987/88*, London, pp. 222, 226.

S. Anargyros, "Michele De Lucchi," in *Intramuros*, 10, January, pp. 14–18.

R. Brusila, "Toimistoon ei enää osteta pelkkiä pöytiä ja tuoleja," in *Kauppalehti*, September 9, p. 10.

S. Carbonaro (edited by), "Silenzio. L'ufficio trasmette! Intervista con Michele De Lucchi," in *Ufficio stile*, 5, pp. 4–7.

L. Cuomo, "Le magnifiche sorti e progressive," and F. Doveil, "L'avanguardia con i piedi per terra," in *Modo*, 98, April–May, pp. 30–33, 34.

M.-L. Kinturi, "Muotoilijan on pysyttävä kiinni arkielämässä," in *Mark*, 8, pp. 54–55.

L. Maunula, "Maailma tarvitsee esineitä, jotka uskaltavat ottaa kantaa," in *Helsingin Sanomat*, September 10.

"Michele De Lucchi luennoi," in *Avorakka*, 9.

"I mobili personaggi," in *Casa oggi*, 153, March, p. 13.

M. Rizzo, "Saranno famosi," in *Business*, 1, pp. 85–90, esp. pp. 85–86.

A. Shugaar, "At the Edge of New Design," in *Capital International*, 11, fall/winter, pp. 104–11, esp. pp. 105–07.

1988

Design heute, exhibition catalogue, Munich 1988.

A. Isozaki (edited by), *The International Design Yearbook 1988/89*, London, pp. 134, 227.

P. Sparke, *Design in Italy*, New York, pp. 199–224.

M. Gastel, "Michele De Lucchi: utopista e realista," in *Donna Design*, May.

"Michele De Lucchi, Italy," in *Designer Journal*, 2, April, pp. 36–37.

B.R. (Barbara Radice), "Michele De Lucchi, New Drawings," in *Terrazzo*, 1, fall, pp. 76–95.

1989

M. Collins, A. Papadakis, *Post-Modern Design*, London.

The Italian Manifesto or The Culture of the Nine Hundred and Ninety-Nine Cities, on the occasion of the 39th International Design Conference in Aspen (Colorado), June 13–18, 1989.

O. Tusquets Blanca (edited by), *The International Design Yearbook 1989/90*, London, pp. 83, 117, 222.

"Önnu Ólafsdóttir, Björnsson, Gledin, í fyrrúmi," in *Morgunblaðið*, April 15, pp. 8–9.

A. Passigli, "Questioni di Styling," in *Epoca*, 2024, July 23, pp. 52–57.

D. Righetti, "Il segreto sta tra l'attaccatutto e il grattacielo," in *Il Giornale*, October 15, p. 3.

P. Runfola, "Segreti," in *Europeo*, 43, October 27, pp. 176–77.

S. Ueno, "Michele De Lucchi," in *Great Design*, pp. 6–11.

1990

K.M. Armer, A. Bangert, *Design anni ottanta*, Florence, p. 229.

N. Bellati, "Michele De Lucchi," in *New Italian Design*, New York, pp. 54–59.

M. Bellini (edited by), *The International Design Yearbook 1990/91*, London, pp. 63, 215, 222.

S. Kicherer, *Olivetti*, London.

Memphis 1981–1988, exhibition catalogue, Groninger Museum, Groningen, pp. 16, 32, chap. 9, pp. 158, 163, 187, 195–96.

A. Pansera, *Il design del mobile italiano dal 1946 a oggi*, Rome-Bari, pp. 87–88, 168.

H. Aldersey-Williams, "Story of Evolution," in *Design Week*, January 26, pp. 14–15.

L.B., "Les créateurs italiens entre usines et musées," in *Le Monde*, March 16, p. 9.

A. Boisi (edited by), "Michele De Lucchi 'maestro' del design," in *Interni*, 405, November, pp. 120–28.

"Italian Architect visits Australia," in *Corporate & Office Design*, fall/winter, pp. 253–54.

A. Mariella, "Itineraire d'un enfant doue," in *Mobilis agencement*, 4, June–July, pp. 65–68.

"Michele De Lucchi," in *Wood Pro*, 8, pp. 41–43.

"Michele De Lucchi, 'Een museum is een plek voor plezier,'" in *Vrijdagbijlage*, January 19, p. 25.

"Photography meets Design," in *Mensch & Büro*, May, p. 26.

P. Räty, "Lasin takana de Lucchi," in *City*, 5, p. 9.

P. Stirling, "Outrageous Memphis," in *Listener*, May 7–13, pp. 4–5.

J. Welsh, "Fall in Milan," in *Building Design*, September 14, pp. 24–25.

1991

AA.VV., *Il disegno delle cose*, exhibition catalogue, Florence, pp. 267–78.

AA.VV., *Mobili italiani 1961–1991. Le varie età dei linguaggi*, exhibition catalogue, Milan.

"Michele De Lucchi," heading in G.C. Bertsch, M. Dietz, B. Friedrich, *Euro Design Guide*, Munich, p. 54.

F. Shimizu, D. Palterer (edited by), *The Italian Furniture*, Tokyo, pp. 41–44.

B. Esik, "Fotografin tasarimla Bulusmasi," in *Tasarim*, 19, pp. 113–19.

L. Farrelly, "Dancing girl and the death of marketing," in *Blueprint*, October, p. 12.

E.M., "1980–1990 a Parigi una valutazione critica del progetto d'arredo italiano," in *Domus*, 727, May, p. 16.

"Michele De Lucchi," in *Icon Design & Architecture*, 29, 5, pp. 30–35.

"Michele De Lucchi," in *Impression*, March–April, pp. 34–35.

"Michele De Lucchi," in *Plus Architecture + Interior Design*, 12, pp. 82–87.

S. Milesi, "Techniques Discrètes. Le design mobilier en Italie 1980–1990," in *Casa Vogue*, 235.

A. Mosca, "La casa in cerca di poesia," in *Corriere della Sera*, May 4, p. 39.

A. Nulli, "Techniques Discrètes. Le design mobilier en Italie 1980–1990," in *Progex*, 6, June.

A. Oedekoven, "Trendwende: Zurück zu alten Stilen," in *Form*, II, p. 10.

P. Pfeufer, "Un maestro du design," in *Maison & Jardin*, September, p. 330.

1992

B.E. Bürdek, *Design*, Milan, esp. pp. 100–03 (original title *Design: Geschichte, Theorie und Praxis der Produktgestaltung*, Cologne 1991).

S. Kicherer, *Michele De Lucchi*, Milan.

"Michele De Lucchi," in *Creazione: Milano*, exhibition catalogue, The Museum of Modern Art, (Japan), 2, pp. 49–52.

A. Putman (edited by), *The International Design Yearbook 1992*, London, pp. 80, 220.

M.C. Tommasini, M. Pancera, *Il design italiano protagonisti opere e scuole*, Milan.

C. Blauensteiner, "Ein designer meditiert," in *Kunsthandwerk e design*, I, January–February, pp. 4–6.

C. Braga, "Competere col design," in *Management*, February, pp. 58–66, esp. pp. 63–64.

S. Kusch, "Sicherheit, so weit das Auge reicht," in *Horizont*, 51–52, December, p. 16.

F. Minervino, "Progetti di nozze tra cose e natura," in *Corriere della Sera*, February 6, p. 7.

"Seldstbedienung=Self-service dell'oggetto anonimo," in *Domus*, 737, April, pp. 113–19.

"Top Ten," in *Md*, 3, March, pp. 70–75, esp. p. 72.

A. Trimarco, "Non solo moda, questa è arte," in *Il Mattino*, September 29, p. IV.

E. von Radziewsky, "Ein Philosoph des Designs," in *Architektur & Wohnen*, 2, April–May, pp. 152–56.

1992–93

"25 anni di Casa Vogue," in *Casa Vogue*, 247, December–January, pp. 48–52.

1993

A. Buck, M. Vogt, *Michele De Lucchi*, Berlin.

H. Höger, *Ettore Sottsass jun.*, Tübingen-Berlin, pp. 48–53.

A. Pansera, *Storia del disegno industriale italiano*, Rome-Bari.

B. Radice, *Ettore Sottsass*, Milan.

B. Sipek (edited by), *The International Design Yearbook 1993*, London, pp. 43, 56, 206–07, 209, 219.

U. Brandes, "Der Computer in der Hand. Interview von Michele De Lucchi mit Richard Sapper," in *Richard Sapper. Werkzeuge für das Leben*, trans. by *Ufficio stile*, 4, 1982, Göttingen, pp. 150–56.

"Erfinder einer neuen Welt," in *Horizont*, December 17, p. 56.

G. Finizio, "Future Design," in *Ottagono*, 107, June, 1993, pp. 75–82.

M. Ghersi, "Nuovi itinerari per la creatività," in *AD*, April, pp. 66–73, esp. p. 68.

K.S. Leuschel, S. Kusch, "Sicurezza und Bellezza," in *Hoch Parterre*, 1–2, January–February, pp. 16–17.

"Michele De Lucchi über die Trends der neunziger Jahre (nr. 51/1992)," in *Horizont*, October 22, p. 54.

A. Pansera, "Verso un nuovo immaginario," in *Il bagno*, 129, October, pp. 146–150.

"Die Zeit der Happenings ist vorbei," in *form*, 144, pp. 28–29.

M. Zetti, "La forma e la sostanza," in *Tempo economico*, 339, November, pp. 86–95.

1994

R. Arad (edited by), *The International Design Yearbook 1994*, London, pp. 97, 107, 143, 216.

N. Bornsen-Holtmann, *Italian Design*, Cologne 1994.

"I materiali. Intervista a Michele De Lucchi," in *Abet laminati*, catalogue.

"Michele De Lucchi," in *GQ*, 21, 11, pp. 156–57.

V. Pasca (edited by), "Minimalismo come complessità," in *Annual Casa*, pp. 26–33.

A. Rawsthorn, "Talent needs intelligence too," in *Financial Times*, June 13, p. 8.

D. Sudjic, "From left field to mainstream, e William Payne, Design is no longer enough," in *Blueprint*, April, pp. 34–36.

A. Tangvald-Pedersen, "Han Tegner Fremtiden," in *VG*, July 19, p. 22.

1995

T. Hauffe, *Design*, Cologne, pp. 139, 151, 154.

J. Nouvel (edited by), *The International Design Yearbook 1995*, London, pp. 46, 118, 204–09, 227.

A. Pansera (edited by), *Dizionario del design italiano*, Milan 1995.

C. Gardner, "Prophet of profit," in *Design*, summer, pp. 32–37.

H. Jatzke-Wigand, "Michele De Lucchi: 'Wir Europäer besitzen das Potential für Gestaltungen in Design und Architektur,'" in *Wohnrevue*, 7, pp. 64–70.

"Michele De Lucchi: 'Los noventa están siendo la década del miedo,'" in *El País*, May 18, p. 46.

S. Makino, "An interview with Michele De Lucchi: 'Let's talk about what design can do,'" in *Spazio*, November.

C. Reinewald, "Michele De Lucchi a long way from Memphis," in *Man*, 23, November, pp. 110–15.

K. Schmidt-Lorenz, "Cooperazione DL," in *Design Report*, 6, pp. 68–70, and idem, "Ein Archiv für die Zukunft," in *Design Report*, 7–8, July–August, pp. 44–45.

S. Vanmaercke, "Michele De Lucchi Architectes et designer: créateurs de formes mais aussi de comportements," in *Tendances*, September 21, pp. 127–28.

A. Zabalbeascoa, "'El diseño de los noventa debe prefecer seguridad' a firma Michele de Lucchi," in *La Vanguardia*, May 18, p. 62.

1996

A. Branzi (edited by), *Il design italiano 1964–1990*, exhibition catalogue, Milan.

S. Casciani, *La fabbrica dell'arte*, exhibition catalogue, Milan.

L. Lazzaroni, *Trentacinque anni di design al Salone del mobile 1961–96*, Milan.

A. Mendini (edited by), *The International Design Yearbook 1996*, London, pp. 108, 198, 224.

C. Morozzi, S. Da Ponte, *Mobili italiani contemporanei*, Milan.

M. Bradaschia (edited by), "Michele De Lucchi. Design e architettura nell'epoca dello Zeitgeist," in *d'Architettura*, 15, pp. 6–7.

M.–F. Holemans, "Michele De Lucchi: de tijd provoceren is voorbij" and "Le temps n'est plus a la provocation," in *Designers weekend*, 5, April, pp. 2–3.

I. Nottrot (edited by), "Michele De Lucchi: neue Philosophie wichtiger als Farben und Formen," in *Luxembuerger Wort*, September 5, pp. 6–7.

"Nur zum Besitzen," in *Stern*, 49, p. 154.

V. van De Vliet, "De Lucchi volwassen geworden," in *Het Parool*, November.

P. Young (edited by), "A million miles from Memphis," in *The Globe and Mail*, July 18.

1997

P. Starck (edited by), *The International Design Yearbook 1997*, London, pp. 66, 110–11, 116, 119, 150, 183, 224.

AA.VV., "Second Conference of the Peterberger Management Forum," in *Films Report Special*, January, pp. 1–4.

ceb, "Oscar dank Mut," in *Kunst Zeitung*, June 11.

AB. Del Guercio, "Né pietra, né acqua," in *Interni*, 467, January–February, p. 32.

A. Demirsoy, "Design-Pokal wandert nach Italien," in *Westdeutsche Allgemeine*, May 29.

"Design-Team des Jahres," in *Md*, 8, p. 54.

"Italien gewinnt Design-Oscar 'Radius,'" in *Handels-magazin*, June 26, p. 22.

M. Jonna, "Le quattro bellezze degli oggetti," in *Casaviva*, 9, p. 54, September, p. 54.

D. Meyhöfer, "Ingenieur, Handwerker, Narr: Michele De Lucchi," in *Zug*, May, pp. 24–26.

C. Morozzi, "Trois generations au Vitra Design Museum," in *Intramuros*, 70, April–May, pp. 20–23.

"New Insights," in *Tools of Success. Newsletters of the Petersberger Management Forum*, January, pp. 4–5.

"Petersberger Management-Forum," in *Verpackungs-Rundschau*, 1, p. 24.

L. Pianzola, "Design per l'ufficio oggi," in *Habitat Ufficio*, 85, pp. 78–80.

"Studio De Lucchi. New working communities," in *Congena Texte*, 1, pp. 13–18.

"Designteam des Jahres," in *Design Report*, 9, September, p. 20.

E. von Radziewsky, "Die Liebesäpfel des designers," in *Architektur & Wohnen*, 4, August–September, pp. 65–74, 169–70.

1998

AA.VV., *Moderne Klassiker*, suppl. to *Schöner Wohnen*, Hamburg, pp. 32, 164, 167, 202–03.

A. Mendini, "Laudazio," in *Programm Das Design-Team des Jahres 1998*, Verleihung des *Radius* an das Philips Design-Team, pp. 6–11.

R. Sapper (edited by), *The International Design Yearbook 1998*, London, pp. 75, 99, 136, 224.

H. Bering, "Design ist eine debatte über den wert von produkten," in *Md*, 1, January, pp. 97–101.

P. Darge, "Michele De Lucchi Design moet onzichtbaar zijn," in *Wonen*, 7, February, pp. 78–82.

"Design is Total Communications, Studio De Lucchi," in *Design*, Design Venture in Italia issue, 242, 8, pp. 126–31.

"Michele De Lucchi über Design, Raum, Büros, Unternehmen," in *Office Design*, 5, October, pp. 16–26.

C. Morozzi, "Michele De Lucchi, ricomincio dal design," in *Interni*, special issue, 3, June 5, pp. 94–98.

J. Teunen, "Waarom? Daarom!," in *Eigenhuis & Interieur*, 3, March, p. 79.

1999

G. Gramigna and P. Biondi, *Il design in Italia dell'arredamento domestico*, Turin, pp. 178–81.

J. Morrison (edited by), *The International Design Yearbook 1999*, London, pp. 81, 82, 223.

C. Neumann, *Design in Italia*, Milan (original edition Cologne).

C. Trini Castelli, *Transitive Design*, Milan, pp. 61, 64, 105, 108.

S.T. Anargyros, C. Hamaide, "Échelle humaine," in *Libération*, 6, October.

"Aperta la rassegna sul designer Michele De Lucchi," in *La Stampa*, November 13.

L. Barberis (edited by), "I disegni di De Lucchi esposti all'archivio storico Olivetti," in *Il nostro tempo*, November 7.

P. Bricco, "Arte senza computer. De Lucchi a mano libera. Proposta per un dibattito," in *La Stampa Torino sette*, November 12, and idem, "Luci, fax, disegni, una matita: c'è il caro Michele," in *Diario*, 50, December 15–21, p. 55.

S. Carbonaro, "Emotionale Vernunft. Die Werke und Projekte von Michele De Lucchi," in *DBZ*, 7, pp. 65–72.

S. Casciani, "Grande interno pensante," in *Abitare*, 385, June, pp. 84–93.

ri. co., "Disegnare?," in *la Repubblica*, Turin, November 17.

F. Di Bartolomei, "Il computer aiuta ma c'è la matita," in *Messaggero Veneto*, February 13, p. 10.

D. Gariglio, "I disegni di De Lucchi in mostra nella villetta Casana," in *La sentinella del Canevese*, November 11, p. 7.

H. Höger (edited by), "Michele De Lucchi. Essere irriverente per andare più in profondità," in *Domus*, 819, October, pp. 54–63.

F. Irace, "Il mercato dei concorsi," in *Abitare*, 383, April.

F. Maffioli, "Il designer dalla matita facile," in *Il Giornale*, December 17, p. 47.

"Mit dem Fragen fängt das Denken an," in *Horizont*, 6, pp. 76–77.

E. Morteo (edited by), "Ufficio diffuso ufficio domestico, home office," in *Panorama Interni*, 1, April 9, pp. 06–09.

G. Perlasco, "De Lucchi … a mano libera," in *Ivrea*, November 12, p. 9.

S. Ricci, "Disegnare ancora … a mano libera," in *Varieventuali*, 21, November 17, p. 11.

2000

4:3: 50 Jahre italienisches & deutsches Design, exhibition catalogue, Bonn.

S. Annicchiarico (edited by), *1945–2000 Il design in Italia*, Rome.

E. Karcher, "Michele De Lucchi," in E. Karcher, M. von Perfall, *Italienisches design*, Munich, pp. 203–08.

I. Maurer (edited by), *The International Design Yearbook 2000*, pp. 78, 83, 91, 128–29, 228.

C. Morozzi (edited by), "Michele De Lucchi," in *Stile italiano*, Rome, pp. 64–65.

I. Adler, "Verwicklung und Verheissung," and T. Reuschling, "Wenn der Toaster zur Skulptur wird," in *Italienische und Deutsche Design*, June, pp. 1, 2.

M. Ajello, "Ciampi 'rivaluta' le onorificenze di Stato," in *Il Messaggero*, June 11, pp. 6–7.

L.B., "Milan Rendez-vouz du gotha mondial de la mode et du design," in *Enjeux*, July–August, p. 119.

R. Ferruzza, "Scrivania addio," in *Gente Money*, 4, April, pp. 116–18.

"Michele De Lucchi cinque cose," in *Domus*, 831, November, p. 144.

P. Pan. (Pierluigi Panza), "Sottsass: ma quei designer pensano troppo al mercato," in *Corriere della Sera*, April 11.

M. Portanuova, "Col pennarello in cda," in *Il Mondo*, June 30, pp. 94–101, esp. 95–96.

"Up to date. Design," in *Confort*, 42, pp. 6–7.

2001

AA.VV., *Aldo Cibic, Michele De Lucchi, Massimo Iosa Ghini*, exhibition catalogue, Münster, pp. 22–39.

A. Colonetti (edited by), *Grafica e design a Milano, 1933–2000*, Milan.

H. Höger, *Michele De Lucchi Architektur Innenarchitechtur Design*, Stuttgart-Munich.

Olivetti 1908–2000, Archivio storico Olivetti, Ivrea.

S. Polano, *Achille Castiglioni tutte le opere 1938–2000*, Milan.

M. Vitta, *Il progetto della bellezza*, Turin.

G. Darugar, "Michele De Lucchi. Design extrême," in *Résidences décoration*, 38, p. 26.

M. De Cesco, "Ti ridisegno la vita," in *Specchio, La Stampa*, weekly, 269, April 7, pp. 28–37, esp. pp. 30–32.

L. Ferrari, "Il filosofo della luce," in *Io Donna speciale casa*, enclosed with *Io Donna, Corriere della Sera* weekly, 14, April 7, pp. 48–49.

M. Kern, "La teoria delle quattro fasi. Intervista a Michele De Lucchi," in *Cda*, 1, January, pp. 54–59.

"Michele De Lucchi, Disegnare a cavallo di un'idea," in *Il Sole 24 ore, Nuovi Segni*, insert, design competition, Monday, April 2, pp. 1, 6.

R. Pasero, "Michele De Lucchi: io, l'eco designer," in *Vita*, 14, April 6.

P. Schwab, "Exemplarischer Vertreter seiner Generation," in *Design report*, 12, pp. 8–9.

C. Staib, "Design ist stets mehr als Design," in *Wohnen*, 11, November, pp. 32–33.

R. Tessa, "L'architetto che ama l'industria," in *la Repubblica, Affari & Finanza* insert, February 19, p. 36.

M. van Gessel, "Michele De Lucchi," in *Residence*, 9, September, pp. 32–33.

2002

R. Lovegrove (edited by), *The International Design Yearbook 2002*, London, pp. 34, 82–85, 128, 144, 220.

S. Suardi, *Michele De Lucchi. Dopotolomeo*, exhibition catalogue, Milan.

A.-M. Fèvre, "Tendances Design 2. Le design pour un monde durable," in *Signes de Sienne*, 6, June, pp. 17–19.

E. Gandolfi, "Michele De Lucchi. Il bello è utile," in *Ottagono*, 154, October, pp. 42–53.

t. m., "Dobbiamo imparare ad amare l'industria," in *la Repubblica*, August 31, p. V.

"Micheles Handarbeit," in *Md*, 4, pp. 56–57.

L. Ogna, "Progettista della modernità," in *Brava casa*, 6, June, pp. 67–68.

F.-C. Prodhon, "La première chose…," in *AD French edition*, *Spécial Italie*, 21, April, p. 34.

K. Schmidt-Lorenz, "Michele De Lucchi: Zeichner aus Passion," in *Häuser*, 1, November, pp. 8–9.

"Wie, Form von Hand," in *Süddeutsche Zeitung*, 62, March 14–20, p. 4.

2003

A. Bassi, *La luce italiana. Design delle lampade 1945–2000*, Milan.

P. Zec (edited by), *Who's Who in Design*, 2, Essen, pp. 126–27.

A. Bassi, "Michele De Lucchi: il mio progetto," in *Auto & Design*, 138, February, pp. 71–75.

G. Bosoni, "Non c'è lampada senza lampadina," in *Modo*, 227, pp. 46–50.

F. Bulegato, "Un laboratorio ideale," in *diid. disegno industriale*, 5, pp. 82–91.

A. Colonetti, "De Lucchi. Il mio design nasce in un pollaio," in *Corriere della Sera Design*, suppl., April 5, p. 3.

A. De Angelis, "Light & Technology," in *Modo*, 227, pp. 41–45, and idem, "Intervista a Michele De Lucchi," in *Modo*, 230, pp. 49–56.

M. Gabbiano, "L'architetto che voleva portare la luce in banca," in *la Repubblica, Affari & Finanza* insert, March 31, p. 27.

"L'indice degli spazi," in *Ufficio stile*, abstract from the conference "Spazi del sapere," November 25, 2002, Milan Triennale, January, pp. 8–9.

"In senso industriale: De Lucchi a Parigi," in *Abitare*, 427, April.

A. Matarrese, "Sono senza disciplina e piaccio ai francesi," in *Panorama*, December 11, p. 27.

"Mr Design," in *Pass design + entertainment milano*.

P. Panza, "Gli architetti: subito un museo del design," in *Corriere della Sera*, April 7, p. 49.

L. Piana, "Aiuto mi si è ristretta la scrivania," in *L'Espresso*, April 23, pp. 158–63, esp. p. 163.

S.R., "Après-Memphis, Michele De Lucchi," in *Architecture intérieure cree*, 308, April–May, pp. 4–5.

M. Romanelli, "Italian (after the heroes)," suppl. dedicated to Italian Style, in *The New York Times*, May 16, pp. 2–3.

L. Salza, "Padroni di casa," in *Capital*, April, pp. 126–27.

L. Saporito, "Il cuore del design: Michele De Lucchi sperimentatore a modo suo," in *Sur la terre*, 14, p. 67.

R. Tessa, "Re-design," in *la Repubblica, Affari & Finanza* insert, October 23, p. 7 and idem, "De Lucchi per un anno al Boubourg," in *la Repubblica, Affari & Finanza* insert, November 17, p. 27.

2004

"Aprire e chiudere. Lo scenario per le scelte. Intervista a Michele De Lucchi," in G. Mazzocchi, A. Villani (edited by), *Sulla città, oggi*, Milan, pp. 73–80.

G. Bosoni, "Intervista a Michele De Lucchi," in *Architettura degli interni*, 4, April, pp. 11–12, 20–22.

F. Bulegato, "Il made in Italy al Salone del mobile: chiavi di lettura proposte da un designer," in *Casa Vogue, Vogue* suppl., 644, 19, April, pp. 10–11.

"Conversazione con Michele De Lucchi," in E. Del Drago, *La Triennale di Milano. Design territorio impresa*, Rome, pp. 11–18.

"Michele De Lucchi," in *Axis*, 6, June, pp. 13–19.

M.P., "Michele De Lucchi," in *OFX, Office System*, special supplement to *OFX*, 5, November–December, p. 46.

G. Pettena, "Radical Design: ricerca e progetto dagli anni '60 ad oggi," in *Arte architettura ambiente*, 7, July, pp. 26–28.

L. Prandi, "La logica della produzione," in *Box*, 45, April, pp. 154–58.

P.R. (Paolo Rinaldi), "La libertà di creare," in *OFX*, 77, pp. 94–97.

C. Simenc, "La lampe est mon object préféré," in *Le Journal des Artes, Luminaire,* dossier, 1, April 30, p. 21.

P. Tamborrini, "Le due anime di Michele De Lucchi," in *Il giornale dell'architettura*, February, pp. 35, 37.

"Tasarimin katkisi küçüktır!," in *art+decor*, 135, June.

"Voice of creator from Italy: Michele De Lucchi," in *Photon*, 4.

Writings by Michele De Lucchi

1977

"Seminario della premeditazione," in *Eco d'arte moderna*, 1, January–February, pp. 16–18.

"Un po' d'architettura ufficiale," in *Eco d'arte moderna*, 2, March–April, p. 19.

with P. Bulletti (edited by), "Siamo in crisi da sempre," in *Eco d'arte moderna*, 4–5, May–June, p. 28.

1978

"Cibo Italian style," in *Modo*, 6, January–February, p. 3.

"Manuale del piccolo punk," in *Modo*, 7, March, p. 4.

"Il bello umido, Arte in francobolli componibili" and "Per il ponte? Dentro il Centro," in *Modo*, 8, April, pp. 5, 8, 74.

"Achille Castiglioni, Gio Ponti, Marco Zanuso," in *Laica Journal*, Italian Art issue, 18, April–May, pp. 29, 51, 59–60.

"Hollywood-style, Piccole architetture volanti e Allusioni fragili," in *Modo*, 9, May, pp. 4, 6, 71.

"Microurbanistica da biliardino e Caminelettrico offresi," in *Modo*, 10, June, pp. 4, 73.

"Piatti, torte, budini o Ufo?" and "Cianografica in facciata," in *Modo*, 11, July–August, pp. 4, 76.

"In punta di piedi, Per non confonderli, A scuola ridotta: design di arredo per l'infanzia" and "L'entomologo falegname," in *Modo*, 12, September, pp. 4, 5, 21–26, 73.

"Zoccolo a vela," in *Modo*, 13, October, p. 9.

"Avanti a tutto colore," in *Modonotizie, Modo*, suppl., 13, October, p. 13.

"Architettura metereologica, King Kong non ha peli sulle gambe" and "Al mio letto è cresciuta una sedia," in *Modo*, 14, November, pp. 11, 12, 68–69.

1979

Intervention at the 2nd ISIA exhibition/conference in Rome, October 24 and November 9–29, 1978, Centrokappa, Noviglio, in *Atti del convegno*, pp. 49–50.

"Senza fissa dimora" and "Non tutti i divani riescono col buco," in *Modo*, 17, March, pp. 5, 71.

"Scusi, le peso?," in *Modo*, 18, April, p. 10.

"Architetture di quaderni," in *Modo*, 19, May, pp. 49–52.

"Una casa con bagno soggiorno" and "La 'Stanza del banale,'" in *Casa Vogue*, 95, June, pp. 126–29, 163.

"Io sono un'autarchica sedia," in *Modo*, 20, June, p. 71.

"Intrappolati lentamente," in *Modo*, 22, September, p. 71.

"Criticare la musica per suonare il mondo," in *Modo*, 23, October, pp. 71–73.

"A Imola Archimede fa piovere i sassi dalla luna," in *Modo*, 24, November, pp. 25–29.

"Autore: io, il sole e un po' di vento," in *Modo*, 25, December, p. 71.

"Old and new aspect on environmental reduction," in *Space Design*, December.

1980

"Prefabbricato funzionale con colonnato optional," in *Modo*, 26, January–February, pp. 39–43.

"Al villaggio in casa propria," in *Casa Vogue*, 104, March, pp. 202–03.

(edited by), "Il caso 'Vela blu,'" in *Casa Vogue*, 108–09, July–August, pp. 116–19.

"Appunti di architetture tropicali," in *Casa Vogue*, 110, September, pp. 362–67.

"Il corpo del televisore," in *Donna*, 6, September.

1981

"Gli uffici sono paesaggi e l'orizzonte è lontano," in *Abitare*, 199, November, pp. 48–56.

1982

"L'ufficio è elettronico e fa bip-bip," in *Ufficio stile*, 4, June, pp. 20–22.

"L'era della scrivania elettronica," in *Domus*, 631, September, pp. 50–52.

1983

"Il ruolo del design nell'arredo come strumento di lavoro," in *Mobili per ufficio* (Olivetti Synthesis), pp. 38–39.

"Il posto di lavoro attrezzato," in *Sumo*, 2, March–April, pp. 76–79.

"Ergo Enjoy," in *Design*, April.

"La rivoluzione degli accostamenti cromatici," in *Interni*, 330, May, pp. 16–17.

1984

in Christina Ritchie and Loris Calzolari (edited by), *Phoenix New Attitudes in Design*, exhibition catalogue, Phoenix, Toronto, pp. 28–29.

"Per un ufficio più comunicativo," in *Casa Vogue*, 148, January, pp. 114–17.

1985

"De Lucchi, Michele," in *Contemporary Landscape from the Horizon of Postmodern Design*, exhibition catalogue, The National Museum of Modern Art, Kyoto, pp. 50–51.

1987

"George Sowden e Nathalie Du Pasquier," in *Du Pasquier & Sowden, Tempi moderni, 13/87*, exhibition catalogue, February 20–March 13, Rome, pp. 4–7.

"Introduzione," in Michele De Lucchi (edited by), *Solid*, exhibition catalogue, Milan, pp. 11–15.

1988

"Nuovi elementi nel progetto dell'oggetto. Design primario," in A. Cannella (edited by), *ADS. Design per lo sviluppo, Atti del corso di conferenze per studenti di architettura e di ingegneria, architetti, ingegneri e operatori del settore della progettazione industriale*, Palermo, December 13, 1982–May 31, 1983, Florence, pp. 44–55.

1989

"Agenda," in S. Calatroni (edited by), *Lettere segrete. Antologia di scritti e di oggetti di design*, Milan, pp. 87–90, 201–04, 254.

Aspen, text from the conference, June.

"Commento," in G. Varchetta, *Relazioni. La passione dello sguardo. Quarantasei fotografie commentate*, Milan, pp. 26–27.

"Due stili, due case," in *Casa Vogue*, 206, March, pp. 126–39.

"Export di cultura del progetto: esperienze giapponesi," in *Domus*, 710, November, pp. 17–18.

1990

"Ettore Sottsass che non è il mio maestro," in *Maestri: Musatti, Carlson, Berio, Sottsass*, Milan (later in *Ettore Sottsass*, exhibition catalogue, Milan, 1999, p. 34).

"Machines, Objects and Architecture," in *George J. Sowden designing 1970–1990*, exhibition catalogue, Musée des arts décoratifs, Bordeaux, pp. 149–81.

in *Terrazzo*, 5, autunno, pp. 28–29.

1991

"Angelo Micheli," in Patrizia Catalano (edited by), *Angelo Micheli. Le tracce del progetto*, Galleria Schubert, Milan, p. 2.

1992

with A. Castiglioni, *Elegant Techniques. Italian Furniture Design 1980–1992*, exhibition catalogue, Milan, pp. 6, 52–59.

"The world of industry and furniture design in Italy," in *Elegant Techniques. Italian Furniture Design 1980–1992*, exhibition catalogue, Milan, pp. 6, 52–59.

"Presentazione," in *M. Christina Hamel, una zebra a pois, arredi in ceramica*, exhibition folder, Galleria Colombari, Milan.

"I Designer si raccontano. Michele De Lucchi: confessioni di un architetto," in *Casa Vogue*, 239, March, pp. 88–92 (published under the title "Private Gedanken," in H. Höger, *Michele De Lucchi Architektur Innenarchitektur Design*, Stuttgart-Munich 2001, p. 9).

1993

"Spaghetti al pomodoro," in AA.VV., *Il design italiano da mangiare*, Assarredo, n.l.

"Il designer Michele De Lucchi racconta la scoperta del lago Sirio, suo rifugio ora non più segreto," in *Casa Vogue*, 249, March, p. 28.

"Design: Style to Reflect a Personality," in *Dartamation*, 1, March, p. 17.

"Direzionali," in *OFX Guide 1993*, monographic issue dedicated to Head Offices, suppl. to *OFX Office International*, 9, September–October, pp. 32–33.

1994

"Möbel, Lebenstil und Technologie in Italien," in *Digitaler Möbelbau*, Stuttgart, pp. 73–75.

"Il colore che c'è e che non c'è," in *Domus*, 775, October, pp. 105–07 (also in *I colori della vita*, conference proceedings, Turin, August 27–28, Turin, p. 104).

1995

"Symposien und Stadtmusikanten," in *Standort Gestaltung*, 5 Jahre Designförderung Bremen 1990–1995, Bremen, p. 22.

"Un manifesto programmatico," in *Interni*, 448, March, pp. 58–63.

1996

Oltre gli schemi delle culture d'azienda, transcript of talks at the Assemblea di Centromarca, "Marca, discontinuità, evoluzione," Milan, July 3.

"Lavoro e libertà," in *Interni*, Il Contract, pp. 3–11.

1998

"Sui tasti della storia," in *Il Mondo*, 44, October 30, pp. 135–37.

1999

"La realtà va presa in giro," in B. Finessi (edited by), *Su Munari*, Milan, p. 147.

"Fuori dal mondo," in *Abitare*, 385, June, pp. 94–97.

"Der Mensch und die Arbeit in der Zukunft," in *Büro '99*, special edition of *DBZ*, 819, October, pp. 38–40.

"Krusten brechen auf," in *Mensch & Büro*, 6.

"Onvision," in *Modalità Friendly*, 0, pp. 80–85.

2001

"Synligt genbrug i design (The visibility of recycling in design)," in *Re-f-use*, exhibition catalogue, Dansk Design Center, pp. 14–15.

"Introduction," in idem (edited by), *The International Design Yearbook 2001*, London, pp. 8–13.

"Il design in Olivetti. Una tradizione che non tramonta," in *La sentinella del Canevese*, April 19, pp. 25, 31.

"La sfida dell'arditezza," in *Crossing*, 2, June, pp. 56–57.

2002

in S. Suardi, *Dopotolomeo*, Milan.

"Artemide et moi," in *Designer's days*, exhibition folder, Paris, May 30–June 2.

"La mia 'Produzione Privata,'" in *Artigianato*, 45, April–June, pp. 10–13.

2003

A mano libera disegni senza computer, exhibition catalogue, Ivrea.

"Conversazione sulle esposizioni," in A. Abruzzese, M. De Lucchi, F. Galdo, *Il Palazzo di Roma*, Rome.

"Design è tante cose," in *Design–italia.it magazine*, 2000–03/1, p. 9.

in *Martine Bedin*, exhibition folder, Galleria Roberto Giustini, Rome, April–May, p. 27.

1951

Born in Ferrara, November 8

1973

Performance Designer in General, 15th Milan Triennale, September 20

1973–76

Founder and promoter of the Cavart group seminars in Padua

1975

Graduates in architecture, Florence school of architecture (with a dissertation on *Vertical Housing*, supervisor Adolfo Natalini)

1977

Moves to Milan

1978–80

Exhibits his products at the Alchymia exhibitions, "Bau.haus I" (1979) and "Bau.haus II" (1980)

1979

Begins work for Olivetti Synthesis, brought in by Ettore Sottsass

1980–87

Founder and designer of Memphis. The first exhibition of the Memphis collection opens on September 18, 1981 at the Arc '74 showroom, Milan

1980–94

Opens a practice in Via Borgonuovo, Milan, next to Sottsass Associati; in 1984 moves to Via Vittoria Colonna, together with Angelo Micheli and Ferruccio Laviani. Nicholas Bewick, Pio Barone Lumaga and Torsten Fritze join the firm as commissions increase. In 1987 the firm moves to Via Goito; in 1994 it takes up premises at Via Pallavicino 31

1990

Founds Produzione Privata, design firm and workshop employing Italian craft workers

1992

Director of design at Olivetti (until 2002)

1996

Opens a branch of the firm in Rome

1997

Divides the practice into two separate firms: Studio Architetto Michele De Lucchi (aMDL) and Studio & Partners with Nicholas Bewick, Torsten Fritze and Emilio Torri, with premises on Via Lanzone, Milan (De Lucchi left this firm in 2001)

2000

With Mario Trimarchi founds the Studio Grafico Fragile (today with Mario Trimarchi, Frida Doveil, Ottorino Ermacora)

Receives the honorary title of Ufficiale della Repubblica Italiana for "achievement in the fields of design and architecture"

2001

Appointed full professor of Industrial Design at the Faculty of Design and Arts, IUAV, Venice

2003

The Centre Georges Pompidou in Paris acquires a large number of his drawings and models, installing them in two rooms in the permanent museum of the Beaubourg, inaugurated on November 18, 2003

"Cavart Seminars," Italy, 1973–76

"Michele De Lucchi. A Friendly Image for the Electronic Age," Tilburg (The Netherlands), 1985

"Disegni dell'estate," La Pola gallery, Ginza, Tokyo (Japan), February 26–March 2, 1991

"Sitz. Avantgarde," Design Zentrum Nordheim-Westfalen, Essen (Germany), April 4–May 4, 1991

"Michele De Lucchi," La Fenice gallery, Osaka (Japan), November 6–22, 1992

"Design Team of the Year," Essen (Germany), 1997

"Crudités," Galerie Binnen, Amsterdam (The Netherlands), June 3–July 6, 1997

"Michele De Lucchi and his Produzione Privata," La Sala Vinçon gallery, Barcelona (Spain), May 21–June 20, 1998

Exhibition at the Lakis Gavalas gallery, Thessalonica (Greece), 1999

Exhibition for the presentation of the "A che cosa servono i vasi da fiori?" collection, Studio aMDL, Milan, April 14–17, 1999

"Luci nel silenzio," Studio aMDL, Milan, April 12–16, 2000

"Michele De Lucchi. Ready Made 2001," Studio aMDL, Milan, April 4–9, 2001

"Black & White," Produzione Privata and Mandarina Duck, Mandarina Duck showroom, London (Great Britain), July 6–27, 2001

"A mano libera. Disegni senza computer," Olivetti and Telecom Italia Ivrea (Turin), November 12–December 19, 1999; Hamburg (Germany), February 7–March 10, 2002

"Die Hand in Architektur und Design," Galerie für Angewandte Kunst des BKV, Munich (Germany), March 15–April 20, 2002

"Chaos and Order – Love and Hate," photographic works by Klaus Oberer and studies of new forms by Michele De Lucchi, Studio aMDL, Milan, April 10–15, 2002

"Michele De Lucchi: Dopotolomeo," Regione Val d'Aosta, Church of San Lorenzo, Aosta, June 8–October 13, 2002

"Dans le sens industriel," La Galerie d'Architecture, Paris (France), March 18–April 19, 2003

"Traces, of Nature, Time, Hand and Spirit. Michele De Lucchi and Ernst Gamperl Explore their Favorite Materials: Wood and Glass," Studio aMDL, Milan, April 9–14, 2003

"Artemide and Me," Yamagiwa Livina, Tokyo, Yamagiwa Osaka (Japan), September–November 2003

"Designobjekte und Unikate aus Italien," Hilde Leiss Gallery, Hamburg (Germany), October 30–November 19, 2003

"Leon Tarasewicz meets Michele De Lucchi," Galleria Rubin, Milan, April 11–May 22, 2003

"Michele De Lucchi," Centre Georges Pompidou, Paris (France), November 18, 2003–October 30, 2004

"Geometries at Will," Studio aMDL, Milan, April 14–19, 2004

Objects and drawings by Michele De Lucchi are present in the permanent collections of various international museums, such as the: Art Center College of Design, Pasadena, California; Centre Georges Pompidou, Paris (France); Centro Legno Arredo Cantù (CLAC), Collezione Storica del Premio Compasso d'Oro-Adi, Cantù (Como); Milan Triennale, Collezione Permanente del Design Italiano 1945–1990, Milan; Design Museum, Ghent (Belgium); Design Museum, Helsinki (Finland); Galleria Nazionale d'Arte Moderna, Rome; Museo Alessi, Omegna (Verbania); Museo Kartell, Milan; The Israel Museum, Jerusalem (Israel); Musée des Arts Décoratifs de Montréal, Quebec (Canada); Musée des Beaux-Arts de Montréal, Quebec (Canada); Museo Nazionale della Scienza e della Tecnologia Leonardo da Vinci, Milan; Museum of Design, Thessalonica, Macedonia (Greece); Museum für Kunst und Gewerbe, Hamburg (Germany); Netherlands Architecture Institute-NAI, Rotterdam (The Netherlands); Civica Galleria d'Arte Moderna-Sezione Design, Gallarate (Varese); Stedelijk Museum of Modern Art, Amsterdam, (The Netherlands); Vitra Design Museum, Weil am Rhein (Germany); National Museum, Poznan (Poland); Museum für Gestaltung (Switzerland).

Awards

1987

Haus Industrieform, Germany (Tolomeo lamp, Artemide)

Shortlisted Compasso d'Oro–Adi (Rossana 214 kitchen, RB Rossana; Delphos office system, Olivetti Synthesis)

SNAI–Oscar des Architectures d'Interieur, France (Tolomeo lamp, Artemide)

1988

Arango International Design

Competition, USA (Tender lamp, Bieffeplast)

Deutsche-Auswahl, Design Center Stuttgart, Germany (Tolomeo lamp, Artemide)

Good Design Award, Japan (eyeglasses, Charmant)

Netherlands Industrial Design Foundation Award. Holland (dispenser Kleberoller, Pelikan)

1989

Compasso d'Oro-Adi (Tolomeo lamp, Artemide)

Design Plus, Germany (dispenser Kleberoller, Pelikan)

1990

Design of the Year, Popeye magazine Japan (Epoca watch, Lazy Susan)

Shortlisted Swan Industrial Design Award (Bancacontinua ovunque, Olivetti)

Smau Industrial Design Award (automatic bank teller CD 6300, Olivetti-Siab)

1991

Office Design Eimu (Segmenti office accessories, Kartell)

Shortlisted Compasso d'Oro-Adi (Segmenti office accessories, Kartell; Paper On office stationery, OlivettiBaltea; CD 6300 automatic telling machine, Olivetti–Siab)

1992

Design Innovationen, Design Zentrum Nordrhein-Westfalen, Germany (Sigma lampada, Classicon)

1993

Design Preis Schweiz, Switzerland (Sigira lamp, Classicon)

1994

IF Award for Good Industrial Design, Germany (Philos 44 laptop, Olivetti)

IF Award for Good Industrial Design, Germany (multimedia kiosks, Olivetti)

Shortlisted Compasso d'Oro–Adi (Sintesi bathroom accessories, Interform: Echos laptop, Olivetti)

Shortlisted Smau Industrial Design Award (Echos laptop, Olivetti)

1995

Design Innovetionen. Design Zentrum

Nordrhein-Westfalen, Germany (MS 6050 automatic telling machine, Olivetti)

Design Plus, Germany (Ginger e Fred salt and pepper shakers, Rosenthal)

Smau Industrial Design Award (Envision computer box, Olivetti)

1996

D'Excellence Marie-Claire Maison, France (Tolomeo lamp, Artemide)

IF Award for Good Industrial Design, Germany (Tolomeo lamp, Artemide)

IF Award for Good Industrial Design, Germany (JP 170 inkjet printer, Olivetti)

Smau Industrial Design Award (PR2 bank printer, Olivetti)

1997

Design Innovationen, Design Zentrum, Nordrhein–Westfalen, Germany (Deutsche Bahn ticket counter; Sistemare filing system, Mauser Office)

Design Team of the Year 1991, Design Zentrum Nordrhein-Westfalen, Germany

ID Annual Design Review, USA (Acquatinta lamp, Produzione Privata; Domestic Chips, Olivetti; Eidos and Pegaso office systems, Olivetti Synthesis)

IF Product Design Award – Best of Category, Germany (Deutsche Bahn ticket counters)

IF Product Design Award – Excellent Design. Germany (Deutsche Bahn self-service ticketing system)

1998–99

Good Design Award, USA (Allavoro office chair, Mauser Office)

1999

Goed Industrieel Ontwerp, Holland (Chair no. 1 chair, Kembo)

2000

Creative Distinction Award–EDA European Design Annual (graphic design of the volume *Olivetti 1901–98*, Olivetti)

Design Innovationen, Design Zentrum Nordrhein-Westfalen, Germany (Attivo 480 chair, Mauser Office)

Design Innovationen, Design Zentrum Nordrhein–Westfalen, Germany, Roter Punkt für höhe

Design Plus Light+Building, Germany (Dioscuri lamp, Artemide)

Designqualität (Dioscuri lamp, Artemide)

IF Product Design Award, Germany (Attivo 480 chair, Mauser Office; Jet Lab 600 multifunction fax, Olivetti)

Innovationenpreis, Architektur und Office, Germany (Attivo chair, Mauser Office; Sistemare filing system, Mauser Office)

Shortlisted Smau Industrial Design Award (Modifon computer, ICS)

2001

Compasso d'Oro-Adi (Artjet 10 printer, Olivetti)

Designpreis des Landes Nordrhein Westfalen-Ehrenpreis für Productdesign, Germany (Palme outdoor lamp, Artemide)

IF Product Design Award, Germany (Tolomeo off–center lamp, Artemide; Palme outdoor lamp, Artemide)

Internationaler Designpreis–Baden Württemberg-Fucus Mobilität, Germany (Tolomeo off-center lamp, Artemide)

Observeur du design-Produit sélectionné-APCI. France (Tolomeo micro lamp, Artemide)

Shortlisted Compasso d'Oro-Adi (Poste Italiane corporate identity, con Fragile; Poste Italiane post office branches; Jet Lab 600 multifunction fax, Olivetti; Palme outdoor lamp, Artemide; packaging for electronic products, Olivetti, with Fragile)

2002

Designpreis der Bundesrepublik, Germany (Palme outdoor lamp, Artemide)

Reddot Design Award, Design Zentrum Nordrhein-Westfalen, Germany (Logico lamp, Artemide)

2003

Finalist Medaglia d'Oro alla Committenza Privata, Milan Triennale (Poste Italiane)

Reddot Design Award, Design Zentrum Nordrhein-Westfalen, Germany (Tolomeo mega lamp, Artemide)

2004

Design Plus Light + Building, Germany (Logico mini-suspension lamp and Castore lamp, Artemide)

Reddot Design Award, Design Zentrum Nordrhein-Westfalen, Germany (Castore lamp, Artemide)

Shortlisted Compasso d'Oro–Adi (Banca Intesa corporate identity, with Fragile; Castore lamp, Artemide)

Studio aMDL collaborators

Simona Agabio
Werner Aisslinger
Sezgin Aksu
Felipe Alarcao
Marco Ammannati
Davide Angeli
Manuela Antonante
Taku Arai
Bastiaan Arler
Patrizia Attene
Susanne Backer
Julia Bald
Nicholas Banks
Jonathan Barnes
Pio Barone Lumaga
Paolo Bassetto
Luca Bellingeri
Nicholas Bewick
Alberto Bianchi
Marcello Biffi
Stephanie Blaasch
Emanuela Botter
Aida Bucci
Matthias Burhenne
Brigid Byrne
Michele Caja
Massimo Canali
Eric Castets
Stefano Chiabrera
Alessandro Chiarato
Nicoletta Colombo
Alvaro Conti
Mara Corradi
Michael Corsar
Adolfo Dalla Tea
Alessandra Dalloli
Daniela Danzi
Nora De Cicco
Paolo De Lucchi
Carlo De Mattia
Augustus De Vree
Monica Del Torchio
Marco Della Torre
Gladys Escobar
Zaira Faravelli

Barbara Farina
Lisa Farmer
Paolo Feroleto
Francesca Ferroni
Filippo Flego
Torsten Fritze
Paolo Fromage
Matthew Fuller
Gabriella Furlan
Elisa Gargan
Hanno Giesler
Marco Gillio
Bruna Gnocchi
Adriano Gregoris
Christian Hartmann
Hans Hoeger
Denise Houx
James Irvine
Mercedes Jaén Ruiz
Alexander Fraser Kenneth
Johannes Kiessler
Sanae Kimura
Geert Koster
Masahiko Kubo
Luca La Torre
Giovanna Latis
Ferruccio Laviani
Frederic Le Court
Antie Le Petit
Annelaure Lesquoy
Christine Licata
Maria Mancini
Michele Marozzini
Massimiliano Martini
Simona Martino
Aya Matsukaze
Olivier Maupas
Markus Melzer
Sergio Menichelli
Giovanni Battista Mercurio
Angelo Micheli
Fabiola Minas
Penny Morgan
Gianluigi Mutti
Matteo Nannucci

Alberto Nason
Laura Negrini
Amabilia Nichetti
Philippe Nigro
Ida Osnaghi
Francesco Otgianu
Filippo Pagliani
Laura Parolin
Eliana Pasquini
Giusy Pedone
Paola Pedretti
Lanfranco Perotti
Claudia Pescatori
Manuela Pighetti
Carlo Pintacuda
Enrico Quell
Livio Rabasco
Gerhard Reichert
Martin Reichuber
Roberta Rizzoli
Erminio Rizzotti
Nathalie Rossetti
Daniele Rossi
Michele Rossi
Mario Rossi Scola
Stefan Samson
Katia Scheika
Andrea Schiff
Christian Schneider
Steffen Schulz
Casper D. Schwartz
Federico Seymandi
Paola Silva Coronel
Trond Sonnergren
Silvia Suardi
Akiko Takaichi
Tadao Takaichi
Anna Telesca
Caterina Terribile Chianese
Laiza Tonali
Etien Veeman
Claudio Venerucci
Francesca Vincenzo
Paolo Zass

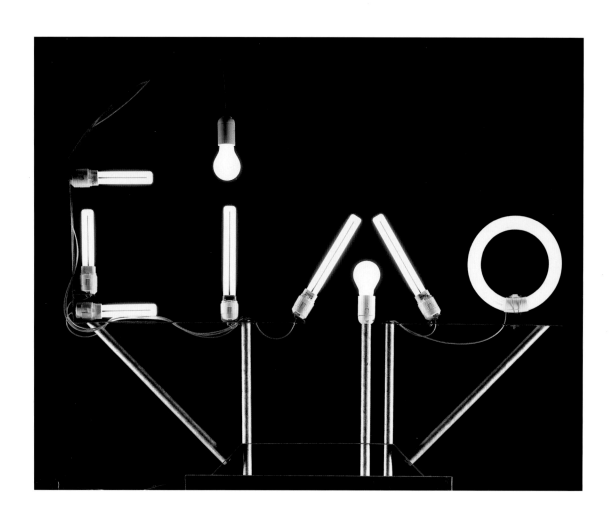

Photo credits

All the illustrations in this volume come from the Michele De Lucchi studio, which has authorized publication.

Among the others, we wish to acknowledge photos by:

Madjid Ashgari, pp. 174, 175

Aldo Ballo, p. 83

Gabriele Basilico, pp. 209–11, 220–25, 260, 261, 273, 291, 293

Chris Broadvent, p. 133

Piero Brombin, pp. 23, 24

Federico Brunetti, pp. 152, 155, 171

Santi Caleca, pp. 71–73, 75 bottom, 98, 99, 188–91, 251, 252, 253 top left and bottom, 254–59, 274–77

Mario Carrieri, pp. 146, 238

Centrokappa, p. 93

Paola Silva Coronel, pp. 268, 269 bottom left and at right

Nora De Cicco, p. 118

Jacopo De Lucchi, pp. 34, 35

Michele De Lucchi, pp. 26–31, 62, 104–11, 120, 121, 130, 131, 169, 239

Ottorino De Lucchi, pp. 32, 33

Diego Erti, p. 25

Pino Guidolotti, p. 203

Paolo Manusardi: pp. 7, 11, 14, 15, 18–21, 42, 44, 45, 48, 66, 67, 80, 82, 84, 133 bottom left, 134, 138, 142, 168 at right, 197 bottom, 207 bottom, 242, 243, 290

Giorgio Molinari, p. 47

Nacasa and partners, pp. 140, 141

Alberto Novelli, pp. 232, 233, 248, 249, 262, 263, 282, 284–89

Matteo Piazza, 176, 177, 179–81

Mayer und Kunz, pp. 182–87

Peter Ogilvie, p. 55 top right and bottom

Michele Rossi, p. 112

Luciano Soave, p. 74 top

Studio Azzurro, p. 49, 55 top left, 56–59, 76, 77, 173

Studio Koller, pp. 192–193

Tadao Takaichi, pp. 100–103

Luca Tamburlini, pp. 60, 87, 89, 114, 115–17, 119, 122, 123, 125 top, 126–28, 144, 145, 159 at bottom, 160–165, 196, 197, 212, 213, 217, 219, 226, 230, 231, 234, 246, 247, 253 top right, 264–67, 269 at top, 270–72, 278–80, 295

Tom Vack, pp. 61, 91 top and middle, 94–97, 125 bottom, 129, 135–37, 143 ,157

Miro Zagnoli, pp. 88, 201, 281

Holders of rights to any unattributed photograph sources should contact the publisher.